Afro-Mexican Constructions of Diaspora,
Gender, Identity and Nation

Cajoneando, by Ixrael Montes. (Courtesy of the artist.)

Afro-Mexican Constructions of Diaspora, Gender, Identity and Nation

Paulette A. Ramsay

THE UNIVERSITY OF THE WEST INDIES PRESS
Jamaica • Barbados • Trinidad and Tobago

The University of the West Indies Press
7A Gibraltar Hall Road, Mona
Kingston 7, Jamaica
www.uwipress.com

© 2016 by Paulette A. Ramsay
All rights reserved. Published 2016

A catalogue record of this book is available from
the National Library of Jamaica.

ISBN: 978-976-640-579-3 (print)
978-976-640-580-9 (Kindle)
978-976-640-581-6 (ePub)

Cover illustration: Image representing the *Artesa*. Artwork done in Father Glyn Jemmott Nelson's workshop, El Centro Cultural Cimarrón (Maroon Cultural Centre), in El Ciruelo, Mexico.
Cover and book design by Robert Harris
Set in Adobe Garamond Pro 11/14.5 x 27

The University of the West Indies Press has no responsibility for the persistence or accuracy of URLs for external or third-party Internet websites referred to in this publication and does not guarantee that any content on such websites is, or will remain accurate or appropriate.
Printed in the United States of America

Para los afro-mexicanos de la Costa Chica, después de muchos años de investigar su historia, su cultura, su tradición oral con sus décimas y coplas, sus poemas líricos; después de caminar con ellos y escuchar sus cuentos, sus silencios y sus cantos, después de partir el pan con ellos y sentir su profundo deseo de verse y ser vistos en su propia piel de ébano

For the Afro-Mexicans of the Costa Chica, after many years of researching their history, their culture, their oral tradition with its *décimas* and *coplas*, their lyric poems; after walking with them and listening to their stories, their silences and their songs; after breaking bread with them and sharing their deep desire to see themselves and be seen in their own ebony-coloured skin

Contents

List of Illustrations / ix

Foreword *Father Glyn Jemmott Nelson* / xi

Acknowledgements / xviii

Introduction / 1

1. Racial and Ethnic Diversity in Mexico through the Distorted Lens of *Memín Pinguín* / 28

2. Constructions of Gender and Nation in Selected Afro-Mexican Folktales / 47

3. Masculinity, Language and Power in Selected Afro-Mexican *Corridos* / 73

4. Place, Racial and Cultural Identities in Selected Afro-Mexican Oral and Lyric Verses / 107

5. Afro-Mexico in the Context of a Caribbean Literary and Cultural Aesthetics / 135

Conclusion / 157

Photographs / 164

Notes / 175

References / 181

Index / 191

Illustrations

Figures 1–6	Artwork samples from Father Glyn Jemmott Nelson's workshop /	**xv–xvi**
Figure 7	Metal *pueblo de gusto* (2004) /	**xvii**
Figure 8	Map of Mexico /	**xx**
Figure 9	The *Minga* in the Devil Dance /	**26**
Figure 10	Devil Dance /	**26**
Figure 11	Artwork sample from Father Glyn Jemmott Nelson's workshop /	**27**
Figure 12	Artist's representation of the *Artesa* /	**27**
Figure 13	Afro-Mexican girl /	**164**
Figure 14	Woman from El Ciruelo /	**164**
Figure 15	Policeman in the town of Santo Domingo /	**164**
Figure 16	Resident of El Ciruelo /	**164**
Figure 17	Young girl from El Ciruelo /	**165**
Figure 18	Young girl from Santo Domingo /	**165**
Figures 19–20	Women in El Ciruelo /	**165**
Figure 21	Afro-Mexican woman in Punta Maldonado selling typical Costa Chican *champurrado* (made from corn and chocolate [cacao]) /	**166**
Figure 22	Policeman in Santo Domingo /	**166**
Figure 23	Afro-Mexican boy in El Ciruelo /	**166**
Figure 24	Afro-Mexican woman teaching traditional craft /	**166**

Figure 25	People at workshop in Lagunillas / **167**	
Figure 26	Petition made by *México Negro* for black Mexicans to be counted in the 2010 census as a distinct ethnic group / **167**	
Figure 27	Entrance to the town of El Ciruelo / **168**	
Figure 28	Entrance to the town of Santo Domingo Armenta / **168**	
Figures 29–32	Scenes from Cuajinicuilapa in the state of Guerrero / **169**	
Figure 33	Current president of *México Negro*, Sergio Peñalosa / **170**	
Figure 34	Father Glyn Jemmott Nelson with Paulette Ramsay / **170**	
Figures 35–36	Traditional houses in Tapextla / **171**	
Figure 37	Vendor in Cuajinicuilapa / **172**	
Figure 38	Banner on display in the *XI Encuentro de pueblos* / **172**	
Figure 39	Woman in the street in Lagunillas / **173**	
Figure 40	Women in workshop / **173**	
Figure 41	Small library with information on the black heritage of Afro-Mexicans located in the town of El Ciruelo / **174**	

Foreword

Father Glyn Jemmott Nelson

The process of self-discovery in the life of an individual is a necessary step on the road to self-acceptance and with it an ability to harmonize disjointed and conflicting histories, to reconcile past with present, and to celebrate what is unique at each turn on the uneven road to the present. It is the same with nations: each chapter of a nation's history, each tributary that has contributed to its growth, each social and ethnic minority must be accepted and accounted for, as a sign of reparation, albeit symbolic, of past injustices, of recognizing "who we are", and of a collective commitment to equality, for all its citizens in the future.

For Afro-Mexicans, descendants of enslaved Africans brought into New Spain during the first three centuries of colonial rule, recognition and acceptance have been delayed, due to their reduced and scattered presence among more than sixty different "indigenous" groups, but primarily the result of Mexico's self-avowed mestizo credentials. The author of these pages does not dwell for long on the reasons for this delay, nor on the resulting injustices and inequalities black Mexicans have endured. She focuses on their survival; on the tributary role they have played at every moment of Mexico's history; during the early expansion and conquests, driving with their labour, the economic transformations of the colonial period, as "caudillos" and as soldiers in the wars of independence, and in their silent and invisible presence in contemporary Mexico.

Behind the "official" silence and "out of sight" of most Mexicans, much of what was brought from Africa centuries ago has been preserved and continues to reveal itself in music, in regional festivals of Veracruz and along the Pacific Coast, in culinary styles, in their folk dances, language and religious practices and especially in the patterns of association and kinship which have survived, allowing Mexico's Afro-Mestizos – *afro-mixtecos/morenos/prietos* or just plain *negros* – to seek each other out and to continue their search for a place in the Mexico of today.

Paulette Ramsay focuses on Afro-Mexicans on the Costa Chica. In the state of Oaxaca, Afro-Mexicans are to be found in all three political districts which comprise the Coastal Region: Jamiltepec, Juquila and Pochutla, with the largest number in the district of Jamiltepec. Among the villages with a more than 80 per cent Afro-Mexican population are El Ciruelo, Estancia Grande, Rancho Nuevo, Santa María Cortijos and Santiago Llano Grande, El Magüey, San Juan Bautista de Soto, Corralero, Collantes and Lagunillas. Others, with a significant, though not majority black population are Pinotepa Nacional, Santa Rosa, Río Grande and Santa María Huazolotitlán.

A similar situation is to be found in the neighbouring state of Guerrero. There are at least thirty medium to small communities with majority Afro-descendant populations. The largest and best known is Cuajinicuilapa, whose ethnic, social and cultural history has been the subject of a study by Gonzalo Aguirre Beltrán (in *Cuijla, Esbozo etnográfico de un pueblo negro*, 1958). Even Acapulco itself, a city of approximately 1.2 million is home to thousands of Afro-Mexicans. History shows this has been so since the earliest colonial period. One might affirm that generally, the Afro-descendant population is concentrated along the four-hundred-kilometre stretch from Acapulco in Guerrero to Huatulco in the state of Oaxaca, an area they share with the mestizo population and with various indigenous ethnic groups, among them the *Amuzgos, Mixtecos* and *Zapotecas*.

The largest concentration is to be found in the forty villages situated in the area around Cuajinicuilapa in Guerrero and Pinotepa Nacional in Oaxaca. Apart from these settled migrants, everyone in El Ciruelo is Afro-descendant, in spite of the varying "skin complexions" that hit the eye. The saying "in El Ciruelo eleven out of every ten are black" is hardly an exaggeration. The same is also true for the most of the villages on the Costa Chica.

This volume presented by Paulette Ramsay comes at a time when the sons and daughters of Africa throughout the Americas are seeking each other out in a more intense and determined fashion than was common decades ago. One can correctly refer to the latter decades of the twentieth century as a time of "Afro-descendant reunion" in the Americas. The journey inland, which began when our forefathers stepped off the slave ship onto the different shores of Cartagena and Bahia, Santo Domingo and Havana, Portobello and Kingston, Barbados, Mobile and Veracruz, making us strangers to the African homeland and to each other, has reversed its course. It is now a journey of return, out of the urban and rural enclaves where we have been confined and out of the self-imposed silence of many generations, towards new "spaces", multiple meeting places in conferences, expositions and celebrations of a shared religious, social and cultural heritage: the material and spiritual footprints left by Africans in their five-hundred-year journey across America and the islands of the Caribbean.

More than merely academic moments, these reunions are occasions for celebration. Long separated by language and changing national boundaries, Afro-Latin and Afro-descendants generally are meeting each other once more. For a long time shut in and blinded by racial and socially ascribed identities, these reunions provide a space where we can see ourselves "differently", and remind ourselves where we have come from, who we really are and what is really ours as a people.

It should be no surprise that the social and cultural processes that have shaped the identity of black Mexicans attract the interest of a prominent Jamaican scholar; one might venture to affirm that for Afro-Mexicans, the voice of the author and of "others" who have known similar struggles and have made similar journeys, is essential to the struggle to break out of their "silence", as it is for all those attempting the return to the shores where their journey inland began. It is in these diaspora reunions, wherever they occur, where disjointed and conflicting histories, and inherited hurts are shared, where silence is broken, where unseen struggles are recognized, where identities are strengthened and where lingering injustices can be addressed. But more, much more, takes place at these revisited shores: Jamaicans hold hands with black Mexicans. Panamanians and Haitians sit together and share their stories; Brazilians and Colombians, Barbadians and people of the Dominican Republic, Ecuadorians and Guatemalans, Hondurans and Peruvians, Cubans and Trinidadians, in a new language and a vision enriched by sharing, find answers to many of the questions that Ramsay pursues in her book: "questions of place, of belonging, of pride, of national and individual agency and subjectivity". Through close attention to the chapters which follow, the reader is guaranteed a privileged place in an ongoing diaspora reunion.

El Centro Cultural Cimarrón

These photographs of artwork are used with the kind permission of Father Glyn Jemmott Nelson. The images were created by participants in a workshop established and organized by Father Glyn in the town of El Ciruelo, Municipio de Santiago, Pinotepa Nacional, Oaxaca, Mexico, where he worked as the priest of the local Catholic church for twenty-eight years. The workshop was called El Centro Cultural Cimarrón (the Maroon Cultural Centre) and functioned from 1986 to 2007.

Mario Guzman Olivares was co-founder of the centre and an instructor there for more than twelve years. Many of the participants whose artwork appears in this volume were children at the time: Victor Palacios Camacho, Blanca Liévano Torres, Alberta Hernández Nicolás, Santa Obdulia Hernández Nicolás, Diana Laura Carmona Sánchez, Elder Ávila Palacios, Miguel Angel Vargas Jarquin, Martin Hernández Aguilar, Guillermo Vargas Alberto, Balthazar Castellano Melo and Ayde Rodríguez

Figures 1–6. Artwork samples from Father Glyn Jemmott Nelson's workshop (1986 to 2007)

Figure 7. *Metal pueblo de gusto* by Elder Ávila Palacios (2004)

Acknowledgements

This book is the result of many years of research which took me to many places in and outside of Mexico and also brought numerous interesting persons into my life.

I would like to thank the Mona Research Committee (Office of the Principal) for granting me a research fellowship which allowed me time to do much of this research. I am especially indebted to Joseph Pereira, former deputy principal of the University of the West Indies, Mona, who led me to Afro-Mexico when he presented me with a copy of the book *Jamás fandango al cielo* and subsequently, much of the material he had collected during the time he himself spent on the Costa Chica. I also benefited greatly by his own published research (among the first of its kind on Afro-Mexico). He has supported and provided advice for this research from its inchoate stages.

I am very grateful to all those persons who diligently read and commented on different sections of the manuscript: Marvin Lewis, Carl Campbell, Verene Shepherd, Jerome Branche, Melva Persico and Curdella Forbes. I have to make special mention of Anne-María Bankay's and Curdella Forbes's time spent doing careful proofreading of the text. I am grateful for the affirmation of the work provided by Jerome Branche who has included a section of chapter 4 in his forthcoming book and to Michael Niblett and Kerstin Oloff for publishing a section of chapter 1 in their book *Perspectives on the "Other America": Comparative Approaches to Caribbean and Latin American Culture*.

I could not have completed this book without the encouragement of several persons – family members, friends, colleagues and students. I thank Althea Aikens for the many, many hours she spent helping to prepare the manuscript. Peta-Gay Betty and Tamika Maise must be recognized for their help in different ways. I must express sincere appreciation for the interest and encouragement of Ingrid McLaren, Carolyn Cooper, Anne-Marie Pouchet, Waibinte Wariboko and Paulette Kerr. To Elisa Rizo of Iowa State University, who constantly reminded me to "finish that book on Afro-Mexico", I say thank you, thank you.

It was my great pleasure and honour to meet and spend several hours with Father Glyn Jemmott Nelson, who freely shared with me about his multifaceted experiences, living and working for more than thirty years among Afro-Mexicans on the Costa Chica de Guerrero y Oaxaca. I learned so much from him that helped to enhance and shape this book. His dedication to bringing the existence of Afro-Mexicans to the fore will always be remembered and honoured. I will cherish the warm smiles, expressions of appreciation and the love with which I was met in every Afro-Mexican community on the Costa Chica of Oaxaca and Guerrero, once I mentioned his name.

Special thanks to María Elisa Velásquez Gutiérrez for allowing me to use the map, her photograph of the Devil Dance and one image of an Afro-Mexican girl. My heartfelt gratitude to the artist Elder Ávila Palacios for permission to reproduce his representation of a typical setting in which the *corridos* would be sung (figure 7).

I am very grateful to the University of the West Indies Press and its competent editorial team for the work on this manuscript.

Finally, to the many friends I have made in the Afro-Mexican towns of El Ciruelo, Santo Domingo, Tapextla, San Nicolás and Cuijinicuilapa – especially Sergio Peñalosa and his family – I say, *Mil gracias*. I will always remember their generosity and warmth. I wait with them for Mexico to recognize them as full citizens of Mexican nation.

Note about Translations

While I have done most of the translations, I must thank Karen Henry, Bradna McLaren, Peter Bailey and Charles Ball for varying degrees of help with some translations. I also acknowledge Michael Niblett and Kerstin Oloff for their translation of a few verses in chapter 5.

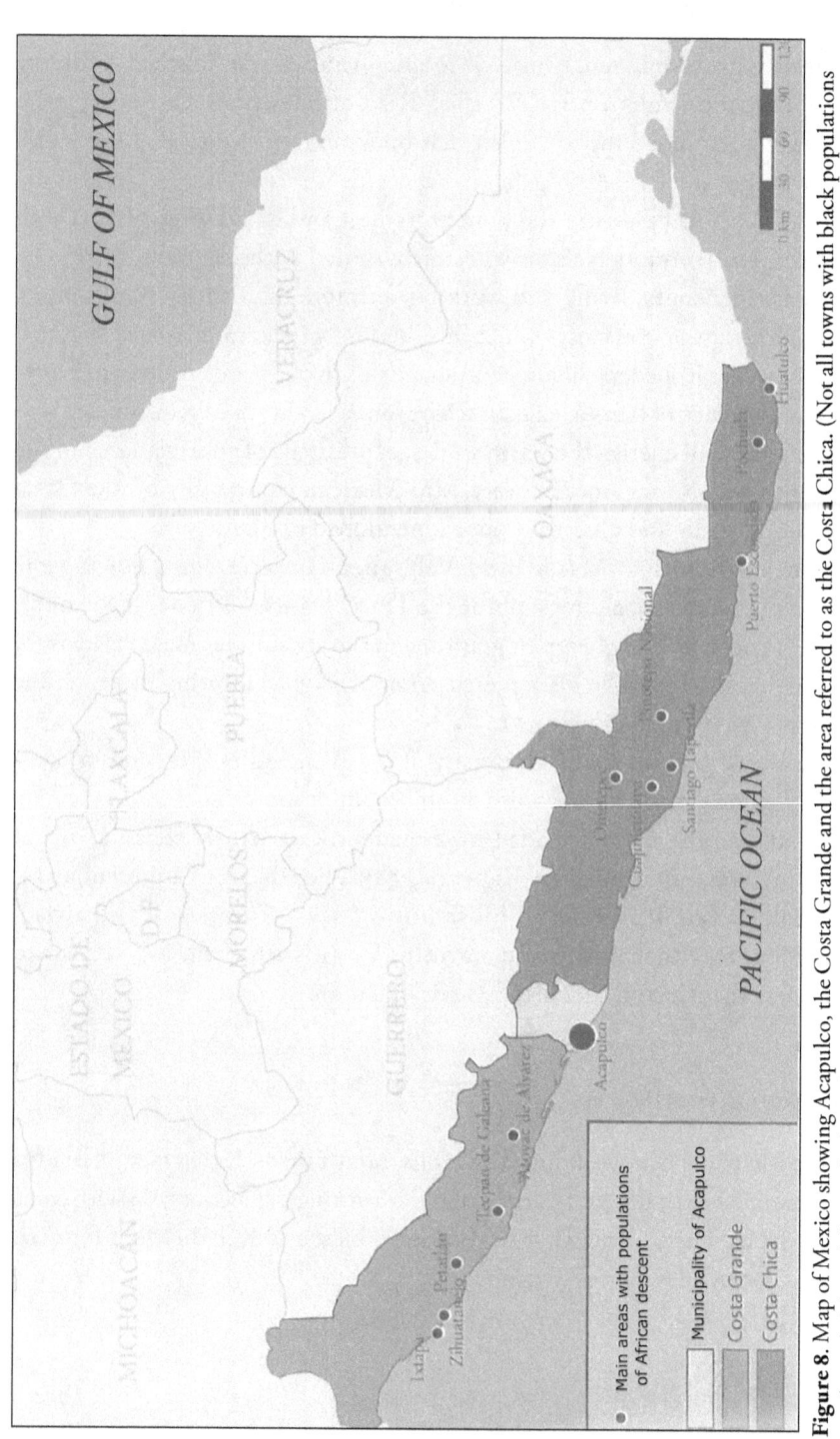

Figure 8. Map of Mexico showing Acapulco, the Costa Grande and the area referred to as the Costa Chica. (Not all towns with black populations are shown.) Adapted from *Afrodescendientes en México* with the kind permission of María Elisa Velázquez.

Introduction

In the nations of Latin America, people of African ancestry are an estimated one-quarter of the total population. The former plantation zones of Latin America were powerfully and irrevocably shaped by the presence of Africans and their descendants.
—George Andrews, *Afro-Latin America*

In the first years of the 21st century, almost five hundred years after the conquest, it is surprising that Mexicans as well as foreigners are still shocked on discovering the black presence in Mexico.
—Ben Vinson III and Bobby Vaughn, *Afroméxico*

From as far back as 1810, the Mexican government ceased the inclusion of ethnic groupings in its census data (Muhammad 1995). Despite this determined attempt to counter perceptions of Mexico's ethnic heterogeneity, the evidence continues to refute the claims of homogeneity. Indeed, the past two decades have produced an increasing amount of material from scholars in various disciplines such as anthropology, film studies, music, dance and cultural studies, to confirm that Mexican racial and cultural identity is neither fixed nor homogenous. Historian George Andrews (2004, 7) forcefully supports this position, by declaring that "Mexico is a multiracial society based on the historical experience of plantation society". This and other similar claims continue to unsettle Mexico's official characterization of the country as one that has been produced by a process of *mestizaje* or the cultural and racial whitening of all other ethnic groups.

Blacks in the Pre-Columbian and Conquest Periods in Mexico

Ivan Van Sertima (1992) declares that Egyptians and Nubians arrived in Mexico as far back as the thirteenth century. As support for this bold claim, he offers the striking similarities between the Olmec heads at La Venta, Tabasco and San Lorenzo and the head of King Taharka, a Nubian-Kushite ruler of ancient Egypt, as well as the resemblance of all of these to traceable features of African tribes. Additionally, Van Sertima (1992) points to the discovery of a "colossal granite head of a Negro" in 1862, on the site of Canton, Tuxtla. Indeed, this discovery led renowned Mexican historian Manuel Orozco y Berra to write about the inescapability and certainty of a pre-Columbian African-Mexican connection (Van Sertima 1992, 24).

Undoubtedly, blacks have played a pivotal role in Mexico from as early as the 1500s. According to Patrick Carroll (2001, 26) "they participated in virtually every major thrust into the colony". The highly celebrated Mexican anthropologist Gonzalo Aguirre Beltrán established in his book *La población negra de México 1519–1810* (1972) that the importation of blacks into Mexico began with Hernán Cortés in 1519, and Juan Cortés was the first African slave brought to Mexico by Hernán Cortés. Luz Martínez Montiel (1992, 41) also supports this claim in her assertion that the introduction of the first African slaves in Mexico began with the expedition led by the *conquistador* Cortés. Other historians also concur that on 21 April 1519, when Hernán Cortés disembarked for the first time in Veracruz, the three hundred Africans, or *ladinos*,[1] who accompanied his team of *conquistadores* during his expeditions were the first Africans to land in Mexico. Blacks who accompanied Hernán Cortés and Pánfilo de Narváez were considered auxiliaries and "personal slaves" (Herrera Casasús 1991). Although historians have, for the most part, treated Africans as auxiliaries in the Spanish conquistadorial mission to Mexico, the number and presence of these Africans made the conquest group formidable, while their active participation aided the Spanish subjugation of the Nahuas and the eventual conquest of Tenochitlán, renamed Mexico City (Herrera Casasús 1991, 16). Arguably, then, the conquest of Tenochitlán is not solely attributable to the Spaniards; rather, their victories were gained with the full support of blacks. Despite their contribution to the Spanish conquest in Mexico, blacks were not placed in the same prominent rank as the Spanish, but relegated to a lower position. Moreover, the Spanish did not give blacks the praise or acclaim they deserved or even a passing mention in the history of the *conquistadores*. Instead, the only compensation awarded to the Africans after "major battles fought" (Bennett 2005, 15) were positions as "retainers, soldiers, auxiliaries with booty, freedom, and occasionally even an *encomienda*",[2] which served as an incentive to lure blacks to enlist in future expeditions for the pursuit of fame and glory.

Africans were viewed as auxiliary to the Spanish plans for occupation and colonization. Occupation took place through the settlement by the conquistador groups and the initiation of more migrations into Mexico. The intention of the Spanish crown and church was to "civilize" the indigenous Indians in order to make them more submissive to Spanish control as, in the course of the gradual establishment of Spanish occupation, the need arose for a more pacific form of conquest which was effected through Christianization. However, blacks (*ladinos*) who accompanied the conquistadores were no strangers to Christianity as they had been introduced to Catholicism in Spain, prior to their arrival in Mexico. This had been done to solidify the religious unity necessary for Spanish acculturation. The fact that they also demonstrated familiarity with the Castillan language (Aguirre Beltrán 1972, 157) gave further reason to believe that the Africans had been successfully proselytized prior to their arrival in the New World. So, Christianization and the acquisition of Spanish by blacks were considered to be indispensable to their integration into the Spanish colonial culture.

When the Spaniards first arrived in Mexico, they found major religious and cultural differences in the practices of indigenous groups, which they felt compelled to eliminate by Christianization. The interactions between Spanish and *ladinos* during the conquest period afforded greater social status and "social fluidity" to the latter, but once Spain established its dominion over New Spain this familiarity became dispensable.[3] Thus, blacks such as Juan Cortés and Juan Garrido, who were allies of the Spanish in the conquest of Mexico, were later relegated to a lower status in the social hierarchy. With the arrival of greater numbers of African slaves or *bozales*,[4] Africans became synonymous with slaves and vice versa and, as a result, all blacks came to be regarded as slaves.

The small group of West African blacks who were listed with the Spanish *conquistadores* and who shared in the conquest of Central Veracruz, were placed at a lower social rank than *ladinos* upon their insertion into Mexican society. Patrick Carroll (2001, 80) asserts that this was due to their Afro-ethnic identification in the newly instituted colonial social order.

Blacks in Colonial Mexico

The introduction and increase of enslaved Africans and the dissemination of the ideology of black inferiority by the Spanish in Mexico in the sixteenth century, following the overthrow of the Moors in the Iberian Peninsula, occurred as acts of revenge and psychological annihilation. In the first place, because the Moors who were Africans had occupied the Iberian Peninsula, their defeat was regarded as retribution. According to Ben Vinson III (2004, 24), the Moorish occupation between 711 and 1492, during which the Moors governed large extensions of the peninsula, allowed open and direct international relations between Africa and Spain both militarily and economically. Spain was aided by Portugal in the Granada War, which saw the Moors defeated, while the Spanish regained power and reclaimed their freedom. Spain and Portugal, military allies in the war and economic allies afterwards, subsequently "consolidated their frontiers through the reconquest in the fifteenth century" (ibid., 25).[5]

The need for labour in New Spain, which resulted in the inauguration of the trade in enslaved Africans, was fuelled by both demographic and economic factors. At first, in the course of the conquest, indigenous Indians were initiated into slavery and divided among the soldiers and settlers of the conquest generation. The near extinction of the indigenous population through exploitation and imported epidemic diseases from Europe resulted in the reduction of the labour force. Consequently, the Spaniards' agenda for expansion became severely hindered. Bartolomé de las Casas then declared in 1511 that Africans were needed to "replace the *indio* who was being exterminated at an alarming rate of 4 million within the first twelve years of the conquest" (Muhammad 1995, 164).

Blacks were chosen to fill the gap created by this decline as the need for labour increased (Vaughn 2004, 76). Blacks were considered to be more resilient than Indians, more suited, in particular, for work in the mining and sugar industries. Aguirre Beltrán (1972, 156) asserts that "el indio considerado flaco y débil fue aliviado de la cargá que pesaba sobre sus hombros a costa de los hombres de ébano". (The Indian, considered thin and weak, was relieved of the load that weighed on his shoulders at the expense of men of Ebony.) The preference for African labour was therefore due to their purported strength and inherent industry, which made them more attractive considering that the productivity of one black was worth four times that of one *indio* (Muhammad 1995, 165). Eric Williams (1994, 9) also affirms this view of the blacks' physical superiority and strength by citing an incident in which a Spanish official in 1518 requested the recruitment of blacks judged as "robust for labour, instead of natives, so weak that they can only be employed in tasks requiring little endurance such as taking care of maize fields or farms". Subsequently, there was a massive importation of black slaves into Mexico to meet the growing needs of the mines and plantations. According to Carroll (2001), the number between 1521 and 1639 is estimated to be 50 per cent of the total slaves brought to the Western Hemisphere. Andrews (2004, 16) sums this up in his book when he succinctly states that "the societies and economies of Latin America depended enormously on slave labour".

The Trade in Enslaved Africans to Mexico

Mexico's involvement in the trade in enslaved Africans was so extensive that it outrivalled other colonies. Some researchers, such as Carroll (2001, 26), claim that the large number of slaves needed for Mexico meant that "no matter how hard African rulers tried, they could not keep pace with the Mexican-driven need for slaves".[6] European traders were forced to divert from trading with Congo kings to other means of acquiring slaves which proved more economical and profitable. The source turned out to be interior leaders who were less scrupulous and more avaricious (Carroll 2001). In highlighting the vigorous slave trade that developed in Mexico to meet its labour demands, Andrews (2004, 17) states that "during the first century of colonization (1520–1620), as the Indian population fell from ten to twelve million to less than one million, local slave-owners imported an estimated eighty-six thousand Africans. Then during the 1700s – as the Indian population began to recover, growing to some three million by 1800 – slave imports fell to fewer than twenty thousand, despite the rapid economic growth and increasing demand for labourers."

During slavery, miscegenation was encouraged as a tool of population expansion in underpopulated areas. However, the rapid exponential rate at which Africans interbred with native Indians later created fear among the Spaniards, causing the Spanish to impose restrictions on sexual relations between Indians and Africans. Threatened by a surge of intermarriages between the two groups, the Spanish authorities soon declared exogamous relations illegal. Legislative decrees were issued by Spanish officials to set the parameters for determining social stratification and hierarchical ordering in Mexico's sixteenth-century society (1530–1550s), based on the Hispano-Catholic religion. The demarcation established between Spanish blood and the blood of "the others", ensured that Africans and their descendants were subordinated. David Davidson (1973, 84–85) postulates that these (essentially royalty-driven) caste laws were intended to set out privileges and set "limitations" pertaining to the slaves' place within the society. The church also played a political role by arguing that slavery was acceptable on the basis of Christian principles and practices. However, it may be also argued that the church was really interested in helping to secure and maintain a steady labour supply and evinced bias towards the enforcers of slavery.

Despite the restrictions imposed on miscegenation, relations among Africans and Indians persisted and their hybrid descendants continued to multiply, to the annoyance of the Spanish. The *sistema de castas* was introduced to classify the population born of Indian-African sexual relations. The perception of Africans as enjoying neither acceptable social status nor appropriate ethnicity was bolstered. The social demarcations were enforced by church officials such as priests, whose duty included the registration and record keeping of births and marriages for municipalities and cities.

Race Relations in the Colonial Period

The denigration of blacks during slavery and colonization occurred both on the physical and psychological levels. They were demeaned in various ways that underscored the very negative perception of them held by the Spanish. This was evidenced by the myriad epithets assigned to blacks by the Spanish such as "mala raza" (evil race), "gente sin razón" (senseless people), "gente de mala sangre" (people with bad blood, mongrels). Some researchers such as Jameelah Muhammad (1995, 167) posit that Africans and mulattoes were represented in this negative way as justification for "the brutal oppression to which they were routinely subjected". According to Edith Sanders (1969), these misconceptions followed a long tradition of making a genetic argument in which the black race was depicted as being "sinful" and their progeny as "degenerates", in supposed accordance with their physiognomical characteristics. The colour of their skin and other physical features, such as their Negroid hair, were regarded as indications of their being damned to perpetual "fornication and theft" and set the schema for them to be looked upon with undesirability (p. 522). Blacks in Mexico were not excluded from these specious claims and suffered the consequences of this perception of them as naturally diabolical.

As a consequence, black slaves in colonial Mexico were allowed neither religious freedom nor freedom to practise their own African customs and traditions. Spanish slave-owners completely opposed Afro-Mexican religions or cultural practices associated with African folk beliefs, which were classified as witchcraft, sorcery and divination. Further, little protection existed for blacks in the courts, as there were legal restrictions and limitations to freedom of expression for slaves, even if they were in the right. In a well-researched article entitled "Integration Patterns and the Assimilation Process of Negro Slaves in Mexico", Martínez Montiel (1992, 452) underscores the rigidity of the laws, which prescribed harsh punishment for any slave who "even dared to protest verbally against his master".

Afro-Mexican Marronage, Rebellion and the Movement for Independence

From as early as about 1522, three years after the conquest of Tenochitlán (Mexico City), blacks fled from the service of their masters and were found roaming the Zapotecas region (Aguirre Beltrán 1972, 205). Slaves were driven into a life of marronage by the harsh working conditions in the mines and haciendas. Two thousand slaves, then representing one-tenth of the slave population, allegedly escaped to the mountains in 1579 (Davidson 1973, xiv). In 1609, the Maroon community of Yanga became the first such community to fight for self-government and the right to own land. The Maroon warrior Yanga (known also as Prince Ñanga) conducted concessionary negotiations with the crown's representative and obtained land rights and privileges for his Maroon town, San Lorenzo de los Negros, later renamed Yanga.[7] In 1609, Yanga became the first free town, not just in Mexico, but in the Americas (Martínez Montiel 1992, 452).

Although Yanga is regarded as the most famous Mexican *palenque* still in existence, its Afro-Mexican population is practically non-existent today, partly because most of its residents relocated to the neighbouring town of Mata Clara, but also as a result of racial mixing (Muhammad 1995, 167).

Carroll (2001, 490) maintains that unlike the Ecuadorian Maroons in Esmeraldas who were "absorbed but never conquered", thus managing to maintain some independence, cohesiveness and distinctiveness, Yanga suffered from an untimely "death" due to rapid racial dilution. After the Yanga Maroon community was upgraded to town status in 1609, joint efforts were formalized between the colonial government and Yanga for the recapture of runaway slaves and, as a result, full militia responsibilities were conferred on the town (Vinson III 2001, 22). This military commission was offensive to the Spanish. It was agreed on because of the double benefits: first, the expertise of Maroons was crucial to combat subversive activities and to uncover hideaways or fortresses because of their familiarity with such settings or terrain; and second, the context and means were provided to acculturate Maroons into becoming "obliging citizens in a colonial society" (Vinson III 2001, 22). Their collaboration with this agenda and their subsequent deviation from strictly preserving African identity and ethnicity, resulted in racial amalgamation with the result that they became "racially and ethnically indistinguishable from the other settlements that dotted the area, after a few generations" (Muhammad 1995, 166). However, there are other Afro-Mexican communities which did not suffer the same fate as Yanga, as later discussion will reveal.

Blacks in Mexico constantly rebelled against the oppression meted out to them under the colonial system until it eventually crumbled. The persistence of discrimination against them and the segregation they experienced influenced their involvement in the War of Independence as they chose to fight for social, economic and political equality – equal opportunities and recognition for Afro-Mexicans as part of the nation. Hostilities began with the Hidalgo rebellion of 1810 which eventually spread to the slave plantations of Veracruz. Slaves were encouraged to flee the plantation and join the rebels who were fighting against colonial rule (Andrews 2004, 58).

Without question then, Mexico's independence was won with the aid of blacks who fought in the War of Independence to help free the country from oppressive colonial rule. Blacks readily joined the revolution because they regarded it as a way of ending slavery, as well as gaining national independence. Among the black fighters were Vicente Guerrero – popularly known as *El Negro Guerrero*, who later became president of Mexico, and José María Morelos, who became a general in the War of Independence. The Mexican states of Guerrero and Morelia were renamed in honour of these two black Mexicans.

The struggle for independence was also a fight to end the caste regime in order to establish racial equality. In Latin America the first call to end the caste laws was made in Mexico by Miguel Hidalgo, who was executed in 1811 after leading an uprising. José María Morelos then assumed command of the rebellion. Morelos declared his commitment to racial equality, land reform and the abolition of slavery and led a group of rebels against Spanish troops. Following the execution of Morelos in 1815, Vicente Guerrero continued the guerrilla warfare and eventually succeeded in striking a deal with the Spanish authorities for the caste laws to be repealed (Andrews 2004, 87).

The fight for independence from Spain, which was initiated by blacks, was later taken over by creole elites who took the reins in the final leg of the journey to independence and claimed the glory for the post-independence gains. Carroll (2001, 153) expressly states that the elites "made limited concessions to non-whites that did little more than recognize some of the gains the latter had made in the mid and late colonial periods". The post-independence climate showed greater uncertainty for black mobility and more inclination for "greater equality from the middle sectors of society" (ibid.). Consequently, during the colonial period, disenfranchised blacks received voting rights and the privilege to be elected to public office, signaling a repudiation of the racially and ethnically based inequities of the colonial system" (Carroll 2001, 131).

In 1824, Guerrero was aided into the presidency by free blacks and a mulatto militia. Guerrero and his supporters nourished bitter memories of the Spanish caste laws, Spanish tax collectors and Spanish domination (largely enabled by the caste laws) of wholesale and retail commerce. Once in power, he signed decrees expelling all Spaniards from Mexico, abolishing slavery and barring the importation of goods which competed with those made by local artisans. He angered conservatives who called for "death to the negro" and was eventually executed (Andrews 2004, 94).

Post-independence Mexico witnessed little change in the socio-economic realm. The newly freed slave was still subjected to his ex-master's will, and instability manifested in resentment and hostility. Without education or formal training, economic resources, or security, and unable to find suitable jobs, blacks found themselves increasingly more dependent and locked into servitude. Many sought to remain as servants to their old masters. María Luisa Herrera Casusús (1991, 130) forcefully declares: "El antiguo esclavo sin instrucción, sin educación, carente de tierras y de medios económicos, se sujetó voluntariamente a sus antiguos amos por un sueldo exiguo o por limosna al que iba añido al rencor de su amo." (The former slave, without learning, without education, lacking lands and economic means, voluntarily subjected himself to his former owners for a meagre salary or lived off begging, which only increased the wrath of their owners.) Furthermore, the legacy of the caste laws still influenced the manner in which blacks were treated, even though slavery was abolished.

For decades following the end of the Mexican Revolution in 1910, Afro-Mexicans were excluded from official Mexican discourse on the nation. This was mainly the result of efforts made by José Vasconcelos Calderón, minister of education in Mexico between 1921 and 1924, who buttressed previously existing plans to erase Mexicans of African descent from the history of Mexico. Miguel Alberto Bartolomé (1997, 27) affirms that "after the Revolution of 1910 when the repression of cultural plurality became more intense about the indigenous past despite the rhetorical exegesis about the indigenous past, it was assumed that cultural homogenization was a necessary condition for the configuring of a modern nation". José Vasconcelos Calderón's (1925) famous essay "La raza cósmica: misión de la raza iberoamericana" ("The Cosmic Race: Mission of the Iberoamerica Race") was central to the formulations of modern, post-revolution Mexico's national identity which aimed for the homogenization of all ethnicities under the ideology of *mestizaje*. *Mestizaje* rejected the existence of different races in Mexico, advancing the true Mexican as *mestizo*, which in Vasconcelos's (1925) view was part of a "cosmic race – a sort of synthesis of all known races called to hold world supremacy in the future and therefore, the logically determined referent in the process of national constructions" (Bartolomé 1997, 28). In one of his shocking declarations Vasconcelos (1925, 32) stated: "The Indian, by grafting onto the related race, would take a jump of millions of years . . . and in a few decades of aesthetic eugenics, the black may disappear, together with the types that a free instinct of beauty may go on signaling as fundamentally recessive and undeserving." Visibly black Mexicans were neglected and left in remote areas of the country while popular discourse promulgated the myth that they had eventually become totally diluted and absorbed. Some even claimed that "las características físicas del negro han desaparecido" (the physical characteristics of blacks have disappeared) (Del Toro 1921, 8). This myth became so dominant and masked Mexico's heterogeneity to such an extent that even visibly black Mexicans and descendants of indigenous groups accepted the ideology of *mestizaje* and apparently ended up with no consciousness of race or of themselves as blacks or as indigenous peoples. As Marco Polo Hernández Cuevas (2004, 4) argues: "En México, el discurso de nación fomenta la exclusión del negro. Adultera la memoria y provoca que los retoños de los negros, cautivos de la ideología blanqueadora, por lo regular no sean capaces de reconocerse sino como descendientes de españoles e indios; y precisamente en tal orden." (In Mexico, the discourse of the nation promotes the exclusion of blacks. It falsifies memory and causes the children of blacks – captives of the whitening ideology – in general to be unable to recognize themselves as anything other than descendants of the Spanish and the indigenous population; and precisely in this order.) People of African descent remained in obscurity and abject neglect until the 1940s when Mexican anthropologist Aguirre Beltrán conducted systematic research in communities with African-derived people on the Costa Chica, between the states of Guerrero and Oaxaca on the south Pacific coast of Mexico. Aguirre Beltrán's studies exploded the myth that African-derived persons had been completely erased from Mexico's history through processes such as interracial marriage and that even though population censuses no longer documented the presence of a distinct group of Afro-Mexicans, they still existed. Aguirre Beltrán's first work *La población negra de México* (*Mexico's Black Population*) (1946) was initially well received. However, despite the book's immediate success, it failed to spark interest in the study of the historical role of blacks in Mexico, a fact that Aguirre Beltrán laments in his prologue to the second edition to his book in 1972. In contrast to the state-sponsored research into the conditions of the Amerindian ethnic groups, the Afro-Mexican heritage did not become the focus of governmental research until the 1980s and 1990s.

Since the 1980s and 1990s, a number of persons, mainly academics both within and outside of Mexico, have also challenged misleading reports of previous historians who had been intent on showing that Mexico's non-white ethnic groups comprised mainly *mestizos* – "la raza mixta" (mixed race) – and that soon the transition would be completed "así todos llegarían a ser blancos" (in this way everyone would become white) (Molina Enríquez 1909, 345). Among them are Luz María Martínez Montiel, Colin Palmer, Jameelah Muhammad, Adriana Nariela, Patrick Carroll, Herman Bennett, Guadelupe Casteñon, Carlos Paredes Martínez, Luz María Velasquez, Ben Vinson III, Bobby Vaughn, María Elisa Velázquez and Gabriela Iturralde Nieto. A significant consequence of Aguirre Beltrán's (1972) insistence that *mestizaje* had failed to "vaporize" blacks was the establishment of various projects by the Dirección General de Culturas Populares, which sought to promote research in the various Afro-Mexican communities to preserve those aspects of their culture which still survived among them. These programmes became especially popular in the 1980s and 1990s when collections such as *Traigo una flor hermosa y mortal* (*I Bring Beautiful and Deadly Flowers*), a recording of Afro-Mexican *corridos* sung by an Afro-Mexican band, *Los cimarrones* (the Maroons), *Jamás fandango al cielo* (*Never Again a Party in the Sky*), a collection of Afro-Mexican folktales, were produced and later *Alma cimarrona* (*Maroon Soul*) (1999), a collection of *coplas, décimas* and other poems, was published. The attempts at giving attention to these artistic forms have become more frequent as it appears evident that the Afro-Mexican society is a threatened one. The level of community participation indicates that despite the totalizing system of *mestizaje* and the Eurocentric culture of Mexico, Afro-Mexicans have maintained their heritage of diversity.

Blacks in Contemporary Mexico

Despite the Afro-Mexicans' role in the liberation of Mexico, and their participation in the development of the country and other cultural and societal contributions, they continue to be written out of existence by the failure of Mexican governments to recognize them as an integral part of the Mexican nation. Afro-Mexicans have limited access to civic institutions and little opportunity to participate in the political processes of the country. The official position in Mexico continues to be that Afro-Mexicans have disappeared into history through systematic miscegenation. Even more disconcerting is the perception held by Mexicans regarding the black presence in Mexico. Colin Palmer (1990, 1), in a forceful article entitled "Africa's Legacy in Mexico: A Legacy of Slavery", disclosed after a visit to Mexico in 1990, a general perception held by many Mexicans that "Mexico had never imported slaves from Africa". Undoubtedly, this amnesia regarding Mexico's historical past denies Mexico's blacks their role and place in the country. It is indeed ironic and lamentable that a section of Mexican society, which has played such a central role in the building of the country from the age of the *conquistadores*, has very little traceable history as far as many Mexicans are concerned.

The Mexican government launched a national programme entitled *Nuestra Tercera Raíz* (Our Third Root) in 1989 under the National Council for Culture and the Arts for the purpose of recognizing Africa as Mexico's third root. Under this programme studies were carried out on slavery in the Americas, on the oral and musical traditions, religious beliefs, traditional medicine, and the aesthetic codes of people of African descent. The programme also highlighted cultural activities in communities where the specific cultural forms of expression of people of African descent survive, with the aim of granting them recognition, status and stimulation as a constituent element of natural identity (CERD 1965, 2). However, despite the various promotional activities launched by the Ministry of Foreign Affairs and reports submitted under article 9 of the UN Committee for the Elimination of Racial Discrimination, in 2006 there still were no official statistics of communities of Afro-Mexicans. Moreover, in 2010, the National Institute of Geography and Statistics was still exploring the possibility of including persons of African descent in Mexico as a category. This means that the *Nuestra Tercera Raíz* (Our Third Root) programme was highly unsuccessful since, as late as the twenty-first century, blacks still remain statistically undocumented. One is therefore led to question whether the programme was politically motivated or was undertaken simply to satisfy the United Nations' mandate to end racial discrimination worldwide. In November 2003, the Ministry of Education in Mexico also launched a Multicultural Mexico Project. This involved broadcasts, on free television channels and official satellite channels, intended to highlight Mexico's linguistic, cultural and racial diversity. These programmes ceased in 2006. Today the vast majority of Mexicans are still unaware of any official acknowledgements of the African contribution to Mexican culture. Among those who know of this involvement, their knowledge is limited to recognition that blacks did contribute to some aspects of Mexican culture, but there persists a general lack of understanding that there are still persons of African descent in Mexico.

Impecunious Living Conditions

Several visits to the Costa Chica region by anthropologists and other scholars have confirmed the impoverished conditions in which black Mexicans have lived for decades. In the 1940s, Aguirre Beltrán (1946) conducted research that brought attention to the absence of medical facilities and medical personnel in remote Afro-Mexican communities. He revealed that extremely high rates of mortality existed among women and infants, as a result of diseases such as epilepsy and diarrhoea (p. 180). Presently, some changes are evident, but not on a significant scale. Jonathan Roeder of the *Miami Herald* wrote in October 2007 in a revealing article entitled "Mexico's Blacks Struggle to Unite, Thrive", that municipalities occupied by the Afro-Mexicans are the poorest in the country, with no potable water, with unpaved roads and high rates of illiteracy.

In a memorable interview, Father Glyn affirmed that there have been a few changes since the 1980s as some attention has been given to developing the social services in the areas occupied by blacks. He cites, as an example of improvement, the opening of the Health Centre with a resident doctor in El Circuelo in 1984, the first secondary school that was established in the same town in 1986 amid the paving of the road connecting El Ciruelo to the Coast. However, despite these small achievements, the region remains largely neglected in the twenty-first century, with most of the roads still being unpaved. The impecunious conditions in which Afro-Mexicans continue to reside was again brought to the fore by Archibold (2014), in his observation that "the isolation of the African-Mexican communities, whatever the reasons for it may be, has left many with decrepit schools, roads and services – a neglect and deep poverty that has bred resentment". Indeed, my own visits to many of these communities have revealed the extreme poverty and untenable conditions of neglect and deprivation in which blacks continue to reside on the Costa Chica.

Afro-Mexicans in Mexico's Political Landscape

Mexico's political discourse has been both consciously and subconsciously preoccupied with the exclusion and depreciation of blacks. In fact, claims of homogenization in Mexico are really political ploys designed to exclude some, under the pretence of "racial harmony" and national unity. Indeed, blacks are generally eliminated from participation in the political formation of Mexico by government bureaucrats and others who deem them unfit for such political office. "Afro-Mexicans lack recognition, representation, leadership and participation in the political, economic and educational institutions of their country. While indigenous groups have received national as well as international attention and support, Afro-Mexicans' voices have largely gone unheard" (Muhammad 1995, 178).

The *Partido Revolucionario Institucional* (Institutional Revolutionary Party) led by René Juárez Cisneros attracted a majority membership from among Afro-Mexicans in the state of Guerrero on the Costa Chica in 1999. Ironically, Cisneros himself never acknowledged his Afro-Mexican connections: when he participated in the gubernatorial elections, despite being black and having African ancestral ties, surname and physical characteristics, he never made reference either to his colour or his ethnic affiliation. Vaughn (2004, 89) expressly states:

> En México nunca hubo un dirigente político nacional o estatal que se definiera como negro. Es significativo, entonces, que en 1999 se eligiera como gobernador del estado de Guerrero a un afromexicano de Acapulco, René Juárez Cisernos, del entonces oficial Partido Revolucionario Institucional. A juzgar por sus fotografías en los carteles de campaña y en los sitios web oficiales, el gobernador tiene características físicas similares a las de cualquier moreno de la Costa Chica y su apellido, Cisneros, también apunta a su herencia afromexicana.

> In Mexico there has never been a national or state political leader who has defined himself or herself as black. It is important then that in 1999 an Afro-Mexican from Acapulco in the state of Guerrero René Juárez Cisneros was selected governor of the then official Instiutional Revolutionary Party. Judging by his photographs on the campaign placards and on the official website, the governor has physical characteristics similar to any black person on the Costa Chica and his surname, Cisneros, also points to his Afro-Mexican heritage.

Cisneros was said however, to repeatedly express concern for the plight of the indigenous people, but never mentioned the position of blacks (Vaughn 2004, 89–90). The anthropologist further criticized the fact that Cisneros isolated the largest black community in the state of Guerrero – Cuajinicuilapa – in his campaign, by his failure to even take his campaign to that municipality. Vaughn (2004, 90) stated: "La campaña de Cisneros es un ejemplo de cómo un candidato, en su búsqueda del poder político, se alejó conscientemente de su identidad afromexicana y de cómo la vinculación abierta a la negritud constituye un riesgo político y social en la sociedad mexicana de hoy." (Cisneros's campaign is an example of how a candidate in his search for political power consciously distances himself from his Afro-Mexican identity and how the open link to blackness constitutes a political and social risk in today's Mexico.) Similarly, Randal Archibold (2014) emphasized the ironic reality that "the few politicians with black ancestry who have been elected often play down or deny their family roots, and with intermarriage stretching back to the earliest days of slavery, many Mexicans may be unaware of their African heritage".

The reluctance of Cisneros and many other aspiring Afro-Mexican politicians to openly embrace their African ancestry may be said to reveal the extent to which they also endorse the focus on *indigenismo*. The discourse of *indigenismo* which was the focus of Mexican historiography for decades, promoted the classification of Mexico as being primarily a nation of *indios* and effectively erased blacks from the national consciousness. Given this popular Mexican philosophy of *indigenismo*, any Afrocentric focus would have severely stifled all political ambitions.[8]

Towards a New Discourse on Blacks in Mexico

In his rejection of the discourse of *indigenismo* Vaughn (2004, 83) cites evidence gathered from his own lived experience as well as his extensive research:

> Mis entrevistas y la escasa evidencia documental que habla sobre la mezcla racial en la Costa Chica son consistentes en su caracterización de los pueblos de la Costa Chica como casi totalmente negros. En mi estudio de Collantes no encontré ninguna familia collanteña que identificará un posible linaje indígena, o algún antepasado que hablara un idioma indígena, que llevara ropa tradicional indígena o que proviniera de un pueblo que no fuera negro.

> My interviews and the little documentary evidence, which speak to racial mixing on the Costa Chica are consistent in their characterization of the towns of the Costa Chica as being almost completely black. In my studies of Collantes I found no collanteña families which showed even a possible indigenous link, or some ancestor who spoke any indigenous languages or wore indigenous traditional clothing or originated from a town that was not black.

As demonstration of some measure of acceptance that there is a modicum of black blood in some Mexicans and that the term *indigenismo* excludes blacks from considerations of ethnicity in Mexico, some Mexican academics have conceded to using the term *afromestizo*. The term, however, seems to insist on forwarding the ideology of a mixture of races, which still feeds into the official position of *mestizaje* in Mexico. While it cannot be denied that there is indeed some racial mixing in Mexico, and even in some Afro-Mexican communities, although this is more evident in some communities than others, it must be accepted that there are still persons who are mainly Afro-descendants in Mexico. On my visit to towns such as Santo Domingo, El Ciruelo, Tapextla and Punta Maldonado, I found populations that can be characterized as comprising persons who are undeniably of primarily or completely Negroid heritage. In his repudiation of the term *afromestizo*, Vinson III (2004, 57) categorically states:

> Mexico is the only Latin American country where some scholars still refer to black people as *afromestizo*. Although this term would seem to identify a special characteristic of the Mexican "mixing" in the Costa Chica, individuals recognized today as blacks do not show more particularities of "mixing" than the rest of the black of the African diaspora. In fact, the tonalities of the skin color as well as a wide range of phenotypes are the norm amongst African descendants. Therefore, Mexico is not the exception.

The term Afro-Mexican will be used in this study as an indicator of the acceptance of a position that, contrary to what is commonly believed in Mexico, there are groups of people in Mexico whose existence is not the result of miscegenation which has totally diluted their black blood. Indeed, my study is concerned with blacks who are descendants of slaves who were taken to Mexico during the colonial period and who can still be found mainly along the Costa Chica of Guerrero and Oaxaca and in a small area of Veracruz. My main focus will be on the Costa Chica de Guerrero and Oaxaca.

Besides my own research and personal encounters, one of the most powerful testimonies of the presence of persons of predominantly African descent, in small, remote communities in Mexico is presented by Father Glyn Jemmott Nelson, a Trinidadian Catholic priest who has lived and worked among Afro-Mexicans for more than thirty years. His work has extended way beyond the duties of a priest to include many hours spent trying to raise awareness about blackness among Afro-Mexicans. I have had several engaging and enlightening discussions with Father Glyn, who remains indelibly affected by experiences he has shared with black Mexicans. He explains:

In 1983 I transferred to an indigenous community – San Juan Teitipac – in the state of Oaxaca. After one year there I requested and was allowed to move to Costa Chica on the Pacific Coast where I spent the following twenty-eight years, up to 2012. During my first month in Oaxaca, on getting more precise information on where the black population was located, I travelled there for a brief look around. I spent a few days in the area and there and then decided that this was where I wanted to live and work. I wanted to remain and share the life and struggles of this little corner of Mexico where Afro-Mexicans seem to have been hidden from the world and even from other Mexicans. The then Archbishop, Bartolomé Carrasco Briseño, right away agreed and I moved permanently to the Parish of Santiago Pinotepa Nacional in August 1984. Pinotepa Nacional is a small town (approximately twenty thousand population) with a predominantly mestizo population (55 per cent), a 25 to 30 per cent indigenous Mixteco sector, the Afro-descendant population making up the remaining 15 to 20 per cent.

I remained in the area around Pinotepa Nacional for twenty-eight years. By March of 1985, I moved out of Pinotepa to the small village called El Ciruelo, roughly forty kilometres away. El Ciruelo was almost entirely a black community and sits in the centre of what is the principal area populated by black Mexicans in the state of Oaxaca and the adjoining state of Guerrero. My pastoral duties brought me to a dozen or so all-black communities, and slowly I began to visit for a variety of reasons, the more than forty fully Afro-descendant villages and small towns scattered throughout the area. This area is referred to as Costa Chica of Guerrero and Oaxaca, situated to the south of Acapulco, as distinct from the Costa Grande which refers to the coastal area to the north of the city of Acapulco. (Father Glyn Jemmott Nelson, personal interview, 19 July 2013)

These small black communities referred to by Father Glyn, whose name is well known to all their inhabitants, include:

Guerrero: Cuajinicuilapa, El Pitarroso, San Nicolás, Montesillos, Punta Maldonado, Maldonado, Buenos Aires, Alto de Barranas, Cerro del Indio, Banco de Oro, El Tamarindo, El Tamaic, El Jícaro, El Vaivén, El Quizá, Cerro de las Tablas, Ometepec, El Capricho, Vista Hermosa, Huehuetán, Juchitán.

Oaxaca: Collantes, Morelos, La Boquilla, El Chivo, Corro la Esperanza, Santo Domingo, Tapextla, Lo Desoto, Cortijos, La Estancia, La Culebra, Rancho Nuevo, El Callejón, Lagunillas, El Ciruelo, Rio Grande, Santa Rosa, Cerro Hermoso.

Many Mexicans in other parts of the country continue to be ignorant of these black communities that are so well known to Father Glyn and several researchers, as is evident in the following statement:

> While traveling outside of their communities, black Mexicans say they are stopped routinely by the police and accused of being illegal immigrants from Cuba or Central America. They often endure long stares and even touching of their hair by curious fellow Mexicans. That unfamiliarity comes in part because Mexico's black population, often to escape persecution and discrimination, historically never moved in large numbers to big cities and have kept largely to themselves in scattered communities in three southern states – Oaxaca, Guerrero and Veracruz. (Archibold 2014)

My own research into Afro-Mexican culture and literature has led me to several of these small towns with predominantly black or fully black populations. I have had the distinct privilege of interacting with Afro-Mexicans in the fully Afro-Mexican communities of Santo Domingo, El Ciruelo, Tapextla, as well as with blacks and people of mixed ancestry in Cuajinicuilapa, San Nicolás, Cerro del Indio, Punta Maldonado and Huehuetán.

Afro-Mexicans, for the most part, are involved in small farming for personal consumption. They cultivate crops such as sorrel, corn, vegetables, papaya, watermelon, beans, peppers and cacao. A few who may be considered to be in a slightly comfortable economic position, rear cattle and produce sesame seeds to be sold to large exporters.

Cultural Contributions

Afro-Mexicans have retained and preserved several aspects of their African-derived cultural forms in highly black-populated states such as Guerrero, Oaxaca, Jalisco, Huasteco, Tabisco and Veracruz (Muhammad 1995, 174). The influence of African culture on Mexican music and other cultural forms has been traced by Gabriel Salvador, who uncovers the critical role played by Africans through various phases of the development of Mexico's cultural legacy (Vinson III 2004, 49). With the passing of time and ongoing cultural productions by Afro-Mexicans, there has been a transfer of African musical styles into traditional Mexican music that musicologist Rolando Pérez Fernández (1990) assessed to be "fundamentally the result of the transculturation between the Spanish and the blacks".

The popular musical forms, *tropical, chilena* and *corridos*, found mainly in Pinotepa and other rural areas of the Costa Chica, owe much of their formation to the African influence in the Latin American and Caribbean diaspora. *Tropical,* or more accurately *Acapulco Tropical*, considered to be exclusive to the Acapulco region, has a rhythm characterized as African. These musical genres are adaptations of African cultural forms injected into the broader Mexican culture and bespeak the irrefutability of the African cultural essence and impact.

A powerful musical, poetic and dramatic art form associated with African cultural retention in Mexico is the *corrido*. The *corrido* is generally recognized throughout Mexico as a traditional cultural form associated mainly with the people of the Costa Chica. Each region in which it is practised conforms to the traditional structure, but Vaughn (2004, 86) claims that the Costa Chican *corrido* is distinguished by its particular tone, which he describes as "tono melancólico, acentuado por el uso de claves menores y su contenido violento" (melancholic tone, accentuated by the use of minor keys and its violent content). The *corrido* is commonly practised among Afro-Mexicans in predominantly black communities and is preserved through annual celebratory events along the Costa Chican coast. The performance normally depicts local events such as disputes or assassinations, and even commemorates specific experiences. Muhammad (1995, 174) highlights the importance of the *corrido* in the black communities of this region, which hold annual competitions to display the *corridistas*' talents, as they vie with each other in ballads sung in an Afro-Mexican dialect in either the first- or third-person narrative voice.

The *son jarocho* is a dominant and popular musical form associated with Veracruz, particularly in Afro-Mexican towns such as El Coyolillo. This music has a long history, owing its Mexican origins to blacks who introduced it during slavery. In fact, blacks were derogatorily referred to as *jarocho* when their appearance was considered to be unfavourable and contemptible during slavery. In the records of the nineteenth century, there is evidence of festivities where blacks in Veracruz would assemble in a large street-dance competition which is the basis of the *jarocho*. Ironically, the *jarocho,* a cultural form widely associated with blacks and the geographical areas in which they are concentrated, is said to stand as a regional symbol of identity, irrespective of racial affiliation.

La Danza del Diablo, La Danza de la Tortuga and *El Son de Artesa*

La Danza del Diablo (The Dance of the Devil) is the most acclaimed dance form, which has been performed by Afro-Mexicans in Maroon communities of Costa Chica from the colonial era to the present. It is held in high repute among Afro-Mexicans, but particularly in the Afro-Mexican town of Collantes where it is performed during *Todos Santos* (All Saints Day) in November. It is the most celebrated cultural form in El Ciruelo, Morelos and La Boquilla, as well as in the state of Oaxaca. In the state of Guerrero it is deeply entrenched in the communities of San Nicolás, Lo Desoto and Cuaijinicuilapa. The instruments used in the Dance of the Devil (or Devil Dance) include the harmonica, *charrasca* and *tigrera* (Apodaca 2008, 52). The *charrasca* is a cow's jawbone with the teeth loosened to create a powerful and hoarse (bass) sound as the player rubs the teeth with an ice pick. During my own observation of this energetic dance I found it extremely fascinating to watch this unusual instrument being played. The *tigrera* also referred to as *bote* is a drum with animal skin stretched over the top. The player uses a stick to rub the animal skin over the drum to produce music (ibid.).

The dance involves a group of about twenty dancers and three musicians dancing through the streets, creating an ambience of celebration. It is a masked performance depicting a rebel spirit which needs to be restrained, as the main dancers dramatize the idea of resistance against the status quo. The dancers' masks are usually made from animal skin, cardboard and elastic bands that are painted in accordance with the preferences of the particular dancer or group of dancers. Interestingly, there are analogous messages between some *corridos* and the Dance of the Devil, in the sense that, in both cultural forms, rebellion and defiance are projected as admirable qualities. The devil is depicted as a venerated figure which synchronously symbolizes the evil of the Spanish slavery system. The theme of rebellion resonates with the subversive intent of many of the *corridos*, which protest against oppression by superior and powerful forces.

La Danza de la Tortuga (The Turtle Dance) is another popular ritualized performance in which dancers re-enact the ill-treatment of blacks during slavery. The Pancho figure carries a whip in his role as an overseer who ill-treats black slaves. Every aspect of this celebrative and invigorating dance is arresting and distinctive.

El son de Artesa is a dance in which dancers dance on a wooden trough carved from *ceiba* log, also known as *guanacaste*, a tree which grows in abundance on the Costa Chica and is well known for its huge trunk, ideally suited for making the trough. The trough is usually rectangular with an animal's head carved at one end and a tail at the other. It is placed upside down so that a couple or a single individual may dance barefooted on it. The *Artesa* requires great precision and skill as dancers usually move with agility, ensuring that they do not fall off the surface. The dancers usually dance barefooted to rhythmic sounds produced mainly from their feet tapping on the hollow log, along with music produced by string and wooden instruments, with a lead singer and a group of persons clapping, singing loudly and interjecting their voices into the singing at various intervals with loud shouts.

In the 1980s, Julian Salinas, an elderly resident of San José Estancia Grande, and his wife María Santos, originally from Lagunillas, were celebrated as the two best dancers of the *Artesa*, as well as for having the best memories of the *Artesa* and its importance at weddings and other Afro-Mexican community festivities. These two highly revered elders of the community were indispensable to early efforts to fortify recollections of Afro-Mexican cultural forms in the collective memory, as well as to the staging of actvities designed to transmit special skills and customs to younger generations of Afro-Mexicans (Father Glyn Jemmott Nelson, personal interview, June 2015). Today, the best-known *Artesa* groups are to be found in San Nicolás and El Ciruelo. In fact, the town centre of San Nicolás boasts several carved troughs on display while the mural on the Town Hall depicts two dancers performing the *Artesa*. Both the artwork and the carvings seem to serve as a sort of emblem of their identity as a people.

These African-influenced cultural forms which are associated with Mexico's black communities serve to emphasize that cultural marronage continues to be a defining feature of the Afro-Mexican presence. According to Anita González (2010, 84), "Devil Dancing . . . and Turtle Dancing provide opportunities for Afro-Mexican communities to explore roles of slavery/enslaved, victim/victimizer, even potency/impotency through embodiment."

The intention of this book is to extend the existing research on Afro-Mexico in general, particularly as it relates to the critical analysis of the literary and cultural production of the people of the Costa Chica in southern Mexico. I aim to unsettle official definitions of "nation" in Mexico; to challenge and subvert the selective and Eurocentric view of Mexican identity that has been advanced in Mexican discourse about the presence of blacks in that country.

The small body of literary and cultural material which has been produced in Afro-Mexican communities has received very little attention. To date, I am aware of only a few studies of the *corridos* or ballads, including my own, and of my own published research on Afro-Mexican lyric poetry, oral verses and folktales. Marco Polo Hernández (2000) has examined films in Mexico, which depict the lives of early Afro-Mexicans, albeit by white characters. González (2010) has studied Afro-Mexican dances, in particular the Dance of the Devil, to show how Afro-Mexicans use this form of self-expression to perform their perceptions of their own identities. In this book, I study a wide range of cultural forms: *corridos*, oral and lyric poetry, and oral/folk narratives. I also study the renowned comic series *Memín Pinguín*, which depicts Afro-Mexican characters in various social contexts in which they are also subjects of derogation. Although *Memín Pinguín* is not produced by Afro-Mexicans, I believe it is important to analyse the visual images and their messages. This is the first book which gives detailed critical attention to the literary production of Afro-Mexico.

The nature of the primary material with which I engage requires the application of a variety of theoretical constructs. The interdisciplinary analyses draw, therefore, from cultural studies, gender studies, linguistic anthropology, feminism, broad postcolonial and postmodernist theories, particularly as they relate to issues of marginality, isolation, ethnicity, gender, cultural identity, self-formation, questions of place, belonging, pride in nation, statehood, individual agency and subjectivity.

In chapter 1, I present an interrogation of the *Memín Pinguín* comic series, which, I suggest, contests arguments alleging Mexico's ethnic and racial homogeneity. Through the application of postcolonial deconstructionist theories, as well as close reading approaches to the study of visual and literary images, I argue that the comic series indubitably highlights Mexico's racial and ethnic diversity, but simultaneously treats difference as undesirable given that the character Memín and his mother are depicted through stereotypical racial caricatures that perpetuate racist images of blacks. Although the comic series is not part of the literary or cultural production of Afro-Mexicans, it is important for initiating the conversation about the black presence in Mexico. Furthermore, it presents a striking contrast to the self-portraitures and self-representations of Afro-Mexico.

The discourses of postcoloniality and feminism share intersecting theoretical trajectories, as they both aim to dismantle the damaging ideologies of colonization and patriarchy which have both oppressed, stereotyped and marginalized different groups of persons. Within this frame of reference, chapter 2 considers some of the patriarchal assumptions and stereotypes that underpin the ideological representations of gender and sexuality in selected Afro-Mexican oral narratives. Critical interrogations include the ways in which rituals of hierarchy and power play out between the sexes. Studied also are black male/female relationships, which are depicted to show the ways in which race, class and gender intersect in Afro-Mexican society. Different branches of feminist criticism aid in unmasking the politics of oppression and the structure of domination, which may exist in the narratives on relationships among blacks.

In chapter 3, masculinity and femininity are examined, in the context of social constructionism, as gendered ideologies that are both culturally and socially constructed; and as products of various historical and cultural contexts that influence the way men and women are perceived or define themselves, both as individuals and in relation to each other. The performance of masculinity by Afro-Mexican males in the Afro-Mexican *corrido* is shown to be complex and more than a single subordinated form, or one that is only a response to the masculinity of oppressive white/*latino* governments. It becomes more problematized when examined in light of the interactions with Afro-Mexican female figures, who are also marginalized along with males, under the same oppressive system and sometimes further marginalized by black men in their relationships.

In chapter 4, the concepts of "figured world", "relational identities/positionality" and "authoring", drawn from the interdisciplinary field of cultural studies, are used together to establish the analytical frame. I discuss selected poems which, I contend, reveal a significant level of racial consciousness and identification with the land or region occupied by Afro-Mexicans, as their performers or authors engage in a complex process of self-fashioning. I argue that "figured worlds" are created by Afro-Mexican composers and performers of oral poems to advance views about their membership in the Afro-Mexican community and in Mexico in general. "Relational identities" or "positional identities" are dramatized in works that reveal Afro-Mexicans' declarations about their entitlement to Mexican citizenship. In addition to these ways in which the field of cultural studies constructs identity and agency, broad postcolonial theories related to creative revisionism are further used to underline how the verses advance a new discourse about Afro-Mexicans and their ethnic heritage.

Chapter 5 scrutinizes a selection of verses from the collection *Alma cimarrona*. I argue that the availability of Afrocentric poetry undermines the claim that Mexican culture or ethnicity is one of sameness, as it establishes a new literary discourse within the broader context of Mexican discourse. I contend, as well, that the diversity that these poems add to Mexican culture and the definition of Mexican "nation", locates them within a broader conversation, in particular a Caribbean literary and cultural aesthetics. Moreover, the analyses will reveal that these poems also problematize the traditional configuration of nationality in Mexico, to represent it as one marked by heterogeneity, rather than sameness. My hope is that this research will foster greater interest in the black presence in Mexico and will result in raising awareness of the need for a more inclusive definition of community, nationhood, identity and selfhood in Mexico.

Figure 9. Minga in the Devil Dance (P.A. Ramsay)

Figure 10. Devil Dance (courtesy of María Elisa Velázquez, president of Comité Científico Ruta del Esclavo UNESCO).

Figure 11. Artwork sample from Father Glyn Jemmott Nelson's workshop (1986 to 2007)

Figure 12. Artist's depiction of the *Artesa* (with the kind permission of Father Glyn Jemmott Nelson)

1.

Racial and Ethnic Diversity in Mexico through the Distorted Lens of *Memín Pinguín*

> Diversity, which is neither chaos nor sterility, means the human spirit's thriving for cross-cultural relationship, without universalist transcendence. Diversity needs the presence of peoples, no longer as objects to be swallowed up, but with the intention of creating a new relationship. Sameness requires fixed Being. Diversity establishes becoming.... Sameness is sublimated difference. Diversity is accepted difference.
> —Édouard Glissant, *Caribbean Discourse*

The discussion in my introduction has established the fact that official discourse on nation and identity in Mexico has insisted on homogenizing Mexicans. Many Mexicans have embraced notions of national identity originally defended by Mexican educator and politician José Vasconcelos Calderón, along with Mexico's elites, that the Mexican nation is *mestizo* because descendants of blacks have completely disappeared due to racial mixing. However, as I have shown, there are Afro-Mexicans who are identifiably black even though they may not be officially recognized as such in Mexico.[1] In the mid-twentieth century, attempts were made by some Mexicans in areas such as Veracruz to draw attention to the ideology of *mestizaje*/mixture as "an inclusive ideology of exclusion" – that is, an ideology that completely eliminates and marginalizes Mexico's Afro-derived population.[2] Although not part of any agenda for raising awareness about black Mexicans, the comic book series *Memín Pinguín* is one way in which racial difference and identity are highlighted in Mexico. First released in the 1940s, the comic book series continues to centre its story on the hyperbolized cartoon character of a young black boy and his interactions with his light-complexioned/*latino* peers and Eufrosina, his black mother (who is affectionately referred to as Ma'Linda by Memín).³

In this chapter, I argue that while *Memín Pinguín* overtly offers testimony which contests arguments in favour of Mexico's ethnic and racial homogeneity, it simultaneously betrays ill-disposed attitudes towards blacks as Memín and his mother exhibit a range of stereotypical behaviours, attitudes and values which have traditionally been associated with blacks. The discussion will reveal, too, that the images of both characters are iconographic racial and ethnic caricatures, which reproduce unpropitious images of blacks. In other words, this comic series gives visibility to the black figure and exposes Mexico as a place of racial and ethnic diversity, but simultaneously treats difference and diversity as undesirable identities – a position which must invariably contribute to the entrenchment of negative perceptions of blacks in Mexico.

The central character of the series was created by Mexican writer Yolanda Vargas Dulché (2008a, 2008b), who claims that she was inspired by her childhood memories of the province of Guerrero on the Costa Chica, as well as by black Cuban children, whom she met while she worked in Cuba as a singer for a short time (Valles n.d., 1). Since its first publication in 1947, the series has enjoyed immense popularity in Mexico and in other Latin American countries, selling more than a million copies each week in Mexico at one point (Valles, n.d., 3). The soap opera–like feature, in which each week's episode is a continuation of the previous week's, has held the interest of many Mexicans who have developed a culture of following the storyline and anticipating the outcome of Memín's various escapades and encounters. In fact, Memín has become a household name in Mexico with carnival figures and *piñatas* being created to depict the character. The centrality of this cartoon figure to Mexican folk culture was marked by the decision of the Mexican government, in 2005, to publish a collection of stamps featuring and honouring the character (*El País*, 10 July 2008). The stamps generated much controversy in the United States, due to their publicity on the Internet and the frenzy created in Mexico by the rush to collect the stamps. More than seven hundred thousand stamps were sold in one week. African Americans in the United States, including Jesse Jackson, publicly condemned the stamps which depicted the caricature of a black child with thick lips, a big nose and big ears. So intense was the polemic that President George W. Bush was prompted to issue a White House statement condemning the images as "having no place in the modern world" (ibid.).

The 2005 controversy surrounding these stamps alerted many persons outside of Mexico, particularly in the United States, to the existence of the comics. This attention increased in the United States in 2008 when an African American woman publicly expressed outrage after she discovered a copy in a Walmart store in Texas, where it had been imported for sale to the large Mexican community across the United States border. As a result of this public denunciation which was facilitated by CNN, Fox and other major US networks, the comics were removed from all Walmart stores (*El País*, 10 July 2008). This reaction in the United States evoked anger among many Mexicans, who deny that the depiction of Memín carries any racist connotations. Some of Mexico's most renowned historians, such as Enrique Krause (2005) responded to the charges by pointing to his own conviction concerning Mexico's racial equality and homogeneity. Mexico's then minister of foreign affairs, Luis Ernesto Derbez, asserted that the position adopted by the United States revealed their total lack of understanding and respect for Mexican culture, since the comic had never been the source of any dissent in Mexico, where the achievements of famous Mexicans of African descent are widely acclaimed. Ironically, the images of these outstanding Mexicans, including José María Morelos,[4] second commander of Mexico's rebels in the War of Independence, and Vicente Guerrero,[5] who became president eight years following Mexico's independence from Spain, were not considered for the celebratory stamps despite the significant place of importance they hold in Mexico's history.

Despite this public claim of racial equality in Mexico, it is entrenched knowledge that the official attitude to racial difference in Mexico belies this. Furthermore, the fact that Mexican officials can insist on defending the grotesque portrayal of a particular ethnic group as something positive suggests a disturbing disregard for blacks in Mexico and reveals that, like Memín, black Mexicans are mere clichéd symbols that are not regarded and respected for their differences and distinctive identities. The official position that the portrayal of Memín is not racialized or racist, since Mexicans do not see him in terms of his colour, speaks forcefully to the problem of invisibility of blacks in Mexico (Katz 2007, 7).

We may venture further to highlight a major flaw in the claim, which is that if Memín is non-racialized, then his mother who is depicted in the comic as a black woman could, instead, be any race or could be created as raceless. Indeed, she could be white, Aztec or a Pokémon character. But this is not the case. She is an oversized, corpulent, "Aunt Jemima type" of black woman (Vargas Dulché, 2008a, 2). It seems then that the consistency in phenotype is indicative of an attempt, deliberate or otherwise, to ridicule an entire ethnic group, which is an identifiably Afro-derived one.

Within Mexico itself, there has been no condemnation of the obvious disparaging, even racist treatment of the character. In fact, any protests about the comic series have been based on moral or religious grounds. For instance, in one volume, Memín, who is portrayed in the process of preparing for his first communion, meets a boy who tells him that there is no point in doing so, since as a black person he is already irredeemably condemned, and that is the reason "there are no black angels in heaven" (Katz 2007, 1). Memín reacts to this new information by deciding to abandon first communion and assuming the persona of an extremely unruly and rebellious boy. Several Catholic priests in Mexico condemned the new development of the character, and the creators of the series immediately reformed Memín's image, resulting in an increase in sales.

Visual Rhetoric

Visual rhetoric draws mainly on Roland Barthes's (1964) theories of semiotics and relates to the study of how images are used in the art of persuasion. This includes images in films, photocopies, comics and billboards, to name a few forms. Images may be studied in conjunction with writing, to establish how they work together, or by themselves to communicate a particular meaning or message. The canonical approach to visual rhetoric focuses on six elements, which establish the persuasive and rhetorical aspects. They are:

1. arrangement – whether or not readers can see the visuals clearly and the message they communicate through how they are placed or displaced;
2. emphasis – whether or not certain features are given more prominence than others in size, colour, shape;
3. clarity – whether or not readers are able to decode a message being communicated;
4. conciseness – designs that are clearly reflective of a particular situation;

5. tone – how the crucial elements reveal the designer's attitude towards the subject; and
6. ethos – the particular context.

These features – arrangement, emphasis, clarity, conciseness, tone and ethos – help to determine how the visual images are received, perceived and interpreted. Furthermore, they are critical to the development of any understanding of the role, and political, sociological or philosophical significance of the visual images in any society. Historical considerations, which must be given to these images, would also be illuminated/aided through the application of these six elements.

Visual rhetoric is considered to be a language – designed to persuade and communicate a forceful message. According to Tang (1999, para. 5) "language is culture. Language is the soul of the country and the people who speak it". Without doubt, that culture affects the way people use language to communicate, whether in writing, speaking or through the use of visual images. The implication then, is that people within a given culture will understand the ideology, value systems and attitudes that inform the visual images that are created and produced in their societies, and they will interpret and perceive them in keeping with these values, attitudes and ideology. Indeed, the images of Memín are clearly those of a black person and the distorted pictures of him show a deliberate attempt to derogate him.

Unveiling Hegemonic Constructs of *Memín Pinguín*

Postcolonial criticism involves the "dismantling of European codes" and binaries of opposition as part of an anticolonial and anti-imperial agenda (Tiffin 2005, 99). It involves the subversion of dominant European discourses promoted through the consumption of literary works, films, comics, cartoons or any media characterized by "hegemonic assumptions" and "colonialist relations and representations" about non-dominant groups, races or classes in postcolonial societies.

An important aspect of the deconstruction of language involves the exposure of hegemonic constructs. Postcolonial criticism with its emphasis on the dismantling of binaries of oppression would necessitate the consideration of how visual images are used to further or advance hegemony in society.

This includes the machinery used by a dominant group to advance its views, reinforce its position and insist that its views are embraced by everyone else in society. Herein lies the intricate interlinking of culture and the historical, political and social power relations in a given society and their collective impact on language – visual or verbal.

Colonialist relations and representations are present in texts, visual or written, that "inscribe certain features of European colonialism" as in the case of Mexico, which continues to perpetuate the myth of homogeneity with its imperialistic claims, pushed by a political or new elite. According to theorist Homi Bhabha (2012, 327), racial and cultural homogeneity is a strategy of imperial control. Postcolonial criticism is integral to revealing that the visual rhetoric of *Memín Pinguín* inscribes certain features of European colonialism – that is, "the process by which European powers . . . reached a position of economic, military, political and cultural denomination in areas such as Asia, Africa and Latin America" (Stam and Spence 2005, 109). Additionally, an examination of representation and resistance to the objectification of those considered "others" in European/colonialist discourse is essential as, "resistance in post-colonial criticism is an alternative way of conceiving human history" (Said 2005, 97).

It becomes difficult to deny that *Memín Pinguín* is created from a colonialist mind, that does not resist, but rather is intent on participating in the discourse which constructs Mexican self-image as Eurocentric/European and the non-European as outsider, "an object of spectacle", simultaneously pretending that this is accurate while "masquerading" "as objective knowledge", that portraiture of a Mexican black boy and his experiences. Indeed, Mexico's minister of foreign affairs described Memín Pinguín as "a unique character", but failed to state that this uniqueness lies, for the most part, in the stark and contemptible contrast which Memín represents to other characters in the comic book series (Vaughn and Vinson III, 2005). The analysis of visual rhetoric and the engagement with postcolonial criticism will alert us to the debatable position that Memín is the subject of what Stam and Spence (2005, 108) term, "hostility, distortion and affectionate condescension". The impression that we are expected to accept, or are being manipulated into accepting, that Memín is loved by all Mexicans and, therefore, being represented as an integral part of Mexican culture, will be forcefully deconstructed and exposed for its speciousness.

A comic book series as popular as *Memín Pinguín* is undoubtedly a source of great entertainment. However, an understanding of visual rhetoric and how it facilitates the excavation of underlying meanings, historical facts, political ideologies and broader aspects of the culture in which it is produced seems to lead to the conclusion that, whether consciously or subconsciously, intentionally or inadvertently, *Memín Pinguín* exposes and communicates Mexico's wilful disregard for racial and ethnic pride and understanding of diversity and difference. Mexican blacks are regarded as non-existent, and so it is understandable that Memín, the character, would be portrayed as an enigma – for that is what he would be, in reality, to many Mexicans. The exaggeration of his features makes him the object of ridicule and his constant juxtaposition against human beings of a certain racial phenotype, those who possess "normal" features, suggests his undervaluing. Arguably, the significance of his clearly defined difference coded in his greater resemblance to a monkey would be easily understood by Mexicans, who have come to believe that blacks no longer exist in Mexico or treat them as invisible. A black Memín Pinguín and his mother mean that creature from the past – we used to govern his type; that creature from the past – we diluted his race; or that creature who just happens to be presented as black, but is really a half-man, half-beast conundrum. Regardless of how he is seen, he is likely to be interpreted in consonance with everything that Mexicans have been taught, directly or inadvertently, about Mexican identity.

Memín's Domineering Friends

A deconstruction of Memín Pinguín's relationship with his friends reveals that he depends on their approval for validation. The obviously non-egalitarian nature of this relationship is revealed to be one in which they can command and summon Memín, as they wish, to assist them in difficulties and react in the ways they consider to be appropriate in different situations. The volume *Aventura emocionante* (Vargas Dulché 2008a) presents an episode in which Memín is summoned to assist in the rescue of his friend's father, who has been captured by gangsters. Through his own direct interior monologue and the visual representation, we realize that he is drawn into a potentially dangerous situation by the promise of glory/fame, which he seems to desperately crave for self-validation. Underneath this anticipation of recognition is the sense that neither is Memín important/central to the rescue mission, nor does he have a choice regarding his participation; he "has to" go with Ernesto: "Ernesto me dijo que era muy glorioso rescatar a su papá, y tuve que acompañarlo" (p. 1). (Ernesto told me it would be great to rescue his father, and I had to accompany him.) Even though "tuve que" (I had to) comes as a sense of inner compelling, its force is quickly diminished by the term "acompañarlo" (accompany him) which reduces Memín's position to one of subordination and suggests that he will be a kind of prop – rather than one who will be integral or central to the mission. The visual image of Memín, dressed as a half-naked Native American, with his Native American Indian headgear – complete with feathers and arrows – seems to reinforce this conventionalized image of the "wild" native with the potential to unleash violence at any time. His minority status is accentuated by his visual representation – he is clearly different. While Memín is identifiably black, perhaps the artist has simultaneously and deliberately created a persona who is not only non-latino/white, but also a composite of outsider groups in Mexico, given his clothes and headgear, which are associated with Native American culture. This image serves as a powerful representation of outsiderness.

From the outset of the rescue Ernestillo and Memín find themselves in a difficult predicament at the robber's house. Ernestillo is captured, while Memín contrives a ludicrous trick to detract the robbers, by feigning to be a statue: "Yo me puse como 'estatua' de libertad de los Comanches" (Vargas Dulché 2008a, 1). (I became like Comanche's statue of liberty.) This farce prevents him from falling into a fate similar to Ernestillo and allows him to extricate himself from the trap. Nonetheless, his human qualities are superimposed by inanimateness to the extent of non-recognition by the perpetrators of the crime that is in progress. The dehumanization of the black person is implied in this visual representation of a comic caricature, not so much by the metaphoric transformation of being objectified as a statue – a cold, lifeless replica of humanity – but by the remarkably uncanny exactitude in similitude, so that, to the visible human eyes, Memín remains indistinguishable, unnoticeable and overlooked: "y nadie supuso quién era" (ibid.) (and nobody guessed who he was). The visual representation of the ease and effortlessness with which Memín imitates a statue encapsulates a general perception that Africans and their descendants are necessarily devoid of human attributes, unworthy of acknowledgement and inclusion as an ethnic group. This dehumanizing visual image is further underpinned by Carlangas's vituperative assault on Memín, as he vents his annoyance with him:

> Memín—¡Ya solucioné el asunto . . . ahora sí está solucionado!
> Carlangas—No sigas pensando en tonterías, Memín. ¿Dónde está el agua? . . .
> Memín—No se trata de agua, sino de que allá afuerita está un coche último modelo y tiene la llave puesta.
> Carlangas—¿Y eso qué nos importa, pedazo de animal?
> (Vargas Dulché 2008a, 13–15)

> Memín: "I solved the problem already . . . it is solved!"
> Carlangas: "Stop thinking about foolishness, Memín. Where's the water?"
> Memín: "It's not about water, but that outside there is the latest model car and it has the key in it."
> Carlangas: "And how is that important to us, you little piece of animal?"

This outburst of anger and verbal invective, – "pedazo de animal" (piece of animal) reinforces the usual disrespect with which he is regarded by his friends, who also seem to think it is their prerogative to issue orders to Memín, which they expect him to immediately and unquestioningly obey.

Ironically, despite Memín's apparent warrior costume he is presented/imaged as impotent and useless in the rescue mission. Ernestillo's father is found bound and gagged, and Ernestillo immediately begins to unbind him, at the same time requesting assistance from Memín. However, Memín is portrayed as a bystander, unproductive and unhelpful, except to make inane remarks and mindlessly echo Ernestillo. Through the drawings/visual images we see his failure to respond in a crisis and offer any assistance to his friend, although it is requested. In this sense, the idea is reinforced that Memín is really a useless figure dressed as a warrior. He becomes the subject of ridicule and mockery.

The purpose of this portrayal seems to be to project Memín, the representative of black Mexico, in a manner that implies and represents the cowardice of blacks: their lack of mental capacity to engage in serious discussions on critical matters and their inability to think quickly. Memín lapses into ennui and is dismissed by his friends. Ironically, his real fighting skills are seen only when he is dreaming or imagining himself as dominating in a fight.

The mockery is sustained by Memín's buffoonery, which suggests his insensitivity in the situation. It is obvious that after the physical ordeal experienced by Ernestillo's father, Don Fernando, the old man's limbs would be in a state of atrophy. Memín, observing his slow gait, prompts: "Si puede echar una galopada, sería mejor" (Vargas Dulché 2008a, 6). (If you could just do a little trot, it would be better.) Memín's unfeeling and callous comment, in a situation requiring compassion and empathy, implies a deficiency in both sense and sensibility in the black boy. This negative characterization of thoughtlessness and desensitized attitude accentuates traits of cognitive superficiality and mental and intellectual retardation often seen in colonial discourse about blacks. The response of his friend Ernestillo, along with the picture of shock on the latter's face, suggests Memín's shallowness and ineptitude: "¿Cómo va ya a galopar mi papá, Memín? Tú ya sabes que sufre de su pierna" (ibid.). (How is my father going to gallop, Memín? You know he's suffering with his leg.) This invariably creates a response of antipathy in the reader – far from endearing Memín to the public, it indirectly, as well as subtly, fosters aversion towards him, as one who is insensitive and lacking in compassion.

Memín is further portrayed in an unattractive light in his crude attempts to comfort Don Fernando and awaken him from his state of unconsciousness, the result of a pounding headache: "No se queja por tan poca cosa, que ahorita que choquemos le va a doler más" (Vargas Dulché 2008a, 19). (Don't complain about such a little thing, in a little while when we crash it will hurt worse.) Ironically, Memín is the cause and originator of that pain. His concern is counteracted by nonchalant callousness. Words intended to neutralize the effect of Memín's very own brutish action serve only to intensify it. Memín is therefore seen as a miserable comforter, who instead of assuaging or detonating the pain, effectively manages to produce a more damaging effect and a greater headache. The implication that Memín is a failure at everything he attempts, but above all, basic human fellow-feeling favours the speciousness that underlines the message of the scene. It is the typical racist argument that blacks lack intelligence and that their presence confuses, rather than helps in difficult situations.

Memín: Arrogant, Disloyal

The self-assuming air and arrogance at times depicted in Memín is a focal point of mockery by his friends in the story as well as for the readers. His knack of presuming and pre-empting in situations without substantial support or grounds usually results in his embarrassing undoing. Memín conveniently presumes himself the paragon of bravery, protection and security to allay the fears of Ernestillo's father concerning the police and their involvement in the gangsters' activities: "Usted cálmese señor; no le va a pasar nada ... se lo dice este negro que sabe lo que pasa" (Vargas Dulché 2008a, 27). (Calm down sir, nothing will happen to you, so says this black guy who knows what is happening.) However, the self-assuming nature of Memín is mocked by the caricaturized depiction of a powerless and defenceless, feeble and pusillanimous creature. His self-assured knowledge, "este negro que sabe lo que pasa" (this black boy who knows what is happening) is ridiculed by a sharp censorious riposte from Carlos: "¡Mira tú!" (Look at you!) Here the arrogant "know-it-all" attitude of Memín evokes repudiation. Implicitly the narrator draws attention to the perception held of the black person as a boaster who presumes knowledge yet knows nothing and, on the basis of this presumption, who displays the tendency to unthinkingly blurt out confidences.

Memín is depicted as being more than willing to disclose unsolicited information that is known only to his crew. His eagerness to supply Ernestillo's father with information on the background to his capture reveals his scant regard for codes of honour in friendships. Confidences are treated flippantly and little consideration is given to allegiances to his friends, to consult them before acting out of course: "Si lo quiere, yo le hago la explicación completa" (Vargas Dulché 2008a, 5). (If you want, I will give you the complete explanation.) The injections of these instances of disloyalty serve to expose betrayal of confidences as a prepossessing trait, contingent to a garrulous tendency, in the Negro that requires little promptings, and as such dissuades engagement of friendship with blacks.

A Friendship Drawn along Racial Lines

Memín's inferior position is evident not only in the manner in which his friends try to dictate his actions and make demeaning statements about him and his general conduct, but in the manner in which they constantly make him the subject of abuse and scorn. In volume 154 (Vargas Dulché 2008b), we witness Memín's scolding by his friends, who forcefully reject his opinion of his input in helping Ernestillo's father. In volume 251 (Vargas Dulché 2010d), when Memín's friends' attempts at flirting with a pretty *latina* fail, they unanimously reject his suggestions to retreat, and he finds himself at the receiving end of their insults: "Por seguir la costumbre todos me regañaron" (Vargas Dulché 2010d, 1). (Everyone scolded me as usual.) Inevitably, they perceive their control over Memín to be such that they do not expect him to make choices for himself. Memín decides that despite the failure of his friends to win the attention of the beautiful Chipitas, he will attempt to achieve for himself what his friends could not. Feeling upstaged by Memín's boldness, they order him to abandon his plans to "court" the young lady. Their threats and the readiness with which they are prepared to end their friendship with him speak to the scant regard they have for him as a person and confirm that they do not sincerely regard him as a friend or an equal:

> Los tres amigos de Memín se ofendieron ante su desprecio
> —Perderás nuestra amistad para siempre.
> —Te cortaremas en definitiva.
> (Vargas Dulché 2008d, 1)
>
> Memín's three friends were offended by his ignoring him.
> "You will lose our friendship forever."
> "We will definitely cut you off."

The words they direct at Memín are harsh and revealing of their fickleness and lack of commitment to him, but they reveal furthermore, the extent to which Memín is always pitched against his three friends – none of them ever sides with him. However, it is through the visual images that the strong line of dominion is forcefully made evident as his friends join in a determined attack on Memín, beating him and boxing his ears mercilessly as though he were an insubordinate, an underling.

The Image of the Violent Black Person

Some visual images of Memín as well as his actions depict him as barbaric and given to violence. While a bellicose nature is not featured prominently in Memín Pinguín, instances of or references to violence have typecast blacks as an ethnic group with violent proclivities both at the physical and the psychological levels. Physical violence is depicted through graphic visuals of the "neolithic" behaviour in Memín. These graphic illustrations insinuate that truculence seems a natural way of life for blacks. The very striking depictions in the art work by Sixto Valencia Burgos in *Memín Pinguín: Aventura emociante* (Vargas Dulché 2008a) reinforce the argument that seems to be advanced by Vargas Dulché that blacks naturally consider violence as an answer to resolving difficult situations. When the constant prodding of Memín and his friends prove futile in convincing Don Fernando not to remain at the robbers' den, but to leave with them instead, Memín rationalizes that the use of force is the remedial approach: "¡Por lo que veo este no entiende con las palabras! . . . Tengo que usar la fuerza, no me queda otra" (Vargas Dulché 2008a, 9). (From what I see this one does not understand with words! I have to use force, there is no other way!) The graphic sequel of actions which follows accentuates this rationalization and presents a calculated and covertly devised attack on Don Fernando that employs deception to successfully effectuate it. Assessing the height of Don Fernando and the impossibility of reaching him in order to hit him, Memín, with persistent persuasion, convinces Don Fernando to allow him to kiss him on the forehead. Then, instead of administering a kiss, Memín brutally attacks him with a huge jar on the head, knocking him senselessly cold (Vargas Dulché 2008a, 10–11). The irony of the situation is that this action is supposedly done to show his affection for Don Fernando. The exaggerated visual representation of Memín's action implies an innate brutishness, a tendency to be violent and a level of savagery typical of so-called primitive tribes. The powerful inductive claim being advanced by this picture is that he is uncivilized, uncultured and, above all, not truly Mexican.

The myth of the irrational, uncivilized black person is also perpetuated through the depiction of Memín as being unable to handle compliments. When his teacher praises him for his role in the rescue of Ernestillo's father, he becomes carried away with elation and in a very impulsive act that supposedly exposes his stupidity, he leaps onto the teacher's table like an untrained animal out of control. The striking and clear image of him bearing resemblance to a monkey, leaping through the air and landing heavily on the teacher's desk, and the horrified expression on the teacher's face seem to advance an argument about the low socialization of black Mexicans, even in institutions of learning – by extension, the inability of blacks, irrespective of their ability, to interact or intermingle with *latinos* in similar situations.

The implied claim about violence is further sustained in the illustration of Memín's own reflection on his mother's reaction to his late return home. From the drawing, it becomes clear that he is mortified by the thought of confronting her violent reactions. A contrastive parallel is drawn between the threat of the police and the robbers combined and the threat of Ma'Linda, Memín's mother. Categorically, they generate the same response: fear. However, the degree of fear inspired by Ma'Linda supersedes and eclipses that which the young juveniles presently face. Memín communicates this tangible and paralysing fear of Ma'Linda: "me voy a ocultar de la policía, de los ladrones, y sobre todo de mi Ma'Linda, que en cuanto me 'pesque', me va dar una que no vea" (Vargas Dulché 2008, 26). (I am going to hide from the police, the thieves, and most of all from Ma'Linda, who, as soon as she catches me is going to give me [a beating] you have never seen.) In other words, Ma'Linda is even seen to be far more dangerous than the gangsters, insomuch that she drives an "unholy fear" into Memín just by the thought of being caught by her and the punishment that would be meted out to him by her.

Indeed, inferences of parental violence and abuse among blacks are strong and poignant in the comic series. Memín's fear brings into focus the psychological effect, or damage inflicted on the child and, in effect, places parenting skills of blacks and the role of the black mother in a questionable light. The intimation is that the black home, being the supposed safe haven, is a far greater threat than external threats faced on the streets. The violence epitomized in Ma'Linda outrivals the threat of violence posed by any external agent, such that hiding away is preferable to returning home. The fear is strong, palpable and real enough to provoke Memín's desire of choosing to be vulnerable to criminal elements, rather than face the wrath of his mother. But the force of Memín's words diminishes against the artistic illustration of the heavyset, corpulent mother wielding not a mere strap, but a log with a nail at the end of it, waiting to inflict pain on her son. The detailed illustration of the flogging is made more horrifying by the contrast/distinction presented by the non-violent response of his white/*latino* friends' parents. They embrace and greet their children in a relieved and affectionately civilized manner. Undoubtedly, a sharp criticism and condemnation of black parenting is made through the juxtaposition of vivid images of Memín's mother's brutal disciplining of her son, with the images of the methods employed by his white friends' parents. The frames first depict Memín's mother administering barbaric punitive measures and then moves to the very controlled and "civilized" approach taken by the friends' parents. The juxtaposition provides a forceful reinforcement of Homi Bhabha's claim that civility and self-control are still considered the characteristics of those who are in dominance (Bhabba 1994).

Objectified and Mindless

One of the most notable ways in which Memín and his mother are objectified is in the ways in which the perceived ignorance of blacks is implied through the depiction of Memín and his mother in their unstable relationship. The mother herself customarily speaks derogatorily about Memín, as she mournfully questions God's decision to bestow on her such a useless black child: "Este pedazo de flojería negra que Dios echó en mis brazos como hijo." (This little piece of black waste that God threw into my arms for a child.) Her claim of his *flojería* (laziness) is deliberately supported by the visual image of Memín wasting time in school, behaving like a class clown and refusing to emulate the good study habits of his white/*latino* friends. In contrast to his classmates, who take their studies seriously, he jokes around and tries to suggest that it is the educational system that is useless. He is made a subject of ridicule by the teacher, who painstakingly reads aloud all his incorrect answers to the class. It is a merciless act evoking shock and shame in Memín, who does not anticipate that his nonsensical answers would have been rejected, but boasts to the class that he has scored the highest marks.

Memín's mother is depicted as being even more obtuse than Memín as her illiteracy, along with Memín's deceit of adding a one before his zeros, prevents her from understanding his report card. Memín's creator takes him through a series of unflattering acts to present him as stupid, and to fortify his own pronouncement, which cynically reinforces the myth of the barbaric black person: "¡Soy un salvaje! Soy un animal . . . ! ¿Por que no me dejaron enterrado en Africa?" (Vargas Dulché 2010e, 21). ("I am a savage! I am an animal . . . ! "Why didn't they leave me trapped in Africa?") The visual image of a dejected, deflated Memín, who makes the pronouncement upon himself, renders his self-condemnation even more powerful. The direct link between Memín's confusion of his savagery and his connection to an origin in Africa bespeaks the denigrated attitude that informs the creation of a character who could be regarded as mere object, without any intellectual abilities or grounding in the real world of thinking people.

Representation of Black Femininity

Memín's mother, an extremely obese, illiterate woman with a great penchant for violence towards her child, is the only representation of a black woman in the comics. She is disparaged by her actions, speech, physical appearance and class. In contrast, there are several images of voluptuous young "white" females, including one that Memín himself finds irresistible, but who insults Memín as she rejects his advances. The image of Memín's mother, an unhappy disgruntled, overly corpulent figure that seems to have no purpose outside of the domestic space, betrays the extent to which certain caricatures and stereotypes of the black female resonate in Mexican culture and consciousness.

The contradictory manner in which she relates to her child, expressing unconditional love for him at one point and resentment towards him at another, creates an image of a confused, inconsistent and irrational black mother. The visually unappealing image of the black woman has never been questioned or rejected by Mexico's enthusiastic consumers of this comic series. There have been no calls for other images of black women besides what may best be regarded as an "anthropomorphized" figure, suggesting that there is acceptance of the artist's representation of a black woman. It implies too that that a signal is being sent throughout Mexico in the silent acceptance of this depiction, which reinforces certain myths pertaining to black women specifically, and to blacks more generally.

The question may be asked concerning the reason a comic book series with such blatantly offensive images of blacks, continues to enjoy such popularity in Mexico, despite the public debates which were sparked by the controversy surrounding the release of the stamps and the discovery of the comics in Walmart by an African American woman. Many Mexicans insist that Memín is simply a cultural icon, who is beloved by many for his wit and "picaresque" qualities. One of Mexico's leading writers on cultural matters, Carlos Monsiváis (2005, para. 4–11), declared in response to the controversy sparked by the White House comments about the *Memín Pinguín* stamps and comic, the following: "Memín es un dato pintoresco, no es él inferior, es él diferente, sin más. . . . Los mexicanos de hace sesenta años o del año pasado no habrían tolerado un comic abiertamente racista. Las cómicas de México han sido profusamente machistas pero no anti-negros." (Memín is a colourful figure, he is not inferior, he is different, that's all. . . . Mexicans of seventy years ago or even last year would not have tolerated an openly racist comic book. Mexican comics have been profusely *machista,* but not anti-black.) This stubborn refusal on the part of Mexicans to recognize the ways in which the stereotypical depictions reinforce racist attitudes is disturbing. Arguments about persisting racism in the United States and claims of Americans and other outsiders misrepresenting and misunderstanding Mexican culture do not diminish the negative messages conveyed by the visual representations and the verbal exchanges about Memín.

Nevertheless, one firm admission of the problematic nature of *Memín Penguín* and the tendency to treat it as a benign cultural icon has been provided by María Elisa Velázquez Gutiérrez (2005), director of a project on African heritage in Mexico at the National Institute of Anthropology, who underscores the need to re-examine "con ojos críticos a nuestros íconos de la cultura popular" (with critical eyes on our icons of popular culture). In what must be a very rare declaration in Mexico, she adds, "Existen problemas de racismo y discriminación" (para 6) (problems with racism and discrimination exist). Despite this recognition from someone who occupies a place of importance and understands well Mexican culture and heritage, Velázquez Gutiérrez's opinion may very well never have an impact on the future of *Memín Penguín,* or on the attitude of Mexicans towards this series of comic books and by extension towards blacks. Furthermore, the fact that Afro-Mexicans themselves, for the most part, do not interpret images of Memín as speaking to their own racial marginalization suggests that for a long time there may never be any opposition from Mexico's small black population to the publication of this comic book series. Second, given the forceful defence by the Mexican government of the comic and stamps, it can be inferred that there are powerful forces in Mexico which continue to support promotion of the series because they have no objection to the images and the messages it conveys. This inevitably raises questions of how popular culture may be used by governments to advance certain agendas. According to Katz (2007): "El gobierno de México entiende la importancia de estos cómicos como género útil igual que las estampillas para la diseminación de su punto de vista" (Katz 2007, 8). (The Mexican government understands well the importance of these comics as a useful genre, like the stamps, for disseminating its point of view.) Perhaps the series is really Mexico's subtle way of advancing its position on Mexicanness. If it is not, the implied claim would then be that *Memín Penguín* is about some people who look like him – who are not Mexicans, because there really are no black Mexicans. Either way, the message is demeaning to blacks.

The Child Protagonist and Visual Rhetoric

The series depicting a child protagonist is of particular appeal to young children who are easily influenced by the images presented to them in books and other printed material. Although *Memín Pinguín* has a wide readership, in the main it is children, the chief consumers of comics, who will be drawn to the series. In a well-debated essay on the effects of visual images on children, Elise Detriech (2010, 143) affirms that "visual representations of race and gender are particularly potent when aimed at a child audience, communicating ideas about social constructs to a particularly receptive population". What makes this particularly disturbing is that the social implications of the depictions receive no challenge from any of the written discourse in this comic series. "Socially stratified boundaries", perceptions of racial differences are all implied, as well as explicitly conveyed through the visual tool of the comic book, and all the images belie the claims of racial harmony and homogeneity made by Mexican governments and other officials. Many young Mexican children will be introduced to images of blacks by this comic book series and will have their first impressions and attitudes formed by the visual representations. The effect of *Memín Pinguín* on reinforcing certain myths will consequently continue to be far reaching.

Conclusion

All postcolonial societies are still subject, in one way or another, to overt or subtle forms of neocolonial domination, and independence has not solved this problem. This domination is manifested in diverse ways, including the attempt to impose a preconceived colonialist identity on indigenous and minority groups. The development of new elites within independent societies, often buttressed by neocolonial institutions, the development of internal discussions based on racial, linguistic or religious discrimination, the continuing unequal treatment of the indigenous people in settler/invader societies – all testify to the fact that postcolonialism is a continuing process of resistance and reconstruction (Tiffin 2005, 1–2).

In the case of *Memín Pinguín*, the identity created through the visual images is one of outsidership and alterity. It is an identity that invites the curious gaze of those considered to be Mexicans and leads them to form judgements and devalue those groups or individuals who would identify with Memín Penguín. More importantly, the visual images draw attention to Mexico as a geographical and cultural space, in which issues related to community are berated. In other words, the images of Memín are so blatantly based on colonial ideologies and hierarchal notions of identity, that individual identity and difference find no accommodation. The claim can then be made that, through the work of the artist of the comic series *Memín Penguín*, "the possibility for cross-cultural unity among the heterogeneous peoples of Latin America and the Caribbean continues to be undermined by the legacy of colonialism" (Webb 1992, 151). Indeed, a thoughtful and conscientious deconstructionist reading of *Memín Pinguín* signals the need for cultural decolonization in Mexico.

2.

Constructions of Gender and Nation in Selected Afro-Mexican Folktales

> Race, class, gender and sexuality all remain intertwined with nation.
> —Patricia Hill Collins, *Black Feminist Thought*

This chapter will examine from a postcolonial feminist perspective some of the patriarchal assumptions and stereotypes which underpin the ideological representations of gender and sexuality in a selection of Afro-Mexican folktales. The chapter also seeks to unveil some of the ways in which these representations simultaneously subvert the assumptions and stereotypes. Different representations of Mexican society in the folktales, informed as they are for the most part by colonialist ideologies and the attempts to counter these ideologies, will be explored. Critical interrogations to be made will also include the ways in which rituals of hierarchy and power play out between the sexes in the Afro-Mexican folktale, the dominant images of male and female characters depicted in the folktales, representations of male/female relationships and the extent to which these gender relations seem to reflect the Afro-Mexican world view. This would include the portrayals of how male/female relations instantiate the ways in which race, class and gender intersect in Mexican society. Different branches of feminist thought and theory will aid in unmasking the politics of oppression and the structure of domination that exist in the tales.

The tales to be analysed are selected from the collection of oral narratives entitled *Jamás fandango al cielo* (Díaz Pérez, Aparicio Prudente and García

Casarrubias 1993), translated as *Never Again a Party in the Sky*, which is based on the fable of the turtle joining the birds on a trip to a party in heaven/the sky. The turtle uses borrowed feathers to get to the party, but on the way back, he angers the birds. They take back their feathers, causing him to fall back to earth. After the fall the turtle vows: "Never again a party in the sky." Co-editor of the collection María Cristina Díaz Pérez (1993) claims that the title was used to signify the "magical and imaginary, yet contrived and defensive" world inhabited by Afro-Mexicans on the Costa Chica of Oaxaca and Guerrero (quoted by Father Glyn Jemmottt Nelson in email correspondence, October 2014). This collection was compiled by the Unidad Regional Guerrero de Cultura Populares (Guerrero Regional Unit for Popular Culture) as part of a project which was developed for the purpose of raising awareness of the presence of Afro-Mexicans in Mexico and their contributions to Mexican multiculturalism (Valencia Valencia 1993, 14). The project was undertaken as part of the activities commemorating five hundred years of the "discovery" of the Americas. The tales were narrated by men, women and children ranging from ages eight to eighty. Many tales were simply narrated and recorded, while others were demonstrated for the recordings. The folktales provide an insight into the background of this community's code of conduct, their values, beliefs and general ideals that are upheld (Ramsay 2001, 8).

In the study of these tales, I will draw on feminism in its interaction with broad postcolonial criticism to determine how the narratives allow for marginalized black females to be "reinstated" in the face of the dominant culture. Some of the folktales which will be examined have been narrated by males while others have been narrated by females. It seems problematic to attempt to advance claims or to generalize about how a particular narrative perspective is strictly shaped by the gender of the narrator. Nonetheless, close examination of tales narrated by both sexes reveals a general preoccupation with the desire to discover self, to find some type of fortune and to overcome the vicissitudes of life. The general structure of the tales dictates their unfolding – the protagonist is usually male and the story unfolds around his needs, desires and goals. Both male and female narrators, then, accede to what seems to be a thematic thrust and world view that share consensus among Afro-Mexicans. Female narrators simply maintain the narrative that was transmitted to them, in the same manner in which they were to men. According to Díaz Pérez (1993, 22–23):

> El contenido de los cuentos está determinado por elementos estructurales que se integran en la trama argumentativa de manera más o menos constante, por lo general se inician con la salida del personaje protagónico del ambiente familiar, esta separación es motivada por la muerte del padre, la madre o de ambos, por la necesidad de encontrar esposa, porque los padres ya son ancianos, o bien sólo para ir en busca de suerte. . . . Los personajes, al igual que los lugares y el tiempo, son remotos y se mueven en el terreno de lo abstracto.

> The content of the stories is determined by structural elements which are integrated into the thematic argument in a more or less consistent manner; generally they begin with the departure of the main character from a familiar environment. The separation is motivated by the death of the father, mother or both, because of the need to find a wife, because the parents are old, or simply to find fortune. . . . Characters, like the places and time, are remote and seem to function in the realm of the abstract.[1]

The result of this adherence to a prescribed and "fixed" structure is that the male protagonist becomes the central or focal point of the tales while females are presented in a tangential or peripheral manner for the most part. They are usually significant if the actions of the men are directed towards them, or render their existence important. Usually, they are deemed important to the extent that they are useful to the males and are in keeping with their perceived mode of achieving happiness.

While it must be conceded that the individual tales are not necessarily contrived in keeping with any particular agenda which is aligned to the gender of the narrator, it seems fair to conclude that there is a tendency for a standpoint which promotes the superiority of males and the masculine over females and the feminine to be advanced. Concomitantly, a minority of tales reveal, from time to time, an effort made consciously or unconsciously to be revisionist in the presentation of female characters. This seems to be so in the case of some of the stories narrated by Catalina Bruno, whose name suggests a female narrator. It will be interesting to see the extent to which they dismantle some of the stereotypes of the patriarchal system as they relate to females and male/female relationships.

The Emerging "Norm" and Female "Otherness"

The "societal norm" projected in the Afro-Mexican folktales is one in which positions which embody power and authority are occupied by men. Moreover, the experience of "being" and "existence" seems to be synonymous with maleness. Females are usually introduced by the father or a king in an indirect manner, through one of several formulaic phrases which place a king or a father as the central figure. Additionally, female characters are usually depicted as objects of the verbs in the sentences, as in the following examples taken from different narratives in *Jamás fandango al cielo* (Díaz Pérez, Aparicio Prudente and García Casarrubias 1993):

> "E'te era un hombre que vivía en un rancho con su e'posa." ("El Caballito de virtud", 98)
> This was a man who lived on a ranch with his wife.

> "Se dice que era un señor y era muy rico y tenía una hija muy bonita." ("Tontosoy", 139)
> They say he was a man who was very rich and had a very beautiful daughter.

> "Era una vez un señor que se llamaba Revientacadena tenía su mujer." ("La mojarrita de tres colores", 204)
> Once there was a man named Revientacadena who had a wife.

Ironically, even when the folktales bear the name of a woman as the title, she is still introduced in relation to a male character who is presented as having greater significance in the story. This is the case with the folktale "Blanca Flor" (White Flower), narrated by Catalina Bruno (1993, 75): the title suggests that the protagonist is female but nonetheless begins with the introduction of the male who "discovers" her and brings her existence into focus. "Un papá tenía un hijo y ese hijo se llamaba Juan." (A father had a son and his name was Juan.) Blanca Flor is not introduced to Juan in a direct manner, but focalized through the matter-of-fact third-person commentary/point of view in which three "muchachas" are observed by Juan, before the narrator eventually discloses that "la chiquita se llamaba Blanca Flor" (p. 76). (The youngest one was called Blanca Flor.)

This same tradition of male importance and centrality is again repeated in "Morena" (*Jamás fandango al cielo*, 109), in which the title, a term in the feminine form, promises a tale that will be about a woman, but ironically, the tale commences with an introduction in which the focus is on the male character and his concerns about his future: "Así e' que era un muchacho que, llamaba Puertasiban. Entoce' é'te le dijo a su papá que ya no quería vivir ahí con ello, que él se iba a echar a'ndar, iba a saber tierra" ("Blanca Flor", 75). ("There was a young man called Puertasiban. He told his father that he didn't want to live with him anymore, that he was going to go out and discover the world." The compelling fact is that the young woman, who will be crucial and central to the plot's development, is eventually introduced almost two hundred words into the story.

It is in this world in which male characters are generally more visible – at the bargaining tables, as "brave hearted men" in fights, as leaders in family discussions and decision-making, that female characters are objectified and presented on the margins of the narratives' concerns. The tales, therefore, point to what may be regarded as the twofold process of racial inferiorization and gender subordination, to which Afro-Mexican women have been subjected in reality. Indeed, these representations fully substantiate the assertion made by Ashcroft, Griffiths and Tiffin (2005, 233) concerning the ideological constitution of gender in general, and in many postcolonial societies in particular. Their firm claim is that "in many societies, women, like colonised subjects, have been relegated to the position of 'other', 'colonised' by various forms of patriarchal domination. They thus share with colonised races and cultures an intimate experience of the politics of oppression and regression."

Representations of Patriarchal Ideologies

The intriguing tale, "La mojarrita de tres colores" (The Three-Coloured Bream) in *Jamás fandango al cielo* (*Never Again a Party in the Sky*) narrated by Jesús Robles (1990), is steeped in patriarchal ideologies. The first indication of this is evident in the narrator's depiction of the man and his possessions. We note the fascinating manner in which the woman is itemized in a sequence with his animals, suggesting that woman, dog and mare are all regarded as being equal, on the same level and in terms of their usefulness to the man: "Era una vez un señor que se llamaba Revientacadena, tenía su mujer, tenía su perrita, y tenía su yegua" (p. 204). (There was once a man called Revientacadena who had his wife, his dog and his mare.) This relegation of the woman to a position of unimportance is further witnessed as the man takes advice from a fish on how to take care of his three possessions, "su mujer, su perra y su yegua" (his woman, his dog and his mare). Following his conformity to the fish's advice, the three suffer the same fate, leaving him deprived of his three objects which are obviously equally valued – the woman and his two animals: "Parió la mujer, parió la yegua y parió la perra. / Después se murió la mujer, se murió la perra y se murió la yegua" ("La mojarrita de tres colores"). (The woman gave birth, the mare gave birth and the dog gave birth. / Afterwards, the woman died, the dog died and the mare died.)

There is no indication that the death of the woman/wife – his partner – is a greater loss than that of any of the animals, suggesting what could be deemed an unnatural attitude of classifying animals and woman equally, and inviting the rejection of the ideology which underpins this attitude. The patriarchal psychology which informs this male character's society is sharply presented as we witness his decision, following his losses, to prove his manliness and be awarded with the king's daughter, who herself is depicted as having no right or power to influence the outcome of her own fate. She will be rewarded to a man who is successful in killing the seven-headed snake that is threatening the town's safety. What is particularly untenable about this is the idea that the young girl is being given to a man solely on the basis of his proven *machismo*. She is a mere observer as the negotiations take place among her father and prospective males eager to prove their *machismo* so as to impress the king of their suitability as husbands. This narration forcefully draws attention to the patriarchal attitude, which treats women as inane and incapable of making choices and decisions for themselves. Furthermore, in keeping with the overriding world view established in most of the folktales – there is an urgent desire to prove worth, skill and strength, and to establish independent identities on the part of the male characters, whose actions further instantiate the ways in which patriarchal constructions of gender promote inequality. Additionally, their determined efforts to establish their valour projects patriarchy as an ideology which denies women similar opportunities.

The only characters who demonstrate any levels of creativity or resourcefulness are the males, who attempt to win her as the prize for killing the snake. One very ingenious male character even tries to trick the king into believing that he has been successful in killing the snake, a ploy which proves to be very detrimental. The portrayal of the young woman's responses reflects her fear of the snake, highlighting the stereotypical image of woman as the fearful and timid sex, and reveals as well that she is a mere sacrificial victim of the power of her father to determine when or whether she will be married to a snake-killer. Her own ability to kill the snake is never contemplated as she is regarded only in terms of her marriageability, which makes her a worthy reward for the male who would eliminate the reptile. The story exposes and invites criticism of the sexist ideology that it is acceptable for women to be treated as having no choice in the direction their lives take, or to be used as compensation for man's bravery and subjugating skills.

The same perception of a failure to acknowledge any ability on the part of the female to exercise agency, or display any sense of self is witnessed in the tale "Tontosoy", an intriguing story told by Rodrigo Habana Zárate (1990). Despite the self-characterization implied by his name, "I am a fool", the male character is projected with more autonomy and more insight into life; as well, we are presented with the complexity of his thoughts and his responses to the various challenges which he encounters. The female character, on the other hand, is a pawn in a game her wealthy father plays, promising her to someone in exchange for a favour. When the witch saves the father's life, she requests his daughter as payment, as a wife for her nephew. When this request is not met, the witch places a spell on the daughter by rendering her emotionless, a way of manipulating the situation so that the girl will not be able to marry anyone else: "lo que podemos hacer e' que si la muchacha no se va a casar contigo, ni se va a casar con el otro muchacho porque le voy a robar los sentimientos" ("Tontosoy"). (What we can do is fix it that if the girl does not marry you, she does not marry anyone else because I am going to take away her feelings.) The idea that the girl's feelings are separate and apart from her being and can be readily appropriated by another, to be trained so as to force her to love someone else, is a blatant reflection of the patriarchal characterization of the female and a denial of both the complexity of her emotions and her ability to reject a man to whom she becomes betrothed against her will. Moreover, she marries only when her feelings have been captured by another witch and reinstalled in her; she then complies with the father's desires for her to marry someone else. Even when her feelings are retrieved and returned to her, the overwhelming image is one of a battered young girl who is at the mercy of some brave man who rescues her feelings and returns them to her. The patriarchal ideologies which inform this metaphorical representation of how the woman may be made an object, in a game among those who regard her only for her marriageability, is strongly condemned in the metatext by virtue of its depiction and scrutiny. This condemnation is further galvanized by her decision to marry the person of her choice, once her emotions are returned, an action, which subverts the concerted efforts to control her and force her to marry against her will.

Eco-feminism and Female Empowerment

Eco-feminist literary criticism has proved to be critical to the analyses of the folktales, given that this approach shares some of the broad objectives of post-colonialism and other branches of feminism. One of the broad objectives of eco-feminist literary criticism is to dispel many of the myths about nature, particularly as it relates to the way man (humankind) has dominated nature through ownership, exploration and excavation. This dominance is equated with the dominance of woman by man in that nature has traditionally been seen as having an identity through its owner – man, or humankind, the subject. In this construction of nature it is projected as "other" in the same way that traditional and colonialist approaches marginalize women. According to Legler (1997, 227): "Eco-feminist literary criticism is a hybrid criticism, a combination of ecological or environmental criticism. It offers a unique combination of literary and philosophical perspectives that give literary or cultural critics a special lens through which they can investigate the way nature is represented in literature and the ways representations of nature are linked with representations of gender, race, class and sexuality." Proponents of eco-feminist criticism are not by any means suggesting that nature is equal to woman or vice versa. On the contrary, eco-feminists propose that nature can be regarded as a being with its own existence and its own reality, in the same way that woman has her own identity, which is independent of man. This assertion is clarified by Griffin (1997, 219–20):

> Eco-feminism begins with the fact of natural existence. Even if nature cannot be entirely or accurately contained in language, eco-feminism aims toward the visibility of nature as a reality. With this approach one can begin to understand that the so-called social construction (exploitation, destruction) of nature is implicit and inseparable from the social construction of gender. The equation is not that women equal nature, but that by understanding how and why woman is associated with nature, one can decode many structures of injustice in Western society. The social construction of "race", for

instance, which is also justified by an idea of nature, cannot be separated from ideas of gender. And the reverse is also true.

The folktale "Yoatzin", narrated by Melquíades Domínguez (1990) in *Jamás fandango al cielo* (1993, 71–74) poignantly underlines some of the metaphorical links between gender, race, class and representations of nature. This arresting story begins with the image of the orphan (male) who comes of age and decides that he is now ready to hunt in the deep woods. These woods include an area which he has been brought up to fear: "le habían enseñado que ese bosque era prohibido para él" (ibid., 71). (He had been taught that that part of the forest was forbidden.) But in true young, daring *macho* mode, he decides to engage the forbidden, dispensing with caution. The deer he sees and targets as his prize buck transforms into a woman, then into flowers, then back to a woman, then back again to a deer and finally to a woman again. It should not go unnoticed that her metamorphoses transport her through both aspects of nature – flora and fauna. At the same time, traditional stereotypes of the aggressive and strong male are paradoxically reinforced and undermined, as when it seems the youth will succeed in shooting the deer in a display of his great skill at using his bow and arrow, the deer emerges as a young woman peeping out from a plant. Nature is presented as an equal agent and participant in this tale.

Even so the vulnerability of nature to man's hunting and exploration is immediately signalled in these transformations, while the extent to which man's or male subjectivity is linked to supremacy and ideas of exploration and hunting is also evident. The young male is imaged as powerful and bold, graphically depicted as he is, with the weapon with which he threatens to end the life of a young deer. In other words, the power relations reveal the metaphorical links between gender and nature. The young boy/man has the ability and arms to use force to dominate nature. Still, the construction of the narrative continues to undermine his show of bravado as he discovers that, given his unfamiliarity with the forest, he needs the help of the woman, Yoatzin, to navigate his way around. The power positions become inverted as, despite his possession of treacherous weapons, the symbol of his might, he follows instruction after instruction from this deer/flower turned woman. His helplessness is emphasized as he depends on her vast knowledge of the seasons, the habits of the animals and everything that lives and occurs in the forest. He soon discovers that the instructions she gives to him are not just to emphasize his ignorance and his misguided attempts to conquer her in the forest, but also to lead him through a series of activities which will result in the spell under which she has been placed for decades, becoming broken:

> Se fue siguiéndola, siguiéndola, siguiéndola. Ya en su aldea andaban bu'cando al muchacho, jallaron la huella que pa'llá se había metido. . . . Comió el fruto y siguió la cierva, llegó al lugar 'onde siempre la podía "garrar, entonce" e'taba ella cansada, que ya no podía correr. Él la quiso amarrar como siempre lo hacía, pero se de'vaneció y se fue inconsciente al abi'mo. . . . Cuando de'pertó se vio en una ciudá'y e'taba la cierva aco'tadita junto a él y también e'taba la mujer. Vio la cierva y vio a la mujer, dijo:
> —Pero, parece que me caí en un abi'mo y 'ora e'toy en una ciudá'.
> —Cumpli'te ya con tu deber para desencantarme, porque nadie me quería venir a sacar, yo aquél que comiera el fruto tre' años me podía salvar, pero 'ora ya no soy un embrujó, soy una realida'y e'te e' mi pueblo, mi nación. ¿Tú qué prefieres, que te devuelva a tu nación o quedarte en la mía?
> ("Yoatzin", 73)

> He kept following her, following her, following her. Already in the village they were looking for the young man. They found the path that he had taken. He ate the fruit and followed the deer. He got to the point at which he could grab her, once she was tired and couldn't run anymore. He waited to grab her as usual, but she vanished and he fell and lost consciousness. When he awoke he found himself in a city and there was a deer next to him and there was also the woman. He looked at the deer and he looked at the woman and said:
> "But it seems like I fell into an abyss and now I am in a city."
> "*You fulfilled* your duty to release me from a spell because no one wanted to save me . . . but now I am not bewitched anymore, I am a reality and this is my people, my nation, what would you prefer? Do you want me to take you back to your nation, or do you want to stay here with me?"

On one level, the story seems to lapse into a perpetuation of the notion that woman needs to be rescued and given an identity and meaning to life by man. The same act of liberation which he performs, however, not only transforms her physically, but empowers her to declare her own existence – "soy una realida' y e'te e' mi pueblo, mi nación" (Díaz Pérez, Aparicio Prudente and García Casarrubias 1993, 73). (I am a reality and this is my people, my nation.) So while on the surface it seems that by having broken the spell, he gives her an identity, it is she who identifies herself, her ties to a place and a nation. She declares her recognition of her own experience of being and belonging. The act of speaking or voicing on the part of women has been characterized as an important expression of individual agency and selfhood. In other words, when women speak they assert self-certainness and subjectivity. Here, the woman's act of voicing/speaking her existence, simultaneously debunks the way in which nature is regarded as lacking any agentic force, given its muted state, as here nature is presented as more than "inert matter to be probed and penetrated, but has metaphorical status as a speaker, a live, feeling subject" (Legler 1997, 232).

Moreover, the young woman's new status places her in a position of equality with the male. Her subsequent straightforward question to him highlights her acceptance of his right to the same social liberty, which she has now regained. In other words, she unquestioningly accepts that he possesses his own individual identity, place and people. Consequently, her respect for his sense of belonging to his own people is conveyed by the question: "¿Tú qué prefieres, que te devuelva a tu nación o quedarte en la mía?" (Díaz Pérez, Aparicio Prudente and García Casarrubias 1993, 73). (What do you prefer, to return to your nation or remain in mine?)

Ironically, his response suggests that he is the displaced, confused being, with the result that the contrast between male and female is compelling – she being self-certain, he, having no sense of home or belonging, as his pained retort reveals: "¿Pero allá que tengo? No tengo padres, ni tengo hermanos y tampoco tengo mujer, si tú quieres yo me quedo aquí ("Yoatzin"). (But what do I have there? I have no parents, neither do I have brothers and sisters, or a wife. If you prefer I will stay here.) Interestingly, the biggest overthrow of male entitlement, male self-certainness and dominance in the stories is achieved through her rejection of him. This rejection compounds his feelings of failure, since all his efforts to capture the deer, now woman, have failed and she now denies him the privilege of keeping her as a prize. Her firm sense of self and autonomy is established as she rejects him for having no sense of belonging or connections to a place or people.

Their story poignantly dramatizes the situation of the liberator being rejected by the liberated, who now sees beyond the self-serving acts of rescue. They also point to the ability of women to recover from a situation of oppression, to contest the patriarchal systems that they know, by evolving new and independent identities:

—Pue' aquí te quedará'?
¿Quieres matrinomio?
—¿Cómo vo'a querer matrimonio, con quién?
La mujer enseñaló a la cierva.
—¿Qué yo puedo casarme con una cierva?
—Bueno, ¿qué tú no ibas sigiéndola?

—No me seguías a mí, la ibas siguiendo a ella,
¿No sufri'te por agarrarla?
—Bueno, ¿y cómo me caso con ella?
—Cierra tu' ojo'.
Cerró lo' ojo y cuando lo' abrió había desparecido la mujer, sólo quedaba la cierva.
("Yoatzin", 73)

"Will you stay here?
Do you want to be married?"
"How am I going to marry, whom?"
The woman showed him the deer.
"Can I marry a deer?"
"Well, weren't you following her?"

"You were not following me, you were following her.
Weren't you trying to catch her?"
"Well, how do I marry her?"
"Close your eyes."
He closed his eyes and when he opened them the woman had disappeared and only the deer was there.

The woman's rejection of the man here is suggestive of an argument for the Afro-Mexicans to have some commitment to identify with their own people on the local level. The intimation is that while there may be a need to establish links and seek acceptance in the wider Mexican community, there is also a need to understand and have a sense of connection to the local community. And so the pattern of opposition, of indecisive woman/self-certain male, is disrupted to present the woman as the one who understands the significance of connection between identity, self and nation. She displays self-knowledge, understanding of her true values and strength by showing that her identity does not depend on, nor is it determined by, an androcentric consciousness. Despite the young man's initial presentation as the one who is desirous of dominating nature and woman, he emerges weak and uncertain, while she is empowered by the development of her autonomous identity and her connection to her nation. Additionally, her shapeshifting may also be regarded as an indication of a protean ability to adapt to different contexts and challenges as well as to control, Legban-like, the terms of representation and signification.

The declaration reveals further that gender relations are important to constructions of nation. Undoubtedly, Mexico's omission of Afro-Mexicans from the national discourse on and construction of nation invariably ignores not just Afro-Mexican males, but also black females and their concerns. Moreover, perceptions and notions of masculinity and femininity are constructed within and supported by nationalist discourse about the non-existence of this ethnic group. Specific notions of manhood and womanhood that are held in Mexico do not include the specificities of the realities of Afro-Mexican men and women. Yoatzin speaks and metaphorically counters and challenges the official position regarding her status as a citizen in her country. Indeed, citizenship is "a multi-tier membership in a variety of collectivities – local, ethnic, national and transnational" (Yuval-Davis 1997, 69). Yoatzin's statement may, therefore, be considered as a subversive attempt to draw attention to the overt ways in which Afro-Mexican women and men are denied civil, political and social rights. It may even be interpreted as a dismissal of the nationalist agenda to ignore Afro-Mexican men and women, and deny their very existence in Mexico.

Furthermore, the narrative simultaneously derides any attempts to regard Afro-Mexicans in derogatory and dismissive terms. The undeniably firm tone and self-certain attitude speaks to an unshakeable understanding of her rights and her status in a country which is her home and, moreover, reveals a deep appreciation for the fact that "membership in a community . . . is bound together by enduring attachment" (Yuval-Davis 1997, 69). In other words, this representation of an Afro-Mexican woman's definition of herself is integrally linked to her understanding of her place within the nation and of how national and ethnic processes help to define her and affect her position in Mexico. It is for this reason that she is unwilling to leave the place to which she is attached and committed to go to a strange land. Her declaration, then, is about who she knows she is; it is about entitlement and her place in the Mexican collectivity. Yoatzin states categorically her understanding of the interlinking of gender, nation and female empowerment. Arguably the most powerful aspect of Yoatzin's declaration is its underlining of the extent to which "men and women do not constitute homogenous categories" (Yuval-Davis 1997, 116). In other words, she is fully aware that she is able to choose for herself and does not have to comply with the wishes of the young male, in the same way that he does not have to comply with hers.

The unfolding of the story also implies a subversion of the masculinist ideology which promoted colonialism in its intent to expand its territory and control the inhabitants of the lands appropriated. The young woman entices the gullible young man with ideas of marriage and later reveals that she has wrongly encouraged him just to teach him the importance of having an appreciation of his own place or village. Her reminder to him simultaneously trounces his misguided regard of her as his possession and his attitude of entitlement which is similar to that displayed by colonialists in their agenda to encroach on and dominate other people and their lands. Indeed, feminism and its critique of colonialism/imperialism are inevitable in the following exchange and reprimand:

>   —Yo seré tu esposa, bésame.
> Al besarla se de'vaneció y de'pertó en la orilla del río abrazando el tronco de un árbol y preguntó:
> —¿'ónde e'tá mi mujer?
> —¿Cuál mujer? Tú no tiene' mujer ni tiene' familia.
>
> —E'taba' soñando. Te hechiza' te porque te acerca' te mucho a la tierra a 'onde no se debe pasar, tú te debe' quedar, tú te debe' quedar en tu aldea.
> ("Yoatzin", 74)

> "I will be your wife, kiss me."
> As he kissed her he vanished and woke up on the bank of the river embracing the trunk of a tree. He asked:
> "Where is my wife?"
> "Which wife? You have neither wife nor family."
>
> "You were dreaming. I put a spell on you because you came too close to the forbidden land, you must stay in your village."

The portrayal of the self-certain woman who emerges at the end of the story, critiquing his ambiguous confusion and simultaneous imperious attitude, recalls and reinforces the processes of transformation she undergoes before asserting her identity as woman – even offering herself to be his wife – and highlights the importance of the process of becoming or self-invention in feminist criticism. According to Edward Baugh (1991, 3–4):

> In the male-oriented tradition of bildungsroman, the hero seeks to assert himself... there is never any doubt that he has a separate self, a privileged niche of selfhood. Woman cannot repose in any such sustaining idea. She finds herself in a world where her identity is determined for her by an androcentric consciousness. She is merely created, not herself a creator. She is, in another feminist formulation, the test written by the male creative mind. She therefore has virtually to invent herself anew.[2]

Indeed, the female's "metamorphosis of self" forcefully advances a feminist view that woman can be released from the confinement and restraints imposed on her by those who invest in patriarchal notions, by becoming what she wants, and by creating new identities. Indeed the sense of independence, freedom and satisfaction she seems to derive from being able to confound the male character as she assumes different forms are unmistakable as she leaves him still trying to figure out where he belongs. They also serve as a powerful rejection of male-imposed and biased constructions of what woman can do or what woman is. Undoubtedly, the juxtaposition of the strong woman against the uncertain, insecure young man is ironic and striking.

The complexity of this folktale arguably rests in its inherent contradictions because Yoatzin's supposed lack of self also places the young man as a victim of the young woman's cunning. In the same way that he attempts to dominate her, her attempts to teach him a lesson are tantamount to seizing an opportunity to dominate him, so we may in fact concede to having a two-way process of domination. In other words, she is not a "pure victim" in the situation, neither is he a "pure oppressor". They both may be seen as "deriving varying amounts of penalty and privilege from the multiple systems of oppression which frame everyone's lives" (Hill Collins 1999, 287).

Female Self-Construction and Survival

Luis Petatán Mariche's (1991) folktale entitled "Juaniquito el oso" (Little John the Bear), immediately establishes the oppositional terms in which gender is traditionally regarded. The male provider and leader goes out to work every day with strict instructions for his wife to follow:

> E'te era un hombre que tenía su esposa, [*sic*] todos los días salía a trabajar, se iba muy temprano, a su esposa le encargaba que fuera en darle agua al caballo, pero temprano. También le decía que tuviera cuida' o porque andaba un animal peligroso que era el oso. ("Juaniquito el oso", 86)

> There was a man who had a wife. Every day he would go to work early, and would tell his wife she was in charge of taking water to the horse, but early. He would also tell her to be careful because there was a dangerous animal, a bear, walking around.

An unambiguous impression of the power positions in which males assign roles to the females, is presented through this narrative. Moreover, the patterns of binary opposition which reinforce these power positions representing woman/man include: provider/receiver, instructor/follower, leader/led are fortified by their alignment with postcolonial binaries such as: governor/governed, oppressor/oppressed. This traditional ideological representation is further reinforced by the barbaric capture of the woman by the bear. The patriarchal suggestion, of course, is that she is captured because she fails to obey the instructions of her husband or ruler who has commanded her to complete her chores early in order to avoid the bear:

> también le decía que tuviera *cuida* 'o porque andaba un animal peligroso que era el oso. Ella así lo hacía, pero un día se le olvidó ir temprano y cuando se acordó ya e'taba cerca el oso, ella pue'se puso a gritar pero llegó el oso y le dijo:
> —¡Apúrate, vámono'!
> ("Juaniquito el oso", 86)

> he also told her to be *careful* because there was a dangerous animal, a bear, around. She did so, but one day she forgot to go out early and by the time she remembered, the bear was near, she started to shout, but the bear simply approached her and said, "Hurry, let's go."

The woman's subjugation continues, as she is placed in the most oppressive situation under the complete tyrannical control of the bear. The narrative becomes an extended metaphor of the inherent violence of colonialism/imperialism, in its reflection of such an exploitative male/female relationship of dominance and subjugation. The unfolding of this situation strikingly dramatizes the ways patriarchy functions as a system of unequal power, which requires domination and submission in order to function.

The capture situation of the woman sharply contrasts with the freedom with which male characters who go on a journey in other stories do so of their own volition. In all the tales in which the journey or travel motif is central, the men undertake this journey for the purpose of self-discovery. Here, the woman is forcefully removed from the place she knows and is taken on a journey to become a slave to a savage, wild animal.

The parallel in the social construction of gender and nature is evident in the relationship between male/bear, woman/nature implied in the recognition of the bear as a predatory, ferocious attacker of other species in the natural setting:

> Y que se la lleva a su cueva, en la que vivía él, ahí la metió y en la entrada le puso una piedra grande para que no se saliera sólo él la movía. Así se salía él a cazar, le traía carne, luego ella como no era animal asaba la carne para molerla y él no, así se la comía. ("Juaniquito el oso", 86)
>
> And he took her to the cave in which he lived and put her in there. Then he put a huge rock at the entrance that she could not move it and escape. Then he would go out to hunt, and bring her meat. But since she was not an animal, she roasted it to be able to eat it, but he ate his that way (raw).

There is no reciprocity between woman and bear – it is a relationship of dominance, imposition, oppression and sexual violations. The plight of the black slave woman is poignantly played out in this allegorical tale in which the female is deprived of freedom of choice and of control over her own physical body. Her repeated rape by the bear, the metaphorical representation of the violent dominating male, dualistically connotes the links between gender and nature/ecology. The same images of the destructive effects on the environment which the word "rape" conjures up, when used in relation to nature, are portrayed when it is used to refer to the sexual violation of woman. As Griffin (1997, 225) asserts: "Unwittingly this metaphor [rape] suggests a profound connection between the social construction of nature and the social construction of woman. And simultaneously, it describes the desire to conquer and violate woman and nature and a less evident fear of both."

Echoes of Slavery

The slave/woman slave master relationship is also recalled in the determination of the woman to survive the horrors of her captivity, while strategizing the terms of her freedom. Historical accounts are that slave women often feigned acquiescence by adopting a docile demeanour. Similarly, this woman in the folktale assumes an identity that keeps the bear believing that she has completely capitulated to her subjugation, and this way she keeps him unthreatened and unsuspecting of her quiet rebellion. As in the case of the slave woman, the repeated sexual assault on her body by her oppressive "master" produces a child – a hybrid – "half-man, half-bear" like the mulato offspring, who often was the result of the rape of black slave women by white owners and overseers. Like the many black slave women recorded in history, she protects and nurtures her offspring, despite the nature of the relationship and the brutal figure of paternity responsible for the child. In meeting the daily needs of herself and the child, the woman displays quiet resilience and a strong will to survive the horrors of her imperialistic enslavement. In other words, she uses this "space of negation" as a site of self-construction and self-preservation and quietly defies the bear's strenuous attempts to assume harshness, maleness and masculinity through his subjugation of her. In her quiet and seeming acceptance of oppression, she also demonstrates what Gilroy (2001, 205) characterizes as a "double consciousness – a double vision which ensures that diaspora people are in two places at the same time and maintain a double perspective on reality". This double consciousness/double vision empowers her in the forest where her daily labours bring to memory the servile female labour for which slaves were valued. Indeed, "the defeminism of the black female slave" (Beckles 1999, 10) is reflected in the brutal manner in which the woman is taken to inhabit a cave with a bear, to become concubine, servant, cultivator and provider, and to endure the harsh physical environment in the forest. The birth of her son vividly recalls the manner in which black slave women were not just repeatedly raped, but were forced to reproduce, so as to ensure the continuity of slavery (ibid., 8). In contrast to the slave woman/slave master situation, however, in which the black slave woman produced children to increase the labour crew, the woman in this tale produces a child who becomes the new generation of rebels who eventually secures her liberation. It is this child who comes to symbolize the answer to the Afro-Mexican's dilemma, of finding a way out of the continued oppression and the vestiges of colonialism. He eventually overpowers his father, the bear, the imperialistic colonizer, and gains liberation and independence for his mother. Her quiet collusion with the rebellious son is reminiscent of the ways slave women contested gender oppression, without necessarily launching any violent protests. This rebellious stance helps the young man to develop an attitude which helps to liberate their own consciousness from political structures of control and dominance.

Man/Nature, Man/Woman Co-existence and Harmony

The importance of finding his fortune, for the male protagonist, serves as the main introductory point in the story, "Blanca Flor". In seeking his fortune Juan seizes the opportunity to exploit the weaknesses of a vulnerable young woman. His ironic encounter with her presents an opportunity for him to assert his natural inclination to dominate and control. Juan meets Blanca Flor, who is first disguised as a dove, as she flies from a tree along with a flock of her siblings. Their unexpected transformation is revealed by Juan's comments of incredibility: "¡Qué bonitas palomas! Pero son gentes, cayeron como palomas y 'óra son gente" ("Blanca Flor", 76). (What beautiful doves! But they are people; they fell as doves and now they are people.) The implication of his first identifying them as doves, is that he perceives them with all the metaphorical associations of docility and meekness, thus reinforcing his perception of himself as the dominant controlling agent in the situation. The eco-feminist position is sharply highlighted, as the parallel between the social construction of gender and nature is evidenced in Juan's immediate recognition of an opportunity to dominate first nature, the dove, and then woman, in swift sequence. He immediately devises a way to make the most beautiful of the doves/women vulnerable to his control:

> se desenvolvieron y nomá' hicieron turrrr y ya eran unas muchachas bonitas, pero bonitas, de la' tre', la chiquita se llamaba Blanca Flor. Dice el muchacho:
> —Le vo'a esconder la' plumita a la má'chiquita, e'tá bien bonita.
> ("Blanca Flor", 76)

they came back and barely made a sound "turr" and turned into pretty young ladies, very pretty, of the three the youngest was called White Flower. He said to himself: "I am going to hide the feathers of the littlest one, she is pretty."

In a swift act of deception, he strips her of her feathers and hides them just as man strips nature of its lushness and, in eco-feminist symbolism, strips woman of her power so that he can have mastery over her. Deception then, is a useful tool in winning her confidence and enabling his plan to make her feel a need for him and facilitate his displacement of her. The woman, recognizing her vulnerability in her denuded and featherless state, accepts his invitation to be protected, provided and cared for by him. His sense of power over her is, of course, greatly heightened by her display of her own sense of exposure and vulnerability:

> Blanca Flor se quedó sentada llorando, desnuda, llora y llora, ahí sentada. Al largo rato que se habían ido la' palomas salió él, pero ella no llegó a creer que él le había 'garra' o la' plumita,' solamente él había llegado 'onde e'taba ella.
> ("Blanca Flor", 77)

> White Flower sat naked, crying, crying and crying. She just sat there. A long while after the doves had gone, he came to her, but she did not think that he had grabbed her feathers, only that he had come to her

In his home, an alien space for her, she quietly resists his efforts to redefine her and entrench his particular construct of her identity. He does not return her natural covering, but instead hides them with the complicity of his sister. White Flower finds no joy in the clothes – the new and unnatural covering he stipulates for her – and quietly embarks on a secret project of finding her own clothing. Her relentless search reveals her refusal to legitimate her capture and the choice of clothing dictated to her. It implies, too, the ability of woman to resist male tyranny, and to strategize the terms of her freedom. Her refusal to accept his choice of clothing, furthermore, suggests the rejection of patriarchy and the ideologies that regard women, not as individuals, but as objects, which do not possess the ability to make choices.

The eventual recovery of her original clothing/feathers allows her to fly away. The physical flight of the bird/woman symbolizes the ability of woman to develop her own independent spirit and strategize her mental and emotional escape. Additionally, the ease with which she moves from being woman to bird emphasizes the ability of woman to become whatever is necessary for her to escape or survive oppression. Juan, ironically, does not regard her as being capable of taking control and sees her only for her beauty. Implicit in this attitude is the way nature is often considered more for its decorative function, rather than for its right to exist as a living, agentic subject. Flight facilitates self-assertion and boldness, so that when White Flower allows herself to be re-sought and brought back to his land, the terms of agreement and partnership are different. She is no longer being beguiled into thinking that she needs Juan to save her from a desperate situation, but they agree to work together in a mutual situation of need and willingness to support each other. Their new relationship promotes a paradigm for males and females to relate to each other within a frame of mutual respect, self-certainnesss and recognition of how each has a contribution to make to ensure harmonious and productive interactions and relationships.

Black Feminist Thought and Africana Womanism

Both Black Feminist thought and Africana Womanism constitute two illuminating lenses through which some folktales may be analysed. Black Feminist thought advances the debate concerning ways in which black women should/can foster their own self-empowerment and become self-determining in contexts in which they are victims of a hegemonic domain of power or intersecting oppressions of race, class, gender and sexuality (Hill Collins 1999, 230). Additionally, self-definition is considered to be achievable through the development of a "woman consciousness", or a critical mind, which understands how social institutions, men and various structures of power are organized to oppress black women. The significance of resisting domination to establish individual and group agency, are also emphasized in Black Feminist theories.

Africana Womanism is similar to Black Feminism in its attempts to interrogate gender from an Afrocentric perspective, based on the assertion that mainstream feminism does not accurately reflect the struggles of black women. According to Hudson-Weems (1993) who coined the term, "Africana Womanism" is an ideology created for all women of African descent, is grounded in African culture, and therefore it necessarily focuses on the unique experiences, struggles, needs and desires of Africana women. Hudson-Weems (1993, 31) further declares: "Africana Womanism – rather than feminism, Black Feminism, Africana Feminism, or Womanism – is a conceivable alternative for the Africana woman in her collective struggle with the entire community. It enhances future possibilities for the dignity of Africana people and the humanity of all. In short, the reclamation of African women via identifying our own collective struggle and acting upon it is a key step toward harmony and survival." Africana Womanism has not been embraced by all black women in the academy, for various reasons. One of the most frequently expressed criticisms is its exclusionary premise of compulsory heterosexuality. Notwithstanding these issues, I am interested in the broad tenets of the approach, especially in its similarities to Black Feminism; I am not by any means interested in advancing or rejecting any particular sexual preference.

Several tenets of Africana Womanism are useful to this study and are evident in different folktales which have previously been discussed. For instance, psychological and physical strength are considered to be two important characteristics of the Africana Womanist. This strength is exhibited in the enduring strength of the black female character who is captured by the bear in "Juaniquito el oso" (Little John the Bear) and survives the oppressive conditions, including bearing and nurturing the child of her oppressor until she gains freedom. A second quality of the Africana Womanist – the self-definer – is powerfully delineated in the character of the self-certain Yoatzin, the woman in the forest who boldly declares, "I am reality and this is my nation." Her confident announcement finds and gives substance to Hudson-Weems's (1993, 57) claim that "the Africana womanist . . . defines herself".

Male and Female Collaboration

In the folktale "Morena" (Black Woman) narrated by Catalina Bruno (1990), the black female protagonist whose name clearly signals her race/ethnicity is initially introduced as the daughter of the king who will offer her to the man who guesses her name. She endures this period of uncertainty as male after male fails the test and fails to be rewarded with her. Morena, like other female characters depicted in other folktales, is held up as the objectified prize, waiting to be claimed by some "intelligent" male. Of course, the implication created by the principle of oppositionality on which traditional gender constraints operate is that man is intelligent, thus woman is simple-minded and inane. When she is finally won by one seemingly smart male, Puertasiban, she quickly reveals through her counsel and caution that even though she is not valued for her intellectual abilities, she understands the treacheries and dangers of life. The attempt to affirm the woman's ethnicity is arguably evidenced by Puertasiban's matter-of-fact conjecture of her name using the term "Morena", which in fact turns out to be her name. Morena's ready acknowledgement of this name implies that she is aware of the ways in which her name defines her, in the Africana Womanist mode, and more importantly she is not disturbed by being identified as a black woman.

Morena exhibits characteristics of the Africana Womanist in the way she proves not to be the inane counterpart of the new husband, who endears himself to her by his accidental affirmation of her blackness. She projects herself as a partner who is capable of directing their decisions and choices. She outlines the dangers they face as a result of their inheritance from the king and endeavours to awaken his awareness of the potential threats, which he dismisses to his detriment. The unfolding of the story implies Morena's understanding of male entitlement, sexism and oppression which are expressed by the tyrannical misogynist who overpowers her husband and later captures her and proudly announces his personal creed: "Las mujere' son el Diablo. . . . Por es' o no te tienen confianza. Lo hombre' a la mujere' " (p. 113). (Women are the devil. . . . That is why men do not trust women.) It is undoubtedly held up for scrutiny and condemnation, and his subsequent destruction serves as a suppression of this belief.

The woman consciousness which some Black Feminists suggest is necessary for vanquishing hegemonic ideals is implied by Morena's subsequent collaboration with her husband to secure his release and also hers. Additionally, "Morena" displays two important characteristics of the Africana Womanist, as typified by Hudson-Weems (1993). First, the long wait and collaborative planning of their individual escape from their captor shows her as working in collaboration with the male for liberation. As Hudson-Weems (1993, 61) states: "The Africana Womanist invites her male counterpart into her struggle for liberation, and parity in society, as this struggle has been traditionally the glue that has held them together and enabled them to survive in a hostile society."

The second Africana Womanist quality displayed by Morena is her genuine desire for positive male companionship. Once Morena realizes the sincerity of the young man who guesses her name and is rewarded with her, their situation becomes more palatable and they show respect for each other as individual human subjects. Once they rid themselves of the tyrant, she encourages a relationship based on mutual affection in which they are supportive of each other – "an important part of a positive Africana family" (Hudson-Weems 1993, 66).

In the humorous but thought-provoking folktale "La ranita" (Little Toad), also narrated by Catalina Bruno (1991), the king's three sons go out to seek their wives and fortune. The first two sons meet women who have physical challenges – the first being blind and the second being without hands. The reaction of both men to the women's physical defects poignantly reveals their attitude to females and the domestic or utilitarian role they perceive women should perform in order to indicate their worth. The first son who finds a blind woman declares: "no hay muchacha' solamente e'ta ciega, ¿qué voy a'cer?" (p. 93). (There is no girl, only this blind one, what am I going to do?) Undoubtedly, he equates her femaleness with her physical attributes and ignores all the other noteworthy or commendable qualities she may possess as a woman. The same is true for the second son who seems to be mainly preoccupied with the woman's inability to serve him and perform manual work. He initially dismisses her with his pained question: "¿Pa' que' me va servir? Pue' pa' nada" (ibid.). (What use does she have to me? None at all.)

In contrast, the response of the third son to the toad that he finds points to the important reasons for which women should be valued and valorized. This son listens to the toad and allows himself to be guided and instructed by her, to his own benefit. This way, the woman, who has been trapped in the body of the toad, emerges and proves to be a self-certain, strong, confident woman. She is embraced in her state of so-called ugliness as she demonstrates innovativeness, confidence, creativity and, more importantly, an interest in the well-being of others. As a result, she eventually brings satisfaction to the prince, who does not reject her on the basis of superficial physical appearances or lack of value/worth.

Interestingly, the ugly toad-turned-woman proves to be more beautiful than the other two women, as she performs different tasks that produce transformations in the life of the young man's family. Considerations of outward appeal and physical perfection are dismissed by the king's acceptance of her and by his son's willingness to take her home, alongside the human sisters-in-law who turn out not to be humane in their treatment of others. The dualistic representation of the toad-woman conveys the ways in which humanity can benefit from even the least valued aspect of nature, and similarly revalorizes woman, not for any notions of beauty based on external physical attributes, but to reconstruct her as a person who is equally capable as the male, to make a contribution to family and nation building. It underlines furthermore, a critique of the way in which women are valued for physical beauty, as defined by patriarchy, and what men consider to be appealing and vulnerable.

Finally, the analyses of the folktales reveal a complexity of interconnected ideas and issues related to the ways in which the discourse on gender and race intersect with constructions of nation. In other words, a consciousness of the connections among place, belonging and self-construction is implied in the unfolding of some stories. Second, some folktales also develop a politics of empowerment in the way black female characters undermine and subvert exploitation and attempts at domination by their male counterparts.

Several theories provide an effective theoretical frame for illuminating the stories. For instance, eco-feminist criticism facilitates the appreciation of how nature and human behaviour echo each other and help to demonstrate how portrayals of nature can parallel the writing about colonized and oppressed people, including the exploitation of women and especially black women under patriarchy. The erasing of the definite lines between nature and humans, symbolizes the erasure or the blurring of lines between man and other or woman, and between self/subject and other. The projecting of nature as subject often symbolically establishes female agency/subjectivity and the rejection of patriarchy.

The folktales suggest that the politics of woman's empowerment also involve a consciousness of how, when black men participate in social institutions that seek to perpetuate black women's subordination, they invariably come to recognize, albeit late, that they themselves are also victims of a wider oppression involving issues of place, belonging and identity, and, therefore, need to forge their own independent identities. Male tyranny is often subverted in the tales, while positive portrayals of black women, in their quest for liberation, self-definition and an understanding of their place within the nation, are held up as models of female empowerment.

Without doubt, the discourse on issues of nation, gender and race intersect in variously complex ways. Indeed, these narratives that have been preserved and narrated by Afro-Mexicans intimate that in the same way that the Afro-Mexican community is affected by nationalist projects, processes related to ethnicity and national culture; the relations between men and women are influenced and shaped by several considerations of culture. When black females struggle to foster their own empowerment and establish their identities, this is inevitably influenced by broader constructs of nation, of race and hegemonic domains of power.

3.

Masculinity, Language and Power in Selected Afro-Mexican *Corridos*

"All masculinities, even the most radical and counteractive are ultimately performances of and searches for certainty of self, role and image."
—Curdella Forbes, *From Nation to Diaspora*

"No language is neutral seared in the spine's unravelling. . . . What I say in any language is told in faultless knowledge of skin, in drunkenness and weeping, told as a woman without matches and tinder not in words and in words and in words learnt by heart."
—Dionne Brand, *No Language is Neutral*

The subject of masculinity has generated many critical studies from which have emerged various theories designed to establish understandable structures of analysis of the subject of male identity. Undoubtedly, these studies have underlined the complexity of the term and the inherent difficulties in the attempt to establish common ground among the theories advanced by experts and theorists in various fields. The emasculation theory, first advanced by Frantz Fanon (1970), has been rejected by sociologists such as Tim Edwards (2006), for its failure to theorize masculinity in gendered terms.[1] Edwards draws on Robert Connell's (1995, 71) claim that masculinity is a place in gender relations, the practices through which men and women engage and the experience in body, personality and culture. Indeed, Connell, whose research has been recognized as having established some of the most fundamental concepts for the construction of masculine identities, also dismissed the four broad categories which have long provided the bases for defining masculinity.[2]

The approach to the study of masculine identities which seems to be most widely embraced by many sociologists and specialists in gender studies draws on broad social constructionist theories, which focus on the idea of constructions of gender, including the view that "man" and "woman" are socially and culturally created categories (Jant and Hurdley 2007, 219). Social constructionism is accepted as an effective strategy for defining masculinity because it dispenses with the view that gender differences may be determined by hormones, in favour of the position that gender is not "a fixed category", but accepts "man" and "woman" as socially and culturally created categories (ibid.). This is explicated by Rafael Ramírez (1993, ix) as follows: "Social constructionism acknowledges that all societies establish gender differentiations. The masculine and feminine domains are defined by specific attributes, tasks and symbols. Subjects are recognized as male or female, and are evaluated in compliance with gender expectations. What it means to be a man or a woman is a cultural construction. Although gender constructions are embedded on biological differences, they are not biologically determined." Social constructionists also reject the notion of a one-dimensional understanding of masculinity; arguing for the acceptance of the plurality of masculinities. Connell (1995, 8) advances the view that "some masculinities are hegemonic and dominant while others are subordinated and marginalized". According to Connell (1995, 227), "hegemonic" refers to "the masculinity of those men who control power". He further claims that "hegemonic masculinity is the socially dominant form of masculinity in a particular culture within a given historical period".

In contrast, then, subordinate masculinity would refer to masculinity established by men who do not control power in society. Initially, it may seem that the most appropriate location for expressions of masculinity among Afro-Mexican men would be the subordinate category. However, later discussions will demonstrate that this is not as straightforward as it may appear. Indeed, the idea that even "subordinate masculinity" is not a "fixed" and unmovable category, will also be examined later in the chapter.

Masculinity in a Postcolonial Context

In the Caribbean and other postcolonial societies, masculinity as the quest for individual identity and self-assertion has been linked to the history of struggle against imperialist powers, this including the struggle against slavery and the struggle for nationhood and national identity. Hilary Beckles (2004, 227) has established that from early Caribbean slave society, "the masculinity of enslaved blacks was constructed through interaction with hegemonic structures of white masculinity". This response to slavery, he maintains, has continued into contemporary Caribbean societies in which oppressed/marginalized men are in search of their individual identities and struggle to assert these independent identities. Beckles claims that "Caribbean masculinities are conceptualized and experienced as subordinated and struggling to varying degrees in the post- and neo-colonial context, for the personhood, recognition, visibility, citizenship and power felt to be their birthright" (ibid.). Similarly, Kenneth Ramchand (2004) regards the construction of both masculinity and femininity in Caribbean societies as being linked to their history of enslavement, indenture and colonialism, as a search for self. He expressly asserts that "the constructions of both masculinity and femininity have been ordered by the imperatives of organized systems of oppression and exploitation. Here the struggle of the obscure or obscured person to emerge as a self, to become visible and make a mark in the world, the necessity to find the true self, exists for male and female alike" (p. 312).

Indeed, Kimmel and Messner (1995, 302) both support the preceding views in their claim that masculinism is "not static or immutable but shaped by historical and cultural context". Several characterizations of the historical and cultural contexts of Afro-Mexicans have been presented in previous chapters, to show that Afro-Mexicans themselves battle, negotiate and resist the realities of invisibility, racism, social and economic inequalities on a daily basis. The study of masculinity in the Afro-Mexican diasporic context may, therefore, be treated through the same paradigms as those used for the broader Caribbean, marked as it is by marginalization, displacement, loss, broken histories, exclusion, discrimination and even conflicted interethnic relations and class relations.

Constructions of Masculinity in the Mexican Context

It is now well accepted that despite the application of some broad conceptions of manhood, such as essentialist definitions of the masculine or normative definitions of what men are, or semiotic definitions based on the differences between men and women, there is in fact no universal model that is totally acceptable to all societies. There may be some broad areas of consensus related to issues of dominant/subordinate positions, but generally each society will develop its own concept of masculine identity, based on its social and historical experiences. Alfredo Mirandé (1997, 16) for instance, cautions against any unquestioning embrace of norms that are more applicable to white males than to Mexican men, who have had completely different historical and social experiences.

Mirandé justifies the need for different approaches by highlighting the disparate historical experiences specific to Mexico. The first of these is the pre-Columbian heritage, which placed value on bravery and valour; Mirandé (1997, 49) makes reference to the fact that Hernán Cortés's arrival in Mexico was met by fierce resistance and revolt: "*Machista* tendencies were clearly evident in Aztec society long before the arrival of the Europeans." The many wars which ensued between Aztecs and Spaniards seemed to have fuelled the pride in "manliness" and the hypermasculinity or *super machismo* associated with Mexican men. The history of some cases of triumph of Aztecs over Spanish is believed to have produced great pride in Mexicans, who regard this as an indication of who they are and their ability to defend themselves and protect their sovereignty. Second, Mirandé (1997) claims that, in general, Mexicans' conceptualization of masculinity is also rooted in their Spanish cultural heritage. Before the conquest, Spanish society placed a great premium on masculinity and patriarchy. These values were, in turn, imposed on the Indian population once the Spanish arrived in Mexico.

Not to be omitted from this fundamental debate is the view of Mexico's eminent critic, poet, essayist, philosopher and Nobel laureate Octavio Paz. Indeed, Paz (1994) regarded Mexico's well-debated "cult of *machismo*", as a kind of camouflage of the feelings of powerlessness experienced by Mexican men during the conquest, when they were powerless before the *conquistadores* who raped their women and plundered their villages. In his compelling collection of essays, entitled *The Labyrinth of Solitude*, Paz (1994) frames his analyses of the Mexican character, psyche and self with both psychoanalytic and sociological theories. The philosopher grounds his ideas of how the Mexican's existentialist angst about solitude, death and nothingness also results in a deep sense of impotence and ineptitude. According to Paz (1994, 88), the Mexican display and performance of *machismo* is an attempt to mask this solitude and helplessness produced by Mexico's history, a history which Paz further characterizes as a wound, felt by not just the Mexican nation but by the self:

> El mexicano y la mexicanidad se definen como la ruptura y la negación y asimismo, como búsqueda, como voluntad por trascender ese estado de exilio. En suma, como viva conciencia de le soledad, histórica y personal. La historia, que nos podía decir nada sobre la naturaleza de nuestros sentimientos y de nuestros conflictos, nos puede mostrar ahora cómo se realizó la ruptura y cuales han sido nuestras tentativas para transcender la soledad.

> Mexican and "Mexicaness" are defined as rupture and negation, and at the same time as quest, as a will to transcend this state of exile. In short, as a living consciousness of historical and personal solitude. History, which could tell us nothing about the nature of our feelings and conflicts, can show us now how the rupture was realized and what have been our efforts to transcend solitude.[3]

Aramoni (1965, 280) advances a similar view, which incorporates both Aztec and Spanish patriarchal tendencies as being contributory to the formation of Mexican concepts of masculinity. In other words, in the conquest, two equally *machista* groups met: "they were warring, conquering, predatory, military nations in which men were dominant and women were subordinate".

What seems to be an indispensable component in the debate is that historical events such as conquest, slavery and the movement of groups which have established themselves as dominant in the society have contributed to the establishment of Mexican identities and constructions of both masculinity and femininity. This all finds consonance in Connell's (1995, xxii) declaration that "imperial conquest, neo-colonial and the current world systems of power, investment, trade and communication have brought very diverse societies in contact with each other. The gender systems that result are local patterns, but carry the impress of the forces that make a global society."

Connell's (1995) statement notwithstanding, much of the debate on *latino* masculinity in general and Mexican masculinity/*machismo* specifically focuses on the Aztec heritage or the result of European associations with Aztec groups.

This means that the construction of masculine identities in the African-derived community has been ignored. Arguably, this absence of a theory that extends beyond issues related to the Spanish conquest of Mexico, and the ensuing conflicts between Aztecs and Europeans is reminiscent of Tim Edwards's (2006, 64) theory that in general, studies of masculinity are concerned only with white males. It provides corroboration as well, of Connell's (1995, xxii) view of how the "interaction of cultures" under "colonialism and post-colonial globalisation have linked the making of masculinity with the construction of racial or ethnic hierarchies". Indeed, Connell's position provides explanation of how the interactions between racial groups also influence the construction of masculine identities. It helps to explain, furthermore, the omission of the experiences of black men in definitions of Mexican masculine identity/identities.

The oppression and marginalization that were experienced by Aztecs were also experienced by blacks. In this chapter then, masculinity as well as femininity will be treated in keeping with social constructionism, as gendered ideologies that are both culturally and socially constructed; as products of various historical and cultural contexts that influence the way men and women are perceived or choose to define themselves, as individuals and in relation to each other.

The construction of masculinity among Afro-Mexican males will be explored through the discussion of a collection of Afro-Mexcan *corridos*. The *corrido* is a musical folk ballad which dramatizes different aspects of Mexican history; although, it is primarily associated with the portrayal of events linked to the Mexican Revolution. The *corridos* that will be analysed have been confirmed by Miguel Angel Gutiérrez, specialist in Afro-Mexican cultural expressions, as production of the Afro-Mexican region of Costa Chica. Many of them were published as part of an album entitled *Traigo una flor hermosa y mortal*. Others collected from different sources are included for study here.

One major caveat to much of the scholarly respresentation so far is that the performance of masculinity by Afro-Mexican males in the *corrido* can hardly be considered to be a single subordinated form, or one that is only a response to the masculinity of oppressive white/*latino* governments/groups. On the contrary, it assumes several shades of complexity when examined in light of the interactions with Afro-Mexican female figures in the *corridos*, who are also marginalized along with the men under the same oppressive systems, and sometimes further marginalized, by black men themselves in their relationships.

Studies of the construction of masculine identities in popular songs produced in a similar cultural context are important to the examination of the *corridos*. These studies include the work of Caribbean scholars, such as Kenneth Ramchand (2004) and Gordon Rohlehr (2004), who have discussed the construction of masculinity in popular cultural forms in the Caribbean, including the Trinidadian calypso. The calypso is a traditional form of music which developed as a form of protest against British rule and combines European and African beats. Ramchand (2004) further points to the expression of masculinity in Trinidad as being "historically linked with the figure of the bad-john" – a figure associated with marginalized existence in the ghetto or lower-class Afro-Trinidadian life – or "persons repeatedly flouting colonial attempts to regulate and civilize them" (Ramchand 2004, 313).

Gordon Rohlehr (2004, 336) further contends that in the Caribbean, "the underclass, which tends to be criminalized by elite groups constructs masculinity in terms of resistance, rebellion, aggressiveness, toughness and the style and reputation that are inseparable from any ethnic or violent performance". The discourse of masculinity in the Afro-Mexican *corrido* seems to be similarly constructed on the basis of a particular cultural and historical context of marginalization and, as a consequence, depicts individuals who feel compelled to challenge the status quo, and invert power positions.

Masculinity, Power and Language

Many of the widely held and debated views about power and power relations have been derived from the work of Michel Foucault (1980). Indeed, his contribution to the postmodernist debate concerning definitions of power advances the theory (influenced in part by Nietzsche's philosophy on power) that power is action over action *(une action sur desactions)*. This theory presented a contrast to theories of power advanced by Machiavelli, for instance, based on *jurídico/* political conceptions of power, as well as theories based on class domination advanced by Karl Marx.

Foucault's (1980, 220) view that "power is inextricably linked to subjectivity as people become subjects in and through power relations", is well known. He further defined subject, first as being subject to someone else's control or dependence, and second as "tied to one's identity by conscience or self-knowledge". Although Foucault amplifies his theory on power to include the stance that "power is everywhere, not because it embraces everything but because it comes from everything" (ibid.), the central claim remains the same, that power entails a set of actions performed upon others.

Foucault expresses other characterizations of power which have relevance to the claims being made about how the powerless often find subversive means to assert self or exercise power. Two very potent aspects include the tenets that "power inheres the individual" and that "power occurs in a locus of struggle" (ibid.). Foucault's forceful perspectives on power are central to the discussion of masculinity in the *corridos* because the *corridos* may be characterized as unfolding the discourse of the powerless reinventing themselves as powerful, in order to establish subjectivity.

The preceding claim finds validity in the fact that the *corridos* being studied were created in a context of struggle, in which male protagonists are depicted as recognizing that power does reside in the individual, is immensely enabling and allows the individual the ability to effect change. Moreover, the masculine identities exhibited in the *corridos* underline Foucault's (1980, 92–93) assertion that power is not an institution, and not a structure; it is a certain strength we are endowed with; it is the name that we attribute to a complex strategical situation in a society.

The strategic situation/context of the *corridos* in which the male protagonists are seen to perform powerful masculine roles, draws on the tension and conflict which characterized the different historical periods in which Afro-Mexican guerilla groups (rebels) were overpowered and annihilated by the force of government and other "legitimate" paramilitary troops (Ramsay 2003, 67). The Afro-Mexican protagonists are seen to redefine their identities as powerless victims to become powerful agents of their destinies, through violent retaliations. The *corridos* depict Afro-Mexicans engaging in power struggles and challenging the powerful through the use of power amd might. The analyses of the *corridos* will lead us to conclude that their internal ideology reflects a philosophy that finds substance in Foucault's (1980, 92) philosophy as it relates to power, "as action designed to modify the actions of others", as being inextricably linked to subjectivity, so that protagonists or characters become subjects in and through power relations.

In this vein, both the "Corrido de los Zapatistas de San Nicolás" and "El

Zanatón" seem to dramatize Foucault's (1980, 92) claim that "resistance defines power and resistance is indispensable in the exercise of power". Indeed, in these *corridos,* representatives of the Afro-Mexicans, become powerful by redefining their identities, asserting their subjectivity and resisting their oppressors. They defy the might and force of government troops, despite the seeming impossibility of emerging as winners in such confrontations. It becomes evident that it is through stubborn resistance that they appear as victorious and come to be regarded as powerful fighters. Indeed, they confront the hegemonic and dominant masculinity performed by government troops and emerge as heroes who unequivocally contest the view that subordinate masculinities are usually effeminate or infantile, as they are contrarily projected as heroes and as brave males who take action against mighty forces:

Corrido de los Zapatistas de San Nicolás

Cuando Bruñuela llegó	When Bruñuela arrived
llegó muy desesperado,	he came in desperation
quemando y matando gente	burning and killing people
y sacándola del bajo.	and seizing everything.
Llegando tiró la voz	Arriving he shouted loudly
como persona decente,	like a respectable person
aquí me van a entregar	here they turn themselves in
a toditita esta gente.	all these people.
Ahora si los carrancistas	Now if the carrancistas
andan de ados carilleras,	walk along these tracks
Zapata para pelear	to fight, Zapata
no necesita trincheras.	does not need trenches.
Cuando los vieron tirados	When the mob saw them scatter
Todos pegaron de gritos,	they all began to shout
¡Viva Melquíades Román	Long live Melquíades Román
con todos sus Zapatistas!	and all his followers!
Ya nosotros nos vamos	Now we are ready to go
dijo Everardo Román	said Everardo Román
como a las seis de la tarde	as at six in the afternoon
murió Teodor Montealbán	Teodor Montealbán died.

Ya me voy a despedir	Now I'm going to say goodbye
Con gusto y con muchas ganas,	with much joy and best wishes
¡si me quieren agarrar	and if they want to catch me
allá estoy en La Bocana!	I am there in La Bocana!

Zapata nunca acaba	Zapata never dies
Y se acobardaron todos	and they became frightened
llegando a San Nicolás	on arriving at San Nicolás
y mataron a Don Lolo.	and they killed Don Lolo.

This representation of masculinity gives credence to Rhoda Reddocks's (2004, xxi) assertion that "inter-ethnic relations in [Caribbean] societies are often expressed as a contest among men, where control of political power seems to legitimize claims of citizenship and becomes a symbol of 'manhood' ". The *corridos* reveal a consciousness on the part of the Afro-Mexicans of their exclusion from positions of power and authority. As a result Afro-Mexican protagonists are seen to engage in activities that suggest their recognition that they have a right to selfhood and power. Indeed, the Afro-Mexican males in the *corridos* are delineated as powerful, perhaps not in the same way that their oppressors are, but they attempt to construct powerful identities through their show of bravado. In the context, their construction of masculine identities is concerned with projecting an image of dominance in society as they are presented as overthrowing and defeating forces that are officially regarded as being more powerful in the particular context. Once again, the delineation is consonant with an assertion made by Foucault (1980, 93) that power is not an institution or a structure; it is a certain strength we are endowed with, it is the name that we attribute to complex strategic situations in a society.

Language and Masculinity

In the 1960s, while feminist linguists studied the centrality of language in the construction of feminine identities, the role of language in the construction of masculine identities was ignored. The first call to correct this inexactitude was made by linguist Dell Hymes, who declared that "a focus on women brings to light an aspect of language in social life that has its counterpart for men . . . men's language needs study too" (Hymes quoted in Lakoff 1973, 9). Since then, particularly in the field of social sciences, greater attention has been given to masculinity and its intersections with issues of language and gender. A number of studies have been conducted in the late twentieth century that have established that not only is language one of the resources used to inform the construction of gender identities, but also that men use language differently from women to project particular images and impressions of themselves in order to describe male behaviour and project man as the representative of humanity, and as powerful.

Indeed, language is indispensable in shaping and legitimizing particular masculine identities, since language is also crucial to performance. Moreover, it is generally agreed that language is central in every social situation. Sally Johnson and Ulrike Hanna Meinhof (1997, 22) assert that this is so because both masculinity and femininity are "social processes dependent upon systematic restatement, a process which is referred to as 'performing gender' or doing identity work". Of course, language refers not just to the spoken word, but to other aspects of language usage, which may provide an indication of the gendered identities being projected and the specialized ways in which these identities are presented. Johnson and Meinhof further claim that "language does not simply mirror gender, it helps constitute it, it is one of the means by which gender is enacted" (23).

In the *corrido* the spoken/sung word is important for showing how ideology and speech work together to create the identity male performers want to project. The use of language indicates that the Afro-Mexican male protagonists within the *corridos*, as well as the male narrators of the *corridos*, use a particular repertoire to challenge the status quo, disparage political leadership and promote themselves as competitive, capable, confident men who are concerned with promoting a culturally nationalist agenda, to privilege members, to destabilize the hegemonic masculinity of the society, and to demonstrate that the new masculinity which they are performing/promoting is essentially concerned with exhibiting power. Examination of the language in the *corridos* exposes the intricate ways in which speech and ideology work together to create a particular identity or masculinity. All the discursive language strategies – irony, diction, tone, register, syntax, contrast, restatement, figurative language, among others – accentuate a particular identity, one associated with power.

Language and Violence

The use of language in the *corrido* may be said to be linked to the history of violence of the Afro-Mexicans. Aguirre Beltrán (1972, 19) attributes what he characterizes as "un ethos violento y agresivo en su cultura" (a violent and aggressive ethos in their culture) to the fact that the inhabitants of the Costa Chica region are, for the most part, descendants of Maroons who rejected slavery, established Maroon communities and chose to defend their freedom primarily by violent means. Other historical accounts point to the fact that these descendants of Maroons also combated colonial powers to establish a modicum of independence. Furthermore, according to Ramsay (2003, 69), following the end of colonial rule Spanish jurisdiction was replaced by various foreign entities, and after strategizing and swindling the Afro-Mexicans out of their lands, these foreign entities established paramilitary groups to protect these lands and tyrannize the Afro-Mexicans in the process.

In the context of the counterattacks launched by Afro-Mexican males, language is used to narrate and describe their activities which are designed to defeat the actions of their oppressors. Consequently, their need to appear more powerful extends into the linguistic domain as the language is deliberately crafted to depict the violence which characterizes the power struggle. From one *corrido* to the next, we see that aggressive, political language and the establishment of male identity in this Afro-Mexican context are interrelated. Violence is evident in the speech style and language choices. In "El Zanatón", for instance, the words and expressions used to describe government troops in contrast to those used to describe the Afro-Mexican challengers create a powerful rhetorical concept.

Voy a cantar un corrido	I'm going to sing a *corrido*
señores porque ahí les va.	gentlemen because
les voy a dar a saber	I'm going to tell you what
lo que pasó en Palomar,	happened in Palomar,
donde muieron los guachos	where the bastards died because
por no saberse tantear.	they didn't know how to fend for themselves.
Cuando venían de San Marcos	When they came from San Marcos
venían muy desesperados,	they were very desperate,
pasaron por Las Lomitas	they passed by Las Lomitas

con el fusil preparado,	with their guns ready,
en busca de los Hernández	in search of the Hernández
porque los traiban de encargó.	because they were giving them a hard time.

Al llegar al Palomar	On reaching Palomar
una mujer les habló	a woman spoke to them
se buscan a los Hernández	they were looking for the Hernández
se los juro que por Dios,	she swore to them under oath,
están en el Campo Santo	they were in Campo Santo
bajo palabra de honor.	on her word of honour.

Ay, les dice el fusilero:	Ah, says the rifleman:
sobre aviso no hay engaño,	to be forewarned is to be forearmed,
vámonos pa'l Campo Santo	let us go to Campo Santo
dicen que están esos gallos	they say those chickens are there
si con Constancio me encuentro	if I meet Constancio,
no quedará disgustado.	he will not be upset.

Ay, les dice el fusilero:	Ah, says the rifleman:
cuídense que ahí les va una	be careful because there goes one
soy pescador de la mar	I am a fisherman of the sea
no de esta pinche laguna,	not of this damned pond,
he toreado toros bravos	I have fought fierce bulls
no zanatilla sin pluma.	not a *zanatilla* plant without plumes.

A los primeros balaso'	At the first shots
le gritaban tú le llevas,	they shouted, you carry him,
luego tumbaron a Marcos	then they shot Marcos
y a Alfonso Villanueva,	and Alfonso Villanueva,
pero les quedó Constancio	but Constancio remained
peleándoles pecho a tierra.	fighting them, with his chest on the ground

Ay, les dice El Zanatón:	Ah, says El Zanatón:
por mi lado no hay cuidado,	I'm not worried
ya me tumbé al fusilero	I already shot the rifleman
llevo el fusil a mi lado,	I carry my gun at my side,
y a otros tres compañeros	and three other companions
que aquí quedaron tirado'	who were shot.

Ay, les dice El Zanatón:	Ah, says El Zanatón:
encomienden su alma a Dios	commend their soul to God
encomienden su alma a Dios	commend their soul to God
porque ahí les va El Animal,	because there goes the Animal,
se los juro que por Dios	I swear to you before God
ese sí los va a acabar.	that he will finish them off.
Pobrecitos de los guachos	Poor bastards
ya no jallaban que hacer,	they didn't know what to do
arrancaban pa' las casa'	they started for home
queriéndose defender,	wanting to defend themselves
El Zanatón los búscaba	El Zanatón looked for them
como cosa de comer.	like he would eat them alive.
Pobrecitos de los guachos	Poor bastards
se andaban volviendo locos,	they were going crazy,
arrancaban pa' las huertas	they started for the orchards
queriendo baja' unos coco,	wanting to get some coconuts,
pero al llegar a la barranca	but on reaching the hill
se quedaron otros pocos.	there were a few others.
Pusieron un radiograma	They sent a radiogram message
al Presidente Camacho,	to President Camacho,
que vinieran a saber	to come and know,
a ver como estuvo el caso,	to see how things were,
que vinieran a saber	to come and know
donde murieron los guachos.	where the bastards died.
Bajaron dos aeroplano'	They shot down two aeroplanes
a cargo de un General,	that a general had,
bajaron dos avioneta	they shot down two light aircrafts
a cargo de un General,	that a general had
pero con el Zanatón	but with el Zanatón
ya no quisieron pelear.	they no longer wanted to fight.
("El Zanatón")	

The direct speech of the Afro-Mexican male figures is forceful as in the preceding *corrido* and is in consonance with the agenda to project men who are asserting subjectivity and agency, exercising power over others to counteract and modify actions, which they consider injurious to themselves as Afro-Mexican males/subjects. They make authoritarian statements, which depict them as exhibiting masculine traits such as fearlessness and bravery. Pedro el Chicharrón, the protagonist in another *corrido* by the same name, for instance, is reported to categorically state his dismissal of the perceived might of government troops:

Voy a cantar un corrido	I will sing a corrido
me permitan su atención,	give me your attention;
de esos hombres pocos nacen,	few men like these are born
hombres de mucho valor,	men of great resolve;
el que nace no se logra	those who are born don't last,
como Pedro el Chicharrón,	like Pedro el Chicharrón,
el que nace no se logra	those who are born don't last,
como Pedro el chicarrón.	like Pedro el Chicarrón,
Ese Pedro el Chicharrón	That Pedro el Chicharrón
era hombre y no se rajaba,	was tough and wouldn't back down;
que si el gobierno le caiba	if the government fell upon him
con el gobierno peleaba,	with the government he would fight;
le decía a sus compañeros	he was saying to his companions
que hasta risa le causaba	that it just made him laugh,
le decía a sus compañeros	he was saying to his companions
que hasta risa le causaba.	that it just made him laugh.
Bajaba Zeta Martínez	Zeta Martínez came down
A rumbo de Espinalillo:	on his way to Espinalillo:
"Voy a ver al Chicharrón	"I am going to see Chicharrón;
que lo quiero para amigo,	I want him to be my friend;
me lo encargó el comandante	the commander gave me the job
que lo quiere muerto o vivo,	he wants him dead or alive,
me lo encargó el comandante	the commander gave me the job
que lo quiere muerto o vivo."	he wants him dead or alive."
Cuando el general llegó	When the general arrived
Pedrito estaba sentado,	Pedrito was sitting down,
estaba cuidando las armas	taking care of his weapons,
un ladito de la puerta,	just beside the door,
y de todito el parque	and all of his ammunition

que lo estaba asoleando.	was drying in the sun,
y de todito el parque	and all of his ammunition
que lo estaba asoleando.	was drying in the sun.
Le contesta el Chicharrón:	Chicharrón answers him:
"Dejes de estar molestando,	"Stop making trouble here;
lárguese con esas armas	get out of here with those weapons
ya no me esté usted enfadando,	and quit making me angry;
no vaya a venir el diablo	I hope the devil doesn't come
no vaya a estar achuchando,	and make me lose patience,
no vaya a venir el diablo	I hope the devil doesn't come
no vaya a estar achuchando."	and make me lose patience."
("Pedro el Chicharrón")	

Even in the face of being obviously outnumbered by government troops who are determined to annihilate him, El Chicharrón confronts them with language which indicates his contempt of government soldiers/police and projects himself as fearless, as authoritative and in control of the situation. His fearless attitude is also corroborated by the language narrators employ to characterize him:

Otro día por la mañana	The next day in the morning
su compadre lo invitó:	his *compadre* invited him out:
"Vamos a echarnos un trago	"Let's go and have a drink
pero con ordenamiento,	but in an orderly way;
ahora que estás desarmado	now that you are disarmed
te ayudo en tu sentimiento,	I'll help you through your trouble,
ahora que estás desarmado	now that you are disarmed
te ayudo en tu sentimiento."	I'll help you through your trouble."
Luego sacó su cerrojo	Then he took out his mauser,
también su reglamentaria,	also his forty-five luger,
y le decía a su compadre:	and he was telling his *compadre:*
"De eso ya ni diga nada,	"Don't even speak about that;
voy a tirar de balazos	I am going to fire some shots
por si acaso hay emboscada,	just in case there is an ambush,
voy a tirar de balazos	I am going to fire some shots
por si acaso hay emboscada."	just in case there is an ambush."

Allí dijo su compadre	There his *compadre* told him
Al llegar a la cantina:	on arriving at the cantina:
"Que nos a sirvan una copa	"Serve us each a drink
de mescal o de tequila."	of mescal or of tequila."
El Chicharrón pensativo	Chicharrón was full of thought
porque ya lo presentía,	because he knew what was coming,
El Chicharrón pensativo	Chicharrón was full of thought
porque ya lo presentía,	because he knew what was coming,
Pedro al sentir el balazo	When Pedro felt the bullet
dio la vuelta y luego dijo:	he turned around and then spoke:
"Ya me chingastes, compadre	"Now you have screwed me, *compadre*;
salte a matarte conmigo,	come over and let's have it out,
con esta reglamentaria	with this forty-five luger
van a ser siete contigo,	it'll be eight bullets for you,
con esta reglamentaria	with this forty-five luger
van a ser siete contigo."	it'll be eight bullets for you."
("Pedro el Chicharrón")	

Much of the Afro-Mexicans' use of language in the *corridos* is really related to how they perceive themselves. Thus Pedro el Chicharrón behaves and speaks as if he is in control, even after policemen riddle him with bullets. This matter of self-attribution – a subjective sense of being either masculine or feminine – has been addressed by Connell (1995, 21–27), who states that the matter of individuals attributing certain qualities to themselves is a reflection of how they understand masculine identity in the context.

Ethnic pride and loyalty to the community are strong traits attributed to the male hero, who is usually seen as protecting his community. This is reflected in the regional language used in the *corridos*. The expressive arrangements of some lexical items and metaphors seem to be unique to Afro-Mexican speech as is seen in "El Zanatón" in the phrases such as "no saberse tantear" (they didn't know how to fend for themselves); "porque los traiban de encargó" (because they were giving them a hard time); "no zanatilla sin pluma" (not a zanatilla without plumes); and "ya me chingastes" (now you have screwed me). The use of this non-standard form projects males who share a particular linguistic code, which indicates the extent to which they understand their community. According to Johnson and Meinhof (1997, 9), "this use of language which carries connotations of strength, masculinity and confidence in defying linguistic and social condition is important in establishing particular masculine identities". Loyalty to community established in the *corridos* is an important masculine trait exhibited by the hero character and augmented by the use of the community language.

Language which suggests fearlessness in the face of organized oppression and the use of violence by government forces is also apparent in "La gallinita" (Little Chicken). The hero figure announces his presence to the soldiers who have been sent to capture him, by firing gunshots at them. This way he makes it clear that he is not a coward, but one who will go to any length to protect himself and defend his position. This same commitment to community is communicated about Fan (Juan) Chanito, whom the government tries to bribe because he is seen as this fearless, intrepid fighter. He, however, chooses death, rather than betray the trust of the community he has devoted himself to protect.

Fan (Juan) Chanito

Voy a empezar a cantar	I'm going to start singing
estos versos muy cortitos,	these very short verses,
el día 15 de diciembre	on December 15
mataron a Fan Chanito.	they killed Fan Chanito.
Era jefe de las armas	He was in charge of the weapons
del pueblo de San Nicolás,	of the town of San Nicolás,
había durado siete años	he had lasted seven years
jecutando él no más.	with just him in charge.
Como era hombre muy valiente	As he was a very brave man
el gobierno lo quería,	the government wanted him,
le mandaba parque y armas	they sent him ammunition and weapons
y le daba garantías.	and gave him guarantees.
Juchitán y Huehuetán	Juchitán and Huehuetán
entonces ya no robaban,	no longer stole,
¡ay, decían que Fan Canito	they said that Fan Chanito
con bejuco los colgaba.	would hang them with liana.
Eran las siete 'e la noche	It was seven o'clock at night

Juan estaba en la ramada	Juan was in the arbour
Pero lo estaban espiando	but they were watching him
con las armas preparadas.	with their guns ready.
Vinieron dice escopetas	They came with shotguns
y un calibre 30–30	and a 30–30 calibre rifle
vinieron dos de cerrojo	two bolt action rifles came
y una 380.	and a 380.
La hicieron unas disparos	They shot several times
pero ¡ay, con gran enojo!	but, with great annoyance!
Ay, luego que Fan vivo	Because Fan was still alive
Le quitaron el cerrojo.	they took away the bolt.
Ya no quisieron tirarle,	They no longer wanted to shoot him,
pensaron que estaba muerto,	they thought he was dead,
pero Fan estaba vivo	but Fan was still alive
tenía los ojos abiertos.	his eyes were open.
La gente se amontonaba	The people gathered
donde Fan estaba herido,	where Fan was wounded,
preguntó por sus muchachos	they asked for his boys
que si ya estaba reunidos.	if they had already met.
Ay, luego que se reunieron	Then, after they met
Él les tendió una mirada,	He gave them a look,
Adiós muchachos queridos	Goodbye beloved friends
No me sirvieron pa' nada	You did not serve me in vain
Será que ya se me acerca	Maybe the time is drawing near
o ya se me aranca el alma,	or my soul is being ripped out,
cuídense los más que puedan	take the best care of yourselves
y hagan las cosas con calma.	and do things with calm.
Será que ya se me acerca	Maybe the time is drawing near
el corazón me palpita,	my heart is pounding,
ya se muere Fan Rodríquez	Fan Rodríguez is dying
el gallo de Cosa Chica.	the rooster of Costa Chica.
Su mujer lo acariciaba	His wife caressed him
y estrechándolo en sus brazos,	and while stretching him out in her arms

ya se muere Fan Chanito	Fan Chanito dies
tiene cuarenta balazos	shot forty times
Cuando al fin cerró sus ojos	When at last he closed his eyes
como cuando están dormidos,	as when one is asleep,
ya se muere Fan Rodríguez	Fan Rodríguez dies
Ya me voy a despedir	I'm going to say goodbye
el corazón se me agita,	my heart is pounding,
ya se muere Fan Chanito	Fan Chanito is dead
el gallo de Costa Chica.	the rooster of Costa Chica.

The hero is undoubtedly a "sacrificial lamb", facing death without trepidation or cowardice. The cogent and compelling metaphor "el gallo de Costa Chica" (the rooster of Costa Chica) not only intimates Juan's lack of faint-heartedness, but also implies an unmatched sexual prowess.

Language choice in "El corrido de los Zapatistas de San Nicolás" is marked by poignant diction, strong metaphors, and sharp similes designed to dismiss and disparage leadership positions and the efforts of leaders to oppress and overpower Afro-Mexican guerilla troops as ineffective and weak. The weapons of the *carrancistas* are dismissed as useless toys. The Afro-Mexicans do not need to resort to trench warfare as they can face the enemy head on. The valiant hero figure, El Zanatón, is presented through the image of a predatory animal who can hunt his prey for a meal: "El Zanatón los búscaba como cosa de comer." (El Zanatón looked for them like he would eat them alive.) The efforts of his opponents are presented as the weak actions of "birds" while El Zanatón declares his past feats: "He toreado toros bravos." (I have fought fierce bulls.) The language of contempt used to show how the protagonists in Lupe Ramírez's "El diablo" conduct themselves is also very graphic. The heroes are projected as having total disdain for the government representatives, depicting them as powerless, entertaining "dolls": "Eran los tres bandoleros / Leyenda 'e Caña Hueca / jugaban con el gobierno / como jugar con muñeca." (There were three bandoleros / Legend and *Caña Hueca* / They played with the government like they were playing with dolls.)

Forceful and potent language is employed in the *corridos* for the purpose of raising political awareness or consciousness. Indeed, political consciousness can only be achieved through powerful political vocabulary, phrases and language in general. Graber (1981, 195) outlines five purposes of political language as:

disseminating information, agenda setting, interpretation, and linkage, preparation for the future and past. Without question, close and serious scrutiny of the *corridos* reveals that the language they employ definitely fulfils these purposes, as the *corridos* provide detailed and explicit information about the confrontation and clashes with government troops by all opponents. It cannot escape notice that the language used is "inflated" and provides detailed characterizations of the central characters in terms of "reason", "location", "process" and "time".

"Pedro el Chicharrón" (Pedro the Crackling), powerfully depicts these five uses. The name of the protagonist not only suggests his complexion – *chicharrón* is a colloquial term used in Latin America to refer to a person with very dark skin – but also suggests a level of egotism, arrogance and self-certainty. *Chicharrón* implies, too, the toughness of the pork skin when it is overdone, and the language depicting his feats graphically captures his character in consonance with these insinuations. There is no doubt that his role and character are intended to overthrow the status quo and to confront oppression with bravery. This *corrido* provides his past confrontations, his intentions to put an end to his challenges and celebrates his victory.

Similarly, the well-known *corrido* "La gallinita" (Little Chicken) reveals the five uses of political language. It commences with the presentation of information about the protagonist's audacity and dauntless spirit; then the second stanza announces his agenda:

Me voy a Azoyú Guerrero	I'm going to Azoyú Guerrero
a ver a un familiar,	to see a relative,
y también al comandante	and also the commander
que me quiere desarmar.	who wants to disarm me.
("La Gallinita")	

The information conveyed about his mission indicates that the action he intends to undertake in his encounter with the *comandante* is confrontational and conflictual in nature. The graphic and explicit language provides details of how he initiates the confrontation with his use of violence. The language helps, furthermore, to depict him as a fearless character who places no value on his life, but revels in his reputation as "un valiente" (a brave man) who never surrenders to anyone. Language also effectively delineates an idealized confrontation in which the protagonist, *La Gallinita*, defeats the *comandante* and his men without much difficulty: "a los primeros balazos la policía corrió . . . el comandante está muerto . . . la gallinita lo mató" (*Letras Musicales*). (At the first shots the policemen ran . . . the commandante is dead . . . the little chicken killed him.)

The *corrido* is brought to an end with language that reinforces his bravery, with the connotation that he will continue to be this fearless defender of his honour, and with the unmistakable understanding that the agenda set at the beginning has been fulfilled: "la gallinita mató a un gallo". (The little chicken has killed a rooster.) The direct juxtaposition of *gallinita* and *gallo* renders his achievement even more awe-inspiring and dramatic.

Furthermore, the language of the *corridos* may be characterized as political because it is a language of power, which employs exaggeration to present the Afro-Mexican guerrilla members as invincible and to project the important political needs of the group. To this end, the poetic voices employ name-calling strategies to influence the listerners' judgement of their oppressors and to seduce the listeners into condemning the governenment representatives. The language of the *corrido* is also a language of "illusion" and "ambiguity" because the strengths of the protagonists who are projected are not necessarily real.

The manner in which the Afro-Mexican males express themselves suggests their determination to exercise their rights. In other words, they do not only listen and allow themselves to be spoken to, but they decide to participate by active contribution to the situation in which they find themselves. They demonstrate in this way, their right to defend themselves, giving support to the assertion that "the right to speak depends on the right to be in the situation and the right to engage in particular kinds of speech activities in that situation" (Eckert and McConnell-Ginel 2007, 93).

Fairclough (2013, 2) argues that language helps to maintain power relations in society, so that there is always a connection between language usage and an ideology of oppression, as the more powerful in society often use language to legitimize power relations (p. 2). Undoubtedly, the linguistic development of the *corridos* suggests an understanding on the part of Afro-Mexican narrators and characters of how language is used to maintain the social order, but more importantly of how it can be used to create change. Consequently, these narrators invert the power relations by appropriating very powerful words and expressions so as to communicate their own ideology of self-definition, but also to tip the balance of power in their favour by being the users of the discourse of power. This way, they use language as a forceful alternative to the established or conventional discourse type, in which army personnel, police officers and people who are used to maintaining the power relations in conversations issue the orders. As a result, they create an oppositional discourse or an "anti-language" which dismantles the unequal relations and distributions of power.

Problematizing Masculinity in the *Corrido*

Notwithstanding the skilful use of language to promulgate a particular understanding of Afro-Mexican maleness, the overt representations of masculinity in the *corridos* are problematic. This is due, in the first place, to the fact that the *corridos* present masculine characteristics as the standard of human behaviour in the Afro-Mexican community. Without doubt, because of the emphasis on fighting/violence in which men are involved, the philosophical value system of the *corridos* is essentially masculinist. In other words, the social construction of masculine identity in the *corridos* is embedded in, or influenced by sexism and patriarchy.

Of course, it cannot go unnoticed that the *corridos* have been, for the most part, written by men, narrated and sung by men. All central characters are males, and the females who appear in them occupy minor roles in which they are often disparaged. All perceptions and portrayals of the world of the Afro-Mexicans, as well as images of women in the society being represented, are presented from the male perspective, as John McDowell (2000, 7) confirms when he writes that the *corridos* take us into a "primarily masculine world. . . . Most composers and performers of *corridos* in the Costa Chica are male, and the main audience for *corrido* performance is male as well." This occurrence echoes Keith Nurse's (2004, 5) assertion that often "masculinism, as the hegemonic ideational construct, achieves a logocentric posture" and thus becomes "a pervasive, familiar and powerful narrative by which we organise our understanding of social reality".

Arguably, the relationship between hegemonic and subordinate masculinities may be paradoxical, for even subordinate masculinity can be compliant with patriarchy and sexism. The subjectification of the "other" through difference, stigmatization, stereotyping and so forth has proved to be fundamental to the constitution of hegemonic masculinity. Kimmel and Messner (1995, 19) seem to cogently capture how subordinate masculinities may at times assume hegemonic qualities. They claim that "most masculinities are compliant in patriarchy" and that the marginalization of subordinate masculinities is an essential component to the myth of male power (ibid.). "Most men", according to Nurse (2004, 13), "are not as powerful as they are made out to be. The problem is that they are socialised to see male power and privilege as an entitlement, if not even endowment; this is the essential contradiction in the dominant construction of masculinity."

In the Afro-Mexican *corridos* all images of freedom, agency, subjectivity, resistance, defiance of figures of oppression and injustice are embodied in the Afro-Mexican male protagonists. Consequently, even though theirs may be regarded as a subordinated masculinity, since they form the marginalized group in Mexico, the absence of any association of females with power implies a kind of collusion with hegemonic masculinity, which marginalizes females, projecting them as having no roles to play in the Afro-Mexican community or in maintaining a particular image of Afro-Mexican society. Nurse (2004, 8) characterizes this situation as follows: "The poetics and politics of representation are such that victims can be co-opted by strategies of resistance just as victors display their anxieties and repressed fantasies through the projection of power. This appreciation of the working of power and powerlessness provides a useful framework for analysing the relationship between hegemonic and subordinated masculinities."

This particular construction of masculinity simultaneously suggests that among the Afro-Mexican community only black men can make claims of having any roles in community or nation building. This implied paralleling of men and nation/community building and self-assertion is problematic and recalls Bhabha's (1994) claim that nation building is about public identification and that the "other" the foreigner, is feminized. In other words, this gendering of Afro-Mexican's achievements, affairs and participation in protecting the Afro-Mexican community may be an unconscious/unintended reassertion of dominant masculinity, albeit in a marginalized context. The result is the deliberate or instinctive aiding of sexism and racism as they relate to Afro-Mexican females. Connell (1995, 13) warns of how difficult it is to not aid this agenda in societies that have been moving towards equality for women and subordinated groups.

One of the most notable ways in which the *corrido* reveals collusion between masculinity and sexism is in *Traigo una flor hermosa y mortal* (1975) in which the male protagonist serenades his beloved who is metaphorized as a beautiful flower who turns out to be a disappointment/traitor. The betrayed male is presented as a victim, hurt and wounded by the poisonous flower that has turned out to be beautiful only on the surface. This image of the male being victimized by the female constitutes a sexist and trivial attempt at suggesting that in the male/female relationship, it is the man who is honest and trustworthy, while the female is more likely to be disloyal and calculating. But given the perspective from which this narrative unfolds, we must be suspicious of its honesty and suggestions of a self-effacing character. In the final analysis, no sympathy is lost on this male protagonist, and the attempt to discredit the ability of the female to be loyal is not missed. It is difficult to accept the sense of male victimhood expressed in this *corrido,* which presents a strong sociopolitical message. It is, however, more credible that the males are victims of the political system, given what we know about the historical and political contexts which these *corridos* depict, rather than of the treachery of women, although this is not impossible. Indeed, both men and women are victims in this context, and it would be a contradiction of historical accounting to suggest that women did not contribute in any significant way to the struggles in which Afro-Mexican men engaged to establish the presence of Afro-Mexicans in Mexico and to resist the oppression of wealthy, powerful ruling class *latino* Mexicans.

One of the most powerful *corridos* unapologetically establishes the Afro-Mexican's spirit of autonomy and resistance to striking opponents, achieving this through a very generic masculinism. The fearless hero figure of "La mula bronca" emphatically declares the creed which governs his life of toughness and his rejection of the dominant system of authority: "pa' morir nacen los hombres/no van a estar de esclavitud". (Men were born to die / they will not be slaves.) The use of the term *los hombres* presumes/implies an all-embracing belief that man/male is universal. It betrays, moreover, an acceptance of one of the contentions of feminists that "masculinism is a totalizing philosophical value system in the gender framework" (Barthes 1964). It further underpins the claim proposed by Nurse (2004, 5) that "men rarely see themselves as a gender, and society generally treats masculine characteristics as the prototype of human behaviour, irrespective of time and space". The irony of this lies undoubtedly in the understanding/acceptance that the subversive intent of the *corridos* is for the benefit of a society comprising men and women. But while this is true, it simultaneously strengthens certain myths that men are brave protectors of weak women. Herein lies the tension between two agendas – the one to project masculinity as necessary in resisting hegemonic rule and contesting the subversion of a community's identity and importance to nation building in Mexico and the other to suggest that it is the responsibility of men/males to fight for the freedom of the community, or even that it is men/males who have a right to freedom. "Nationalism becomes, as a result, radically constitutive of people's identities through social contexts that are frequently violent and always gendered" (McClintock 1995, 353).

In a previous study, I argued that the collusion between the subordinate masculinity of Afro-Mexicans and the hegemonic masculinity of the status quo is revealed in the extent to which in the *corridos*, "self-glorification facilitates the restoration of masculine identity. From one *corrido* to the next, an unmistakable correlation between *machismo* and self-praise is established" (Ramsay 2003, 74). Undoubtedly, the display as well as the praise of toughness, the self-consciousness based on confidence in fighting ability is evident in the hero and becomes a means of "channelling undetermined manhood into rhetorical aggression and defiance" (Habekost 1993, 121). So, while, in the work of the *corridos* there is an important quest for self-validation and vindication in a system in which the Afro-Mexican community's understanding of self-worth as a marginalized group is undermined, the agenda is also about masculine validation – establishing manliness as a means of recovering and affirming subjectivity. This sense of synonymity between subjectivity, manliness and masculinity is further confirmed by the negative images of female presented in some *corridos*. In these cases, women are often portrayed in stereotypical images as weeping mothers, disloyal partners who are not deserving of the men's trust or young self-absorbed girls, terrified that they will lose their men, who are often in battle.

This derogation of women is unmistakable in the *corrido* "Prisco Sánchez", in which the protagonist alludes to the intrinsic evil of the coronel's mother, as he is being shot by the coronel and his men: "¡Mal haya quien lo parió!" (Cursed is the one who bore him!) There is a sense in which we may cynically justify this curse since she is the mother of the oppressive *latino* coronel. But the curse simultaneously serves to reveal a general derogation of women particularly as the coronel's father is not cursed. In this same *corrido* we are given an insight into the fact that women often accompanied the guerrilla soldiers as they moved about from one battle scene to the next. Prisco Sánchez is depicted as travelling with a young girl. However, the girl is immediately undermined by the further depiction of her as a traitor: "Estaba una niña, en su compañía / y fue la que le arisó" ("Prisco Sánchez"). ("There was a girl, in his company / and it was she who ratted on him.") Without doubt, this unnamed girl represents the numerous women who in actuality would accompany Afro-Mexican guerrilla fighters, and who would have contributed to the guerrilla movement in one way or another. Even if her role were that of spy, she would have also aided their cause in some way. Nevertheless, the importance of any such supportive role is not highlighted. She may also have been an informant, scout or look-out, who would have been exposed to danger as she performed her roles, but this is not given equal prominence to the situation of Prisco Sánchez, the male, whose bravery is presented in great detail.

Problematic Images of the Mother Figure

In her book *The Mexican Corrido*, María Herrera-Sobek (1990) undertakes an impressive analysis of the images of the social roles of the women and mothers in different *corridos*. I acknowledge her pioneering work in this area and draw on some of her ideas for the discussion in this section. According to Herrera-Sobek (1990, 1–2), who relies heavily on feminist theory for her analyses:

> Analysis of *corridos* yields numerous songs making use of the Great Mother archetype. Appearing in hundreds of folk songs, this archetype has at least three dimensions: good, bad and divine. The passive Good Mother archetype often assumes a weak, weeping personality; she is a helpless and desolate figure tossed about in the turbulent waters of unceasing tears. The active Terrible Mother archetype assumes a negative function. But whether conceived as positive or negative, the Great Mother is associated with a vital dramatic episode in the *corrido*: the death of the hero.

"Corrido de Marín Díaz" acknowledges the role of the mother of the hero/fighter, albeit in a problematic manner:

¡Que vida la de Marín!	What a life Marín lives!
¡Qué vida tan arreglada!	What an amazing life!
Él se ha visto en balaceras	He has been in shoot-outs
y no le han podido hacer nada,	and no one has been able to hurt him,

será por las oraciones que su madre le rezaba. ("Marín Díaz")	it must be because of his mother's prayers

On the surface level, this seems to be a very positive, affirming image of the mother, who has contributed to the success of her guerrilla son's military prowess and bravery. But at the supra-segmental level, we encounter a competing interpretation of the supportive but passive mother, therefore, not a definitively positive role of the mother or female subject.

The future tense *será* suggests a probability, a conjecture that the mother in her passive and pious role (as a person who prays) has contributed to the cause of his demise. But the certainty that characterizes the description of Prisco's prowess is absent, and so while the mother's contribution is acknowledged, it is simultaneously undermined. This subversion is sustained in the final image of the distraught mother who is weeping in fear that her son may be killed. But she is comforted by the brave young son who tells her, "No llores mamacita / que estoy a tu compañía" (Don't cry Mama my dear / I am here by your side.) Of course the same ambiguity shrouds this address of the mother by the son. We question whether or not the mother is alive and is being assured by the fearless son who, despite the overwhelmingly dangerous threat he faces from the enemy's onslaught, believes he will remain invincible, or whether he is is insisting that even if he dies, he will be fine. Either way the utterance speaks to the son's commitment to the struggle to resist oppression and tyranny on behalf of his people.

The son's is a posture that recalls the stance of the protagonist in Claude McKay's poem, "If We Must Die", although the latter holds a more inclusive voice – suggested by the "we" in the famous lines, "If we must die, then let us nobly die." In contrast, in the *corrido* the ideas of resoluteness and commitment are expressed by excluding the female who, though represented in the image of the mother – is an observer.[4]

Disparagement of Afro-Mexican Females

In "La mula bronca" ("The Wild Mule"), the tendency to disparage the female is witnessed through the portrayal of Petra Morgan in very sexist terms. "La mula bronca" is, ironically, the fearless, uncompromising defender of his rights, who is likely to be betrayed only by a woman, a traitor who maintains an amorous relationship with the army general. Those who admire "La mula bronca" warn him of this woman's potential threat to his safety:

Sus amigos le decían	Her friends used to say
cuídate de Petra Morga	beware of Petra Morga
tiene buenas garantías	she's very close
con el jefe de la zona	to the leader of the area
los halló la judicial	the lawmen found them
en la cantina de Chona	in Chona's bar
("La mula bronca")	

In other words, the future of the Afro-Mexican movement of resistance is projected as being compromised by fickle, disloyal women like Petra Morgan. A comparable situation is presented in "Chicharrón" in which the demise of Chicharrón is blamed on a disloyal and therefore despicable woman from his own gang: "La mujer que lo entregó fue de su misma banda." (The woman who turned him in was from his own gang.)

"Tomás Marín" similarly presents a positive image of the male who is concerned about family honour and avenging the violent murder of his family.[5] He launches his own war against the powerful and wealthy, known for murdering helpless peasants for their land. In a show of bravery and manliness, he resists his arrest "como un toro" (like a bull), and survives the vicious onslaught of bullets ordered by the police captain. Ironically, when the shocking news that he is still alive surfaces, all the concerted and organized efforts of the police to find him yield nothing. It is a woman who collaborates with the enemy to bring about his demise. So the image of the female as a betrayer of man is again projected in another *corrido*. The suggestion is that women are unable to support the struggle for social justice and liberation in any meaningful way or are disloyal in love and to the men of their community when forced to make a choice between them and the powerful men of the oppressive army. The implication, moreover, is that the women do not understand the importance of the guerrilla movement for allowing Afro-Mexicans to participate in activities related to nation building.

The most unambiguous image of the female seems to be the figure of the Virgen de Guadalupe. Marín Díaz, after comforting his weeping, frail mother, declares his firm conviction that he will be protected by the *Virgen de Guada-*

lupe, either as he continues his escape from his enemies, or as he is murdered and embarks on the journey into the afterlife. "The Virgen de Guadalupe generally appears as a protective force in the *corridos'* mythic structure" (Herrera-Sobek 1990, 46). This image is not only positive, but it implies the protagonist has more faith in the power of a mythic figure to protect him than he has in his own mother, whom he obviously knows. Furthermore, these positive images of the Virgin are central to the *corrido's* communication of the political struggles of the Afro-Mexicans against discrimination, antagonism and subjugation. Although the cult of the Virgin of Guadeloupe developed during Mexico's period of religious distrust, mainly among the Indian populations, it soon became embraced by mestizos, mulattoes and blacks, who were all disfranchised under colonial rule in Mexico. The experience of "adversity, servitude, subjugation resulted in the search for a source of liberation which the cult seemed to provide without the minority groups turning to the Spanish God who was oppressing them" (ibid.).[6] Marín Díaz's expression of confidence in the Virgin implies the Afro-Mexicans' embracing of Catholic influences while simultaneously modifying/creolizing these influences

A point of contention with the *corridos*, therefore, is the way in which they project and help maintain patriarchal self-identification messages for men. For the most part, the women who appear in the *corridos* seem to stand on the fringes and watch men being attacked and fighting to defend themselves. They cringe and weep in fright and become distractions to the men as they try to ward off assaults from their attackers. In general, there is no real acceptance of the true worth or validity of women to the cause of rebellion. The use of the image of the Virgen de Guadalupe reveals a kind of idealized image of woman as a spiritual guide, but not one who can participate in active real life combat. The contrast of the protective Virgin spirit is the superstitious woman in "Lupe Baños", who warns the male against going out since she takes the barking dogs as a sign that something ominous will befall him. This again is not a particularly positive or redeeming image of the female figure in the *corrido;* she is not projected as one who bases judgements on logic or rationally supported claims, but on superstition, which is, at best, scurrilous.

Glimpses of Phallocentric Masculinity

The masculinity performed in the calypso has been explored by Gordon Rohlehr (2004), who has analysed exaggerated and blatant images of "overtly indulged sexuality" in the calypso in which masculinity is constructed based on the sexual prowess of the male – an overt phallocentricity. While this is less overt and blatant in the Afro-Mexican *corridos,* there is a tendency to equate battle or violent contestation/confrontation not just as an attack against other men, but the very preparation for this battle is often imaged as preparation for sexual encounter.

This is seen in the manner in which arms and weapons are usually compared or conflated with the sexual organ of men. In reference to the manner in which one guerrilla fighter pulls his gun, the phrase, "se la sacan del bajo" is used, to connote a picture of the male organ being put into position. Names such as "el gallo" (cock) – symbol of the phallus – are used quite strategically to imply power and threat. One of the most powerful heroes, nicknamed "La mula bronca" (The Wild Mule), is presented through the length of his tail: "tenía larga la correa" (he had a very long tail). Of course, this image is in keeping with the *mula* metaphor, but it is also symbolically a reference to the male sex organ, a symbol of his masculinity, his strength and intrepidity. This same parallel between the association of masculinity with championship or fights, sexual prowess and superiority, is evidenced in another *corrido*, "Pedro el Chicharrón", in which the fallen hero warns his lover that she will never find satisfaction in the arms of other men, as she will not get to know them as well as she knows him, sexually and otherwise.

Priscilliano cayó adentro	Priscilliano fell inside
Pedrito al pié de una palma	Pedrito at the foot of a palm tree
le gritaba a su querida	shouted to his beloved
te quedas negra del alma	you remain black in your soul
vas a abrazar a otros hombres	you are going to embrace other men
que no sabes ni cómo andan.	and you don't even know anything about them.
Decía Pedro el Chicharrón	Pedro el Chicharrón spoke
cuado estaba agonizando:	when in the throes of death:
"Arrímate, Crescenciana,	"Come close, Crescenciana,
que ya me estoy acabando,	as I will soon meet my end,

te quiero morder el brazo	I want to bite your arm
pa' que te andes acordando,	so you will always remember,
te quiero morder el brazo	I want to bite your arm
pa' que te andes acordando."	so you will always remember."

("Pedro el Chicharrón")

When it becomes clear to Pedro that he himself will die, he demands that his lover/girlfriend get close to him so that he can leave his mark/stamp of ownership – a bite on her leg, so that she will never forget him. The implication is that this indelible scar, his personal or trademark seal, will serve as testimony to other men that she has already been conquered by one greater than all others who succeed him, and that, moreover, she can never forget him and his great sexual prowess. The scar, which will serve as an emblem of masculinity, is to be seen as an aggressive carnivalesque image, and so this fighter is at one and the same time a war hero, albeit a fallen one, but one for whom it took more than five opponents to conquer, and a phallic hero – celebrant of his own prowess. Interestingly, the war/phallic hero is held up as immortal even as he dies physically, for he is immortalized through his aggressive sexual act of biting the woman's leg and leaving her scarred. The act of boasting about violent acts of lovemaking has been described as "an attempt, to not only attract the woman, but to rile and triumph over rival males who are presumed unable to satisfy their partners" (Rohlehr 2004, 339). A similar phenomenon is described by Rohlehr in his discussion of The Mighty Sparrow's calypsoes "Village Ram" and "Congo Man", where he notes that the extremity/violence of these songs, particularly the grossness of the image through which Sparrow represents naked appetite and lust, is aggressively carnivalesque (ibid., 341).

In Search of a Feminist Masculinity

Feminism, in its intersection with postcolonial theory, contends that women are relegated to a position of other, like colonized subjects. Consequently, the broad feminist agenda, like that of postcolonial criticism, is to dismantle all types of oppressive ideology that subordinates women – this includes colonialist thought-systems, which are inherently patriarchal. Radical feminists, in particular, have called for the inclusion of women in the process of undermining the system of domination because women deserve to enjoy some of the same rights men seek for themselves.

I maintain that the *corridos* have established a discourse which places the struggle of males who endanger their lives to establish themselves as independent human beings of fortitude at the forefront, while excluding women and any relevance they may have in the struggle for liberation of Afro-Mexicans. This is a masculinist position, which is essentially about men's right to selfhood. The rhetoric of the *corridos*, then, provides support for bell hooks's (2000, 179) claims regarding male bonding. This powerful feminist literary critic forcefully speaks of male bonding as "an aspect of patriarchal culture, which assumes that men would stick together, support one another and be team players". This declaration was advanced in reference to her experience at a co-educational university where this seemed to be the case. Furthermore, male bonding is seen in the internal/ontological structure of the *corridos* in terms of how they project male characters vis-à-vis women. Males interact with males in a show of camaraderie and bravado. Male bonding is evident in the sexist statements and characterizations of women, both in the male attitudes depicted and the affirmation bestowed on male figures by male narrators. This is an attempt to project Afro-Mexican males as fighting for justice and for the Afro-Mexican community, without portraying women as comrades in the struggle, an observation which also finds resonance in bell hooks's claims that it is not unusual to find men who are radical thinkers, who speak against social injustice, but who are sexist (ibid., 69). In other words, it is possible for some men to be socially aware, but to not regard or reject patriarchy as a type of social injustice.

bell hooks (2000, 70) calls for a visionary masculinity or a feminist masculinity which is typified by "political solidarity" and shared sympathy for common suffering. This visionary masculinity is a reconstruction of that masculinity which is opposed to patriarchy that "encourages men to be pathologically narcissistic, infantile, and psychologically dependent on the privileges (however relative) that they receive simply for having been born male" (ibid.). Indeed, I underline the absence of *corridos* which explicitly highlight an interest in "mutual advancement", in recognition of the shared context of inequality. For if we must/should regard the *corrido* as being about consciousness-raising, then there is a need for women to be depicted in them as being central to a revolutionary movement and as having an awareness of their centrality to a process which is beneficial to men and women alike. Perhaps, some new *corridos* will meaningfully show Afro-Mexican women as integral parts of the process of changing directions in Mexico, as they affect Afro-Mexicans in general. This call may seem contradictory given my previous claims that the *corridos* have been preserved by the community in general. But against the fact that they give voice mainly to men's expressions, the implication, from a feminist position, is that they leave no space for marginalized women to assert their own subjectivity. It can be concluded, then, that the *corridos* allow redefinition of self for men and result in empowerment for men, who rewrite their textual selves, as they give expression to a masculinity which is often compliant with sexism and even racism.

4.

Place, Racial and Cultural Identities in Selected Afro-Mexican Oral and Lyric Verses

San Nicolás I beg you
costeño that I am,
do not forget that I am black
through and through.
   —Francisco J. Zárate Arango, *"Canto a la costa mía."*

Mestizaje is not a synthesis, but rather the opposite ... mestizaje is nothing more than a concentration of difference.
   —Antonio Benítez-Rojo, *The Repeating Island*

The last two decades have witnessed some change in the assessment of Afro-Mexicans and their perception of themselves as people of an Afro-derived heritage. This is due mainly to the research that has been conducted by scholars whose interactions with Afro-Mexican communities have helped to raise awareness of issues of ethnicity and identity among persons within these communities. Recognition must be given to the early work of Aguirre Beltrán (1972), the Instituto Guerrerense de Cultura (Guerrero Cultural Institute), and the Dirección General de Culturas Populares (Department of Popular Culture) in Mexico, which pioneered early research into Afro-Mexican ethnic identities and pointed to some attempts at self-vindication.[1] Moreover, the crucial and historic work done among the people of the Costa Chica by the Trinidadian priest Father Glyn and the ways this work has helped to raise self-awareness within that community cannot be overstated (Sergio Peñaloza, personal interview, November 2014). Indeed, we have seen in other chapters, the manifold ways in which oral narratives, ballads and lyric poems seem to both overtly and covertly construct an Afro-Mexican identity which inexorably counters the official discourse of racial and cultural homogeneity. This chapter is yet another attempt to uncover other ways in which racial and cultural identities are constructed by Afro-Mexicans in their literary and cultural production.

The interdisciplinary field of cultural studies furnishes a particularly useful theory for exploring and interrogating issues related to identity in this chapter. This is so because identity has been framed as a concept that figuratively combines the intimate or personal world with the collective space of cultural forms and social relations (Holland et al. 2003, 5). This significant concept/definition of identity, taken from the field of cultural studies, will be invoked in the discussions of how racial consciousness and place in selected Afro-Mexican creative forms further firm positions about self-formation, self-projection, and issues of citizenship and belonging in Afro-Mexican communities on the Costa Chica.

This determinate, culturally constructed interpretation of identity is advanced by Holland et al. (2003, 271) as an alternative formulation, grounded in practice activity theories and fieldwork. These theories regard identity as being constructed in three different contexts: (1) the "figured world", (2) "relational identities"/"positionality" and (3) the "space of authoring". The term "figured worlds" characterizes the way in which individuals construct reality as they "perceive it or want it to be" (ibid.). A "figured world" is peopled by the figures, characters and types who carry out its tasks and who also have styles of interacting within distinguishable perspectives on, and orientation towards that world. It refers to a socially and culturally constructed realm of interpretation in which particular characters and actors are recognized, significance is assigned to certain acts, and particular outcomes are valued over others (ibid., 51–52).

The second context in which identity is considered as being manifested – "positionality", also referred to as "relational identities" – involves the individual's sense of social place or entitlement. "Relational identities" are performed in different ways – such as the ways people dress, speak, or express themselves and assert who they are in relation to others. Holland et al. (2003, 127) explain the term as follows: "Relational identities have to do with behavior as indexical of claims to social relationships with others. They have to do with how one identifies one's position relative to others, edited through the ways one feels comfortable or constrained, for example, to speak to another, to command another, to enter into the space of another, to touch the possessions of another, to dress for another, or to enter the kitchen of another."

"Authoring" is denoted as the response of an individual or group to the world and situations they encounter. It is "a matter of orchestration, of arranging the identifiable social discourses/practices that are one's resources in order to craft a response in time and space defined by others' standpoints in activity" (ibid., 275). This term is inferred from Mikhail Bakhtin's (1981) philosophy of dialogism, in which he accentuates the value of dialogue or of individuals being able to counter and respond to "authoritative discourses". Elizabeth White (2009, 4–5) sharply characterizes this philosophy of dialogism as follows:

> dialogism represents a methodological turn towards the messy reality of communication in all its many language forms. Emphasis is simultaneously placed on the location of dialogue within the heterglot as the place where opposing forces inter-animate with each other to generate new meaning that goes beyond, and draws from more than the official alone. Inherent within dialogic philosophy is an emphasis on dialogue as an ongoing process of meaning, orality that occurs between people as subjects.

These three concepts will be used together to constitute the analytical frame for this chapter in which I interrogate oral poems which, I argue, reveal a commanding level of racial consciousness and interaction with the land or region occupied by Afro-Mexicans, as their performers or authors unstintingly engage in a complex process of self-fashioning. I propose further that "figured worlds" are created by Afro-Mexican composers or performers of oral poems to advance arguments about their membership in the Afro-Mexican community and in Mexico in general. Relational or positional identities are dramatized by poems which depict the Afro-Mexicans making claims about their entitlement to being regarded in ways that affirm their place in Mexican society. The production of these poems will be treated as the dramatization of Afro-Mexicans' understanding of themselves as blacks and of their attempts to declare who they are, and to engage in the intricacies of self-fashioning.

In addition to these ways in which cultural studies theories construct identity or agency, broad postcolonial theories will be used to underline how the verses proffer a new discourse about Afro-Mexicans and their ethnic heritage. The main aspect of postcolonial discourse on which I will draw is informed by Stephen Slemon's (1988) view of a creative revisionism, which involves the subversion or displacement of dominant discourses. This revisionism "challenges the tenets both of an essentialist nationalism which sublimates or overlooks regional differences of an unconsidered multi-culturalism (mis)appropriated for the purposes of enforced assimilation, rather than for the promulgation of cultural diversity" (Slemon 1988, 157). This is indeed, very applicable to the Mexican context in which all considerations of multiculturality are denied and the discourse of homogeneity promoted.

Racial/Ethnic Pride

In two previous articles in which I discussed Afro-Mexican *corridos*/ballads and Afro-Mexican folktales respectively, I argued that although there were no specific references to blackness in any of these oral forms, the racial positions were encased in the striking posturings, which were similar to the attitudes depicted by other groups of blacks in other contexts, specifically in the Caribbean.[2] However, in many of the *coplas* (verses) in the collections *Alma cimarrona* and *Cállate burrita prieta: poetica afromestiza* (*Be Quiet Little Black Donkey: Afro-Mexican Poetry*) (1992), being studied in this chapter, it is clear that the poetic voice speaks from a position of understanding of a particular ethnic identity and opines in a structured context, best described as a "figured world", which also provides creative reversionings.

Both *Alma cimarrona* and *Cállate burrita prieta* were produced under the auspices of the Mexican Consejo Nacional para la Cultura y las Artes (Mexican National Council for Culture and Arts), in an attempt to promote Afro-Mexican culture. Both were compiled by Mexican anthropologists and ethnographers who have developed an interest in the Costa Chica and its inhabitants. These persons are now well known for the commendable work they have done in bringing awareness to both outsiders and Mexicans of the presence and cultural contributions to Mexican culture by Afro-descendants on the Costa Chica. Moreover, they worked on the projects out of a concern that Afro-Mexican culture is threatened and could be completely lost. *Cállate burrita prieta* was compiled by Francisca Aparicio Prudente, Adela García Casarrubias and María Cristina Díaz Pérez, with additional support from the Unidad Regional Guerrero de Cultura Populares (Guerrero Regional Unit for Popular Culture). *Alma cimarrona* received additional support from the Instituto Oaxaqueño de la Cultura (Oaxacan Cultural Institute) and was diligently compiled by two citizens of the Costa Chica – Augustía Torres Díaz and Israel Reyes Larrea.

Both collections have been validated by compilers and anthropologists as being significant for displaying the richness of oral poetry on the Costa Chica, as well as the centrality of these poems to the African-derived cultural tradition of the people. According to Malinali Meza Herrera (1992, vii):

> Para comprender el fenómeno de la oralidad, entre los pueblos afro-mestizos, particularmente los asentados en la región de la Costa Chica (Guerrero y Oaxaca) necesariamente tenemos que remitirnos a los tiempos coloniales, cuando miles de africanos fueron arrancados del suelo de origen, para ser trasladados como esclavos a plantaciones, minas y haciendas de América. Procedentes de distintas étnicas se vieron de pronto desprovistos de sus referentes culturales, sin tierras, sin dioses y sin lenguas. Enfrentados al silencio tuvieron que reinventar nuevas formas de expresión, copiar algunas y adecuar otras.
>
> Hablar, comunicarse surge como una necesidad imperiosa de sobrevivencia, una manera de burlar al amo, de reírse del yo de ellos mismos. La expresión verbal, acompaña desde entonces, los actos trascendentes de la vida de la comunidad ... tanto hombres como mujeres, niños y adultos crean y recrean esta herencia ancestral.

> In order to understand the phenomenon of orality among Afro-mestizo towns, particularly those established in the Costa Chica region (Guerrero and Oaxaca), we have to refer to colonial times, when thousands of Africans were forced from their homeland to be carried away as slaves to plantations, mines and farms in the Americas. Coming from different ethnicities, they suddenly saw themselves without their cultural references, without their land, their gods and languages. Having to face silence, they had to reinvent new forms of expression, copy others and adapt others.
>
> Speech communication thus became an urgent need for survival, a way of making fun of their master, laughing at him and at themselves. Verbal expression, accompanies ever since, important acts of community life ... men and women, children and adults create and recreate this ancestral heritage.

It is made evident from the testimonies of the compilers that the oral verses are signal definers of the Costa Chicans as a people with an African past and cultural heritage in the manner in which they spontaneously express words, which convey their sense of who they are: "Cuando el sentimiento del costeño es plasmado, nace la poesía, es ésta pues, la herramienta en donde puede expresar su amor, gritar sin furia . . . simplemente un reconocimiento a la vida, a su negra, a su amada Costa Chica" (Torres Díaz and Reyes Larrea 1999, 12). (When the feeling of the coastal dweller is expressed, poetry is born, it is the tool whereby he can express his love, shout without fury . . . simply a recognition of life, of his black and beloved Costa Chica.) The verses were collected from various workshops held in different communities in places such as Azoyú, San Nicolás Tolentino, Cuajinicuilapa, Copala, Maldonado and Huehuetán. People were invited to recite the verses, which were recorded and later transcribed. The compilers assure us that every effort was made to remain faithful to recordings, especially with regard to the popular speech of the people in the transcriptions. Attention was given to the tendency of Afro-Costa Chicans to suppress certain letters at the end of words, such as *D, A, Z, E,* as well as the substitution of *F* for *J* and *H* for *J* among others, which are typical of the local speech.

The oral verses in both collections are rooted in the daily lives of the people and demonstrate the repertoire of verses used throughout the region. As a result, some of the same verses were collected in different communities with slight variations from one to another. They are recited at various social, festive and traditional events in the communities. Such events include different dances, such as *El baile del Toro* (The Dance of the Bull), at wakes, birthday celebrations, family reunions, informal gatherings and even when women are washing by the river.

These oral verses are classified as either *décimas* or *coplas*. The *décima* is a ten-line poem, or a poem with ten-line verses, each of which usually comprises ten to eight syllables, although there are several variations of this form. The *décima* is part of the rich oral tradition of the people of the African diaspora in the Caribbean and Latin America. It is sung as a ballad and used to communicate important information long carried in the memories of Afro-derived people in these places. David Andrade Aguirre (1999, 5) characterizes the *décima* as: "hija legítima del romance y el candombe, heredera de la palabra castellana como de las leyendas fantásticas del África profunda" (legitimate daughter of romance and candombe, heir of the Spanish word as well as of the fantastic legends of deep Africa). They are clearly produced out of a context of oral performance in which an audience and the response of an audience are important. Their verbal artistry or dependence on the effects of words, their dramatic quality, the specific type of rhythm, suggest their grounding in a heritage of oral performance. When read aloud, they forcefully bring to mind Ong's (2000, 14) assertion that "oral cultures indeed produce powerful and beautiful verbal performances of high artistic and human worth". Indeed, it must be borne in mind that these poems have been put in written form only by the compilers and were produced as oral creations grounded in oral speech. Moreover, despite the voice in which they are presented, we get a sense that they are received and understood by a community which owns them in the way that Finnegan (1992, 7) means when she states that "orality belongs to a culture or a whole community as opposed to an individual". The compilers have recorded all the *décimas* and *coplas* without attributing them to any narrator or author in keeping with the view that they belong to the communities.

Attention will be drawn to how these oral poems give expression to both racial and cultural diversity in Mexico. The following lines from the collection *Alma cimarrona* imply a poem written as the result of a cognition or percipience of a specific racial heritage and upbringing in a particular geo-political space that is associated with Afro-Mexican inhabitants.

A mí me dicen el negro	They call me the black one
porque una negra me crió,	because I was raised by a black woman,
y por toda la Costa Chica	and all along the Costa Chica
no hay negro como yo,	there is no black man like me,
porque mi nanita chula	because my sweet mother
con buena leche me amantó.	breastfed me with good milk.

(*Alma cimarrona*, 27)

There is an unequivocal hint of pride in being identified as a black person, but the persona is even prouder of his incomparable and incontrovertible "pedigree" which he traces to his black lineage and the nurturing received from his beloved black mother. This, of course, implies a longstanding tradition of consciously embracing and celebrating a distinct and unique heritage and way of life. The poem derives its forceful meaning from the verbal expressions, the tempo created through the rhyming pattern, and its use of assonance.

In the collection *Cállate burrita prieta*, this same effort at self-affirmation and self-definition is evident. The persona deliberately subverts the stereotypical and dominant discourse about blackness through the projection of positive images. Through the indubious acknowledgement of blackness and elevation of the black male, a discourse about the black race in general and the black man in particular is advanced. The poem's internal structure simultaneously reveals the tension being created by the intentional and deliberate rejection of the expected Eurocentric, biased choice of a white partner, in preference for a black one. Interestingly, the black man is chosen not just for his colour, but for the admirable traits he possesses as the one who is gentlemanlike, romantic and amorous:

De arriba cayó un pañito	A small cloth fell from above
derechito al dura 'nito	right beside the little peach tree
dejé de querer a un blanco	I stopped loving a white man
por querer un trigueñito	because I love a dear black one
tendrá la sangre muy dulce	his blood must be very sweet
y por ser muy hombrecito.	as he's quite a gentleman.
(p. 20)	

Similarly, firm affirmation of the black man is evident in the following *copla* taken from *Cállate burrita prieta*. The black man is a source of hope and refuge:

Negrito de no ser tú	Black man if it were not for you
perdí la e'peranza ya'	I would have lost all hope
porque solamente en ti	because only in you
se encerró mi volunta'.	do I find my will/strength.
(p. 21)	

The black man's supposed/alleged sexual appeal is lauded in the unforgettable kiss, which conveys his great passion and communicates intrinsic joy:

Dicen que el negro e' tri'te	The say the black man is sad
pero yo digo que no e' verda'	but I say it is not true
porque lo' mejore' beso'	because the best kisses
se dan en la o'curida'.	are given in the dark.
(p. 21)	

This is also an attempt to change the conversation about the often conflictual relationship between the black man and woman to project one that is more harmonious and a source of contentment for the woman. The consistent rhyming pattern underlines the message:

Dicen que el negro e' luto	They say the black man is sad
yo digo que no e' verda'	But I say it is not true
porque tu' ojito' son negro'	Because your eyes are black
y se me dan felicida'.	And they give me joy.
(p. 20)	

Underlying commitment to the black man, the supreme choice, is expressed in a spirited, rhythmic *copla,* which declares his beauty. It is interesting that the black man's beauty is compared to a flower – suggesting an endearing personality and a softness that is not often associated with the black male:

Me subí a la punta del barco	I climbed to the top of the boat
adevisar pa' roncón mi negrito e' bonito	in order to look boastfully at my black man, beautiful
como una flor de algodón,	as a cotton flower
no dejo de quererlo	I won't stop loving him
ha'ta botarlo al panteón	until I cast him to the vault
primero le echo la tierra	first, I'll bury him
y de'pué' le pido perdón.	and then I'll beg him pardon.
(p. 20)	

In *Alma cimarrona*, racial consciousness is also boldly expressed in the positive depictions of the Afro-Costa Chican female. The desirability of the black Mexican woman is resolutely conveyed in a spirited *copla,* which dispenses with the mainstream tendency to privilege the appearance or physical attributes of lighter-complexioned women over black ones. The persona earnestly communicates a willingness and eagerness to be close to the black woman and to be united in marriage with her:

De tu boca quiero un beso,	I want a kiss from your mouth,
de tu blusa un botón,	a button from your blouse,
darle a tu nombre apellido	I want to give you a surname
y de ti morenita, el corazón.	and to win your heart, black woman.
(p. 17)	

The persona is obviously proud of his surname, which no doubt indicates his ethnicity, and wants to share this aspect of his unique heritage with the black woman. Evidently his intention towards her is also honourable as he desires to make her his wife. The rhythmic *abab* rhyming pattern reinforces the tone of joyousness which underlies the proposal being made and makes the declaration even more endearing. The poem carries a distinct hint that this voice speaks for a community of black men.

Here, it seems that the issue of how Afro-Mexican women traditionally have been objectified and demeaned becomes a site of contestation as this poetic voice seems to give her dignity – a new "positional identity" in which she is worthy of being or becoming someone's legitimate wife rather than a concubine without legal claims or entitlements. According to Jameelah Muhammad (1995, 177):

> Afro-Mexican women generally work as cooks, maids and domestics. Like black men, they are viewed as objects of servitude – overweight, uneducated, illiterate and poor, and speakers of unintelligible Spanish. Yet black women in Mexico cannot seem to escape the myth of being oversexed. Many historians write about Spanish men's desire to have African women as their concubines. In this way, the black woman's body has become a commodity. She was known as a prostitute in major colonial cities like Puebla and Mexico City. At one point in history the words *negra* and "prostitute" were synonymous. This image has persisted, and is routinely depicted in Mexican comic books.

The seemingly simple proposal by the poetic persona to "give her his name", becomes a powerful and noteworthy attempt to unsettle those disparaging, vocalized constructions of black female identity in Mexico. The idea that the black woman is only good enough to appease the sexual desires of Spanish men – even for monetary gain – is forcefully challenged.

A patently clear restitutive role is intended in the positioning of the black woman in a particularly positive light, in another verse in which she is depicted as one who has the gift of healing and comforting – one who is needed in the life of the black man to make him contented and complete:

Que tendrá mi corazón	What could be wrong with my heart
que no quiere estar conmigo	why it doesn't want to be with me?
yo le pregunto que con quien	I ask it "With who then?"
y me dice que contigo,	and it tells me "with you",
porque contigo? Está dolido,	Why with you? It is hurting,
y cuando lo tienes en tus brazos,	and when you have it in your arms,
negrita linda,	beautiful black woman,
se le quita lo adolorido.	all pain is gone.

(*Alma cimarrona*, 17)

The flirtatious tone gives vocal weighting to the lines and heightens their appeal.

"Relational identities"/"positionality", seem to be spiritedly dramatized in the central role the black woman is presented as having in the black man's life, as is conveyed by another *copla* in which the persona expresses his unmistakable preference for death over life without the black woman:

Negra, negra	Black woman, black woman
sin tu amor no me hallo,	without your love I'm lost,
nada, nada me divierte,	I can't enjoy myself at all,
si a ti te quitan el que me hables,	if the one you speak of takes you away from me,
a mí me han deseado la muerte	they have wished death upon me
mejor que me parta un rayo	it would be better for lightning to strike me
que yo dejar de quererte.	than for me to stop loving you.

(*Alma cimarrona*, 22)

The words of this *copla* are highly dramatic and powerful as a result of the many hyperbolic expressions it employs.

A similar expression of high regard and respect for the black woman is to be found in a verse from *Cállate burrito prieta*. The poetic voice proclaims the black woman as a source of anchoring and stability in his life:

Negra sin tu amor no me hallo	Black woman, without your love I'm lost,
nada, nada me divierte	I can't enjoy myself at all
mejor que te parta un rayo	it would be better for lightning to strike you
para dejar de quererte.	so I could stop loving you.

(p. 22)

Repetition functions as an important discursive strategy of these two *coplas* to highlight their performative nature and the involvement of different individuals in preserving the oral tradition in the Afro-Mexican community. In one collection the *copla* is slightly modified, but the essence remains the same and gives authenticity to its origin and significance, but also shows the competitions between the different communities and how words are passed around and shared in the community's daily life.

Two other *coplas* in *Alma cimarrona* work together to imply that the Afro-Mexican male has assessed the Afro-Mexican woman as someone who is entitled to a particular kind of treatment, given who she is. She is elevated to a position of regality and one deserving of pampering and the finest in life. Here again, we may draw on the concepts of the "figured world" and "relational identities" to comprehend that great value is being placed on the Afro-Mexican woman. The poetic voice has repositioned her as a woman with a social status worthy of stately treatment:

A mi negrita te he de hacer	My black woman, I have to build you
una casita en el viento,	a little house in the wind,
la pared ha de ser de oro	the door must be of gold
y de algodón el cimienta.	and the foundation of cotton.
(*Alma cimarrona*, 23)	

This queenly quality is sustained in another *copla*, which speaks to the beauty of the black woman and points to her as possessing regality. The *copla* simultaneously employs contrast as an effective strategy to indicate how other women of less nobility should be treated:

A las morena' bonita'	For the beautiful black women,
una corona imperial.	an imperial crown.
a la' güera' revolcadas	for the humiliated blonde girls,
una penca de nopal.	a prickly pear pad.
(*Alma cimarrona*, 35)	

The beauty of the black woman is equally lauded in direct contradiction to traditional discourse, which has characterized her as being unworthy of admiration due to her Negroid features:

Bendito sea Dios, Negrita	Praise be to God, black woman
que linda y hermosa te ha hecho	who has made you so beautiful and lovely,
delgadita de cintura	small in waist
y abultadita del pecho.	and voluptuous in breast.
(*Alma cimarrona*, 24)	

The ultimate redemption of the black woman is pronounced through the voice of the female herself, who asserts her own incomparable value:

Me deprecia' por morena	You reject me because I'm black
tiene' toda razón	you are right
entre perla' y diamante'	among pearls and diamonds

la morena e' la mejor.	the black woman is the best.
(*Cállate burrita prieta*, 21)	

While *Cállate burrita prieta* comprises only oral verses – *coplas* and *décimas* – *Alma cimarrona* includes lyric poems; that is, contemporary poems composed by Afro-Mexican authors as well. A very compelling one is "Negrita cimarrona" (Little Black Maroon) from *Alma cimarrona*, which continues in the same vein as some of the *coplas* discussed earlier. It is undeniably, a poem of self-authoring and self-projection, as its architect, Israel Reyes Larrea (1999), portrays the magnificence of the black female in what may be characterized as a meditative ode. Reyes Larrea (1999) expresses strong feelings, personal thoughts and perhaps even a state of mind with regards to the Afro-Mexican woman. The poem becomes an embodiment of the dialectics on race, history and culture and presupposes blackness as a symbol of majesty, even in resistance. The ideology of white supremacy seems to be challenged in the claim of black superiority in this discourse, as the poem connects the Afro-Mexican woman to her African past through her response to the drum, a central instrument in African-derived cultures. The impassioned beat of the drum reverberates in the spirit of Afro-Mexicans and becomes an eternal cadence, awakening the African spirit to alertness:

Ruge el tambor	The drum rumbles
y mi negritilla se emociona	and my little black girl gets excited
sale luego a relucí	she then goes out to show off
su alma cimarrona	her maroon soul
Negra e' su cabellera	Her curly hair is black
cuculuxte la ingrata,	that little ingrate,
su cuerpo de sirena	she has a body like a mermaid
su mirada me mata	her look kills me
Bailar ¡como le encanta!	How she loves to dance!
¿a qué negra, díganme no?	To what black woman? Please tell me.
—Manque sea con charrasca	"Even if it is only with a percussion scraper
como quera bailo yo	I dance anyway."
De tierras muy lejanas	From faraway lands
heredó en su piel, el color,	she inherited her skin, her colour,
la alegría, la bravura	joy, courage
y bailar con sabor.	and she dances with flair.

Ante nada se ejpanta	She's not frightened by anything
e' parte de su cultura	it's part of her culture
les confieso mijhermanoj	I tell you my brothers
¡el no verla me tortura!	not seeing her is torture for me!
Cuando mi negrita habla,	When my black woman speaks,
habla sin temor,	she speaks without fear,
y si es necesario bronquea	and if necessary, she will quarrel with you
¡peleapa' dejeundé su honor!	she fights to defend her honour!
Orgullosa ella ejtá	She's proud
del color achapopotao de su piel	of her tar-like complexion
de su cabecita punchuncha	of her little *punchuncha* head
y de esos labios de miel	and of her lips of honey
Si por negra – dice –	If because I'm black – she says –
me deprecias	you despise me
no maldigas mi color	don't curse my colour
entre perlas y diamantes	because, of all the pearls and diamonds
¡la morena es la mejor!	the black one is the best!
No maldigo mi mulata	I don't curse my mulatto woman
no maldigo tu color,	I don't curse your colour,
pue' de no juyirte conmigo	because if you didn't run away with me
no tendría hoy yo tu amor.	I wouldn't have your love today.
Vengan Diablos y Tortugas,	Let the Devils and Turtles,
Toros, Panchos o Minga,	Bulls, Panchos or Mingas come,
tóquenme un son,	play me a song,
bailaré con mi pardita,	I will dance with my mulatto woman,
mi machete ejta desvainao	my machete is unsheathed
no tenga miedo nadita	I'm not afraid at all
nunca ando descuidao	I never walk carelessly
por si alguién me rejpinga.	in case someone insults me.

(Reyes Larrea, "Negrita cimarrona", 69)

Reyes Larrea apotheosizes the black phenotype that mainstream writers and historians have used derogatorily to define Africans and their descendants. These physical features – hair, skin, eyes and lips – are highlighted, with accolades of appreciation to nullify all tendencies to depreciate them. This way the intransigent strength of the black race of Mexico belies and revises the traditional racial discourse perpetuated through colonialism.

The black woman is presented as the epitome of feminine creation: Negroid hair: "Negra e' su cabellera" (Her hair is black), the mention of which implies its beauty. This noticeable feature is highlighted by the persona in celebration of blackness and in depicting a captivating picture of the black woman's body. Notwithstanding, the beauty of blackness is also linked to the boldness of the black woman as caution is given to the irresistible, but possible fatal effect of an encounter with an Afro-Mexican woman who incubates the Maroon spirit.

In the effort, deliberate or otherwise, to redeem the image of the black woman, fearlessness and a dauntless fighting spirit characterize her. She is celebrated for her indefatigable spirit of resistance and boldness in the face of terror. These traits are presented as inborn, naturally emergent from the African culture, and they typify the black woman as possessing prowess in battle, overthrowing the orthodox view on gender dominance in warfare. This stance is personified both in spirit and in speech, but moreso is actualized in the unstoppable daring that will not allow retreat from any challenge in defence of honour. Reyes Larrea's poem elucidates the historical component attached to black skin colour while presenting blackness as the quintessence of beautiful colour. At the same time, the poetic voice proudly declares Africa as the source and place of black identity formation and the heritage of bravery. The conferring of a rich heritage is embodied in the black skin: richness of colour personifying a fertile earth and a spirit of indomitable courage, the mastery of dance, counterpart to music, enriching Mexico's culture with unparalleled dynamism. The most important aspect to this declaration of beauty, bravery and pride is reflected in the acceptance of the colour of the black woman's skin.

The poetic voice in "Negrita cimarrona" (Little Black Maroon) is still mindful of reality and simultaneously admits the irony of the social context in which the Afro-Mexican woman dwells. For, despite his own pride the *negra* Maroon who is depicted as a paragon of racial beauty, is also seen as repudiated and despised. Staunch resistance in the face of black racial discrimination is vociferously expressed in these lines. The intimation is that there is no justification for prejudice and typecasting of people who are black. The persona condemns the contemptuous utterance and rejects the depreciation of the colour black and black skin in particular. The black woman is metaphorized as the most prized of all precious stones, including white ones; thus the ideology of white superiority is once more rejected.

Indeed, the dogmas of *mala raza* (bad race) and *mala sangre* (bad blood) entrenched in Mexico's ideological racial construct of *mestizaje* (mixed race) enforce a natural tendency for racial delimitation inherent in this stereotypical treatment of the Afro-Mexican in Mexico. Torres Díaz and Reyes Larrea (1999) create this lyric poem to expose the idiosyncrasies of the construct of race. While there is consciousness and appreciation of one's own colour, there is also acceptance of another's. It becomes clear that the framework of intelligibility expressed concerning racial identity and colour incorporates recognition of difference while making allowance for ethnic syncretism.

"Negrita cimarrona" also captures the centrality of music and dance to Afro-Mexican cultural expression. In the excerpt which follows, the poet conveys important ways in which Afro-Mexicans engage in different artistic expressions which are central to their culture:

Vengan Diablos y Tortugas,	Let the Devils and Turtles,
Toros, Panchos o Minga,	Bulls, Panchos or Mingas come,
tóquenme un son,	play me a song,
bailaré con mi pardita,	I will dance with my mulatto woman,
mi machete ejta desvainao	my machete is unsheathed
no tengo miedo nadita	I'm not afraid at all
nunca ando descuidao	I never walk carelessly
por si alguién me rejpinga.	in case someone insults me.

(Reyes Larrea, "Negrita cimarrona", 69)

The explicit references to *diablos* (demons), *tortugas* (turtles), *toros* (bulls) and *mingas* (men disguised as women) clearly signal the persona's familiarity with the performance of specific Afro-Mexican cultural forms; these references signal, as well, how the cultural idiosyncracies associated with them are deeply entrenched. All four figures are the main characters in three of the Costa Chica's main dance forms referred to in the introduction to this book. In *La danza del Diablo* (Devil Dance) and the Turtle Dance, *Panchos* and *Mingas* dance together to perform sacred roles of masculine pursuit of females, even though all the roles are performed by men disguised as women. In both popular dances, rebellion against the status quo is performed in different ways, as turtles, *Mingas* and *Panchos* try to overpower each other. Anita González (2009, 78) explains: "Rebellion in the Turtle Dance is expressed by means of overt sexuality. Generally, the lead Pancho rules over all the dancers, as if orchestrating their mating play. He has the freedom to mount the turtle or the Minga. As in the Devil and bird dances he contains the other dancers without being contained himself. The aggressive behavior is much more subdued in this dance, instead the performers disrupt societal norms in their unconcealed lustful behavior."

In the poem being studied, the implication of the persona's challenge to these figures is that he is not intimidated by the most sexually potent of those famous for their sexual prowess, but is confident of his own physical strength and is determined that no one can/will challenge his position in his woman's life or his ability to ward them off. The reference to his prepared machete invokes the performance of the dances and the various ways in which females are overpowered in this dance space. This presents the male persona as having a paradoxical relationship with the female in which he celebrates her for her blackness but simultaneously establishes male hierarchization. Indeed, he may be seen as projecting more power himself than the *Pancho* figure, normally the one to restrain the other characters which are all drawn from different Afro-Mexican carnivals associated with the Costa Chica. Indeed, the poems play a crucial role in forging linkages between spatial occupation and definitive identity markers of the people of the coastal regions. This poem problematizes Mexico's racial discourse, in which people of African ancestry are considered to be infinitesimal on the landscape, through its privileging of Afro-Mexican presence and culture.

"Pa' mi Nicolasita" (For my Nicolasita), written by Donají Méndez Tello (1999) in *Alma cimarrona*, is a dedicatory poem that illustrates the concept of the "figured world", seen in the deep love and admiration for the black woman that the persona has. There is a sense of awe in response to her beauty, reinforced by the meticulous care given in addressing her, as in the first line of the opening cuarteta: "¡Ay que mi nitare' bonitilla!" (Oh my beautiful black woman!) Méndez Tello (1999) infuses wonderment in the endearment, making the dimunitive form of *bonita* a love language. There is finesse in the black woman's gait, and the poet emphasizes it as a captivating, yet empowering quality:

Mira nomaj qué sensual caminas	Look how sensual you walk
Y me da coraje que te vean los niños	and it makes me angry that the boys look at you
¡Ay mi Nicolasita!	Oh my Nicolasita!

(Méndez Tello, "Pa' mi Nicolasita", 72)

The poem expounds the depth of love that the persona has for his black woman and implies the nuances and textualities of relationships. Such is the deep-felt commitment and love that the persona wants to keep his woman away from the world, so he can be with her without interruption:

Te quiero tanto mi negritilla	I love you so much my little black girl
que yo te pongo un bajarequillo	that I will build you a little hut
pa³ que ejtemos nomaj los doj solitos.	just for the two of us.

(Méndez Tello, "Pa' mi Nicolasita", 72)

The possessiveness that accompanies the portrayal of the woman – "mi negritilla" (my little black girl) – arguably suggests a certain amount of ambivalence; however, this seems to be outweighed by the love the man has for her.

Amid the portrayal of the black man's quest to win the black woman, the poetic voice also reveals a certain level of communal relations and aspects of the livelihood of the people, solidifying the synchronous duality of an autonomously separated community with a collective culture. The implication is that the black man understands the importance of providing for his family and depending on the support of the wider community for keeping the family together. There is no hint of indolence or irresponsibility on the part of the black male, but a sense of pride in building strong family bonds with a wife and increasing the black population. Moreover, the determination to author self, and to project images of blacks in a particular redeeming manner, is evident. Several stereotypical representations of the negligent black man and father are suppressed:

¡Júyete conmigo ahora mejmo	Run away with me right now
y ya dejpué que najca el munchito,	and after the baby is born,
se lo levemos a papacitoj.	we'll take him to Daddy.
Mira, la veredeta que va a tu casa	Look, the path that leads to your house
acompañándola también ejta	is also being trod by my

mi mula prieta que quiero tanto	brown mule that I love so much
y que me ayuda a cargá el mai.	and which helps me to carry my corn.
Anda mi negra no sea jingrate,	Come on my black woman, don't be disagreeable,
júyete conmigo, ni piensejmá	run away with me, don't think about it
que ejte año si Dios me ayuda	because this year, with God's help
toda la siembra del limonar	the entire lemon harvest
será pa' nosotroj doj,	will be for both of us,
Pa' que tengamos otro munchito	so we can have another baby
y al año, otro, nomaj!	and next year, another one and no more.
(Méndez Tello, "Pa' mi Nicolasita")	

Strong awareness of blackness is projected in the *coplas* and lyric poems calling attention to racial consciousness as a sphere of liberation. Black men are positioned to demonstrate that the oppression of Afro-Mexicans stretches across gender lines to include their female counterparts. Images of stately black men accompany images of queenly black women. Each positive address of the black woman, each recognition of her beauty, works to change the way in which black women are perceived and related to and indicates an understanding that any agenda for racial/social legitimation must also include black women. The positive images or proclamations suggest, moreover, an undertaking that black men and women share a common legacy and history of slavery, colonialism and racial oppression, which must inform their self-formation.

A decided aspect of self-definition for black men and success in achieving freedom and gaining access to citizenship must involve validating women as well as men and involve the group as a whole. The positive images point to possible ways in which black men understand that there is a need for the power positions between them to shift so that they participate less in denigrating black women and more in elevating them to muffle the voices of domination and racism against which black women struggle, on an ongoing basis.

Place and Identity

The study of postcolonial societies has also given attention to the role of place in identity formation. Indeed, the oral forms serve as a testament to Mexico's multiculturality, as they reveal a consciousness of a collective culture, language and sensibility, which are used to characterize the Afro-Mexican group and narrate its attachment to a particular region and cultural heritage. The narrators of oral verses and writers of lyric poems in *Alma cimarrona* draw on the versatility of this art form – *décimas* and *coplas* – to express their understanding of who they are. Indeed, the verses reveal the ways in which the poetry is linked to a particular space/place and identifies a group, which is obviously aware of its ethno-racial distinctions in Mexico.

The poem "Canto a la costa mía" (Song to My Coast) gives vocalization that is potent and resonant in soliciting its request. The palm is represented as a powerful communicative device between the land and its people. There is a specifically directed summons to the poetic persona who acts as the immediate oracle, evident from the ensuing verses, to chant songs to the land – to the persona's Costa Chica. The possessive claim to the land shows intimacy and an attachment to it by its inhabitants. Place is undeniably linked to identity formation, and so the poet's musical dedication is not only an expression, but also an extension of identity, embodied in the kaleidoscopic fusion of land and people.

Nature's involvement in broadcasting the tribute to the territory of Costa Chica lends unmistakable force to this poetic form: "El mar arrulló mis versos / en sus olas cadenciosas." (The sea whispered my verses / in its rhythmic waves.) The reverence palpable in the homage is conveyed in the gentleness of the sea's lull. In this sense the poem serves to poetically fuel the oral tradition through the recognition and praise of regionalism – Costa Chica is particularized to be canonized. The persona reveals space as a reinforcement of place, conveying the message of ownership and intimacy with the land and sea:

El mar arrulló mis versos	The sea whispered my verses
en sus olas cadenciosas	in its rhythmic waves
a ti Costa Chica mía	to you my Costa Chica
te dedico algunas coplas.	I dedicate some verses.

(Zárate Arango, "Canto a la costa mía", 52)

While the failure of mainstream Mexico to recognize the Afro-Mexican coastal zone and its people is forcefully underscored, the "Afro-Mexican" coastal flagship is unmistakably clear in drawing awareness to its own existence. The dedicatory lyrics convey the injustice of non-recognition and simultaneously accentuate the unmistakable pride of place and race. The rhythmic cadences and internal assonances of these lines join in the celebration of black selfhood to establish a unique nationalism and regionalism within the broader spectrum of Mexico's denied racial pluralism to reveal *mestizaje* as a denial of regional alignment and distinction.

Regional particularism is pervasive in "Canto a la costa mía" as defining features of towns and locales along the Costa Chica are given prominence. Acapulco is known for its artistic, svelte dancers of *chilena*, a popular Afro-Mexican dance, and for its women of pure coastal blood:

De Acapulco hasta mi tierra	From Acapulco to my land
se ha bailado la chilena,	they have danced the chilena,
orgullo de sus mujeres	proud of its women
de pura sangre costeña.	of pure costeña blood.
(Ibid.)	

Racial pride is marked by reference to the impeccable bloodline of "los costeños" (people from Costa Chica). This conceptualization of "pura sangre costeña" (pure costeña blood) demystifies and debunks the latent underlying colonial stereotype of "mala raza" and "mala sangre" attached to black ethnicities. Without being intentionally antagonistic, the appreciation of beauty visible in the region speaks volumes to the differences in race in reality, against the backdrop of sameness in perceived reality.

Racial consciousness is linked to place in the suggestion that the distinctiveness of Costa Chican women is attributable to their place of origin. Common and dominant along the coastal region is a gamut of beautiful women whose striking beauty is renowned. While the women are celebrated for their beauty, the men are praised for their prowess and bravery: "la cuna de hombres valientes" (the birthplace of brave men) ("Canto a la costa mía", 52, stanza 4). Moreover, the coastal town of Cuajinicuilapa, the area with the largest numbers of Afro-derived people in Mexico, is seen as the birthplace and incubator of outstanding Afro-Mexicans. Black racial identity is endowed with fortitude in these lines, affirming its capacity to produce a special type of men and women:

"De Ometepec se pregona	"Ometepec boasts of having
tener mujeres bonitas,	beautiful women,
Cuajinicuilapa . . .	Cuajinicuilapa, . . .
la cuna . . . de morenas bonitas",	the birthplace . . . of beautiful black women",
"Cuajinicuilapa es bello por sus	"Cuajinicuilapa is beautiful because
mujeres bonitas."	of its beautiful women."
(Ibid.)	

Regional pride and nationhood are highlighted as signal features among Afro-Mexican coastal communities. Place is praised as the heartbeat, the vital life-giving organ of the people. Reverence and adoration are inspired solely by geographical affinity, so there is a duality in identification of people and place. A sense of being is integrally embedded in place, while there seems to be no separateness between place and people: identity with nationhood becomes synonymous with identity with region. In other words, the geographical region evokes a distinctive identity and character in its people:

San Marcos mi corazón,	San Marcos my love,
te canto por ser costeño,	I sing to you because I'm a *costeño*,
es la única razón	that's the only reason
del canto de este cuijileño	for the song of this *cuijileño*
(Ibid.)	

This deep attachment of Afro-Mexicans to their natural environs bears an indelible imprint of racial consciousness: "costeñoque soy" (I'm a costeño), and "moreno del corazón" (black at heart) are, without doubt, treated synonymously. The coast is where their identity is conceived and lived, and an allegiance is forged that surpasses time and the ephemeral, and entering an almost spiritual realm where the natives' claim to the coastal region is preconditioned by the fact of their being Afro-Mexicans. This is voiced in the request and earnest desire not to be forgotten as a true and committed Mexican of African descent. The community is undoubtedly deeply rooted in the geographical locale:

San Nicolás yo te pido	San Nicolás I ask you
como costeño que soy	like the *costeño* that I am
que no olvides lo que he sido	not to forget that I have been
moreno del corazón.	black at heart.
(Ibid.)	

Pride in region highlights pride in nationhood in a consummate climax resonant in the final stanza of the poem. Moreover, the women of the region are made out to be emblematic of the beauty of the region, thereby emphasizing their value to the region and the country, even though this may be viewed as an unwelcome way of typologizing women in traditional patriarchal terms:

Cuajinicuilapa es bello Cuajinicuilapa is beautiful
por sus mujeres bonitas because of its beautiful women
es un pueblo guerrerense it is a Guerrero town
¡Orgullo de Costa Chica! the pride of Costa Chica!
(Ibid.)

A similarly enthusiastic ownership of place and the firm suggestion that ethnicity is linked to the place occupied mainly by blacks in Mexico, is expressed in the following *copla* from the same collection, *Alma cimarrona*:

Soy de puro Costa Chica I am pure Costa Chica
donde reinan los guerreros, where the Guerrero people rule,
donde los hombres where the men
¡son hombres! are men!
y las mujeres, ¡mujeres! And the women, women!
Donde no nacen maricas Where no homosexuals are born
y los que nacen ¡se mueren! And those that are born, die
(p. 33)

Here, the persona orchestrates self-formation structured on the knowledge of place of origin and a particular understanding of black sexuality as one which unapologetically embraces heterosexuality. All three contexts – "figured world", "positionality" and "authoring" – are intricately tied to these lines. The persona creates a world – an "as if" world – as if it were established/given that once these factors converge – place, blackness and a particular sexual orientation, it is understood that this is a bona fide Afro-Mexican. A strong sense of entitlement, understood in the context of "relational identity", is evident as the persona implies how he expects to be understood and regarded. The voice of the "I" unmistakably disrupts the official monologic, authoritative discourse of Mexico, to author itself in a particular way that is inextricably linked to a particular place and cultural outlook.

The affinity of Afro-Mexicans to the land where the coastal regions are emblematic of Afro-Mexican's ethnicity and cultural identity seems evident in Efraín Villegas Zapata's (1999) "Costa". The poem particularizes the region by identifying its unique feature so that place is not just a geographical or spatial reference but an embodiment of human existence, codified by a collective genetic component, determinant of a people and a rich cultural heritage. The opening *cuarteta* (quatrain) reveals a picturesque view of the coast and coastal life. An interconnection between the landscape and the people is immediately distinctive:

Costa canción y caricia	Costa song and caress
borrascosa como el mar	stormy like the sea
donde vive sin matar	where you can live without killing
la vida se desperdicia	life just drifts along
(Villegas Zapata, "Costa", 53)	

The affectionate address in line one, buttressed by the musicality of the alliteration, exposes a sense of suavity and subtleness, which is immediately compared, paradoxically, to the unpredictable and turbulent quality of the sea, "borrascoso" (stormy). The beauty of the land is also paralleled to the longevity of life, which unfolds unhurriedly in a natural trajectory, "donde vivir sin matar/ la vida se desperdicia" (where you can live without killing / life just drifts along). The spirit of the coast is consuming and prepossessive of its occupants, and a sense of cultural aliveness and inherent vibrancy underscores the zeitgeist of the coast to the extent that everyone is captivated by its irresistible magnetism:

La costa es pasión que asfixia	The coast is a passion that suffocates
tiene el vicio de bailar	it has the vice of dancing
se entrega todo al amar	it surrenders all when in love
como una ingenua novicia.	like a naive novice.
(Ibid.)	

Again, we see that the oral tradition is an integral part of the everyday life on the coast and is infused with mundane activities and survival strategies. The stance of the troubadour is militant, dignified, demonstrating the indomitable fighting spirit of African-derived Mexicans. It is this position that becomes a dramatization of what he imagines every Afro-Mexican person to be asked to do:

Montado en un cuaco briosco	Mounted on a spirited scrawny horse
pajerero y bailador	frisky and dancing
sale un negro trovador,	out comes a black troubadour,
con un machete filoso	with a sharp machete
para defender su honor.	to defend his honour.
(Ibid.)	

The image of a proud warrior poised in readiness for battle "con un machete filoso" (with a sharp machete) is evoked as evidence of the passion for life among coastal dwellers.

"Costa" (Coast) depicts a vivid picture of a region luxuriant and diverse in resources, people and culture. Each place is distinguished by its particular feature, which is an eclectic blend of definitive racial characteristics that ultimately unite culture and people. Villegas Zapata celebrates each coastal region for a particular product for which it is known, suggesting that there are strong linkages between the land and the activities of the Afro-Mexicans.

Pochutla huele a café	Pochutla smells of coffee
y Puerto Ángel a marisco	and Puerto Angel of seafood
Pluma Hidalgo es gallo arisco	Pluma Hidalgo is a wild rooster
pelea sin saber por qué.	it fights without knowing why.
(Ibid.)	

Regional distinction is further embodied in its particular products such as coffee, which is aromatic, potent and black, reflective of the land and its people. There is also seafood, evoking the arresting scent of the ocean and publicizing the dominant trade and skill of the region. Pluma Hidalgo gives homage to the Afro-Mexican freedom fighter and hero, whose fighting spirit is immortalized in the identity of coastal Afro-Mexicans.[3] The metaphorical comparison underlines the proud nature intricately interwoven with the fighting spirit, and its atavistic appearance produces a constant zeal for revolution unheeded by external factors. The specific reference to Hildago along with the observation "pelea sin saber por qué" (fights without knowing why) is perhaps a reference to the manner in which the revolutionary was annihilated as he attempted to bring about equality for all Mexicans in the pre-independence period.

"Costa" (Coast) undoubtedly draws pointed attention to the people of the region in celebration of nationhood, racial pride and unity. The distinctions among the people of different areas are marked to disrupt stereotypical perceptions of them as one indistinguishable group, which lacks any specific and distinctive qualities, abilities or traits. Sola de Vegas is therefore recognized for its women whose exceptional beauty is matched only by their own flamboyance. In contrast, the women of Juquila are noted for their religious dedication and pious acts:

Sola de Vegas es mujer	Sola de Vegas is a woman
muy bonita y veleidosa	very beautiful and fickle
Juquila es mujer piadosa	Juquila is a pious woman
que Milagros sabe hacer.	who knows how to perform miracles.
(Ibid.)	

Music and dance, vibrant and powerful art forms of the African legacy, epitomize cultural expression in the Afro-Mexican coastal regions. Both artistic expressions are seen as the heartbeat of the people and their existence is meaningless without these. Performance art is seen as an outlet, as well as an inborn expression of identity, which unifies the group:

Se puso luego un fandango	Then they played a fandango
un violín y un bajo quinto	a violin and a *bajo quinto* guitar
cantaba el negro más pinto	the most handsome black man was singing
una chilena de rango,	a famous chilena,
yo lo zapatié en un pango	I tap-danced to it on a river ferry,
y hasta cimbraba el recinto.	until the area shook.
(Ibid.)	

Conviviality marks the atmosphere in which Afro-Mexicans, through music and dance, perform the identity they want to project of themselves. According to Anita González (2010, 2), "performance allows humans to clarify and articulate their history through embodied expressions. By 'becoming' through either masked impersonation, or crafted improvisation."

The way in which both oral poems and lyric ones are imbued with rhythmic quality and musicality is undeniable. These qualities not only speak to the African religious heritage of the Afro-Mexican people and how the Afro-Mexicans have preserved aspects of their Afro-derived culture, but also recall the centrality of these qualities to their African ancestors from whom they inherited them. In attesting to the great appeal of music and rhythm to African slaves and their descendants in Latin America, during and after slavery, George Andrews (2004, 29) writes:

> Music and dance were healing on almost every level, a balm for body and mind. The graceful movements of dance, movement done purely for pleasure and enjoyment, were the antithesis and direct negation of the pain and exhaustion of coerced labor. And when performed collectively, as they usually were, African *sons* and dance removed,

at least for a moment, the degraded social status of slavery and created alternative, deeply healing senses of person and peoplehood.

Historically, rhythm, music and dance made life bearable and provided a modicum of self-affirmation. Even after centuries of being exposed to Catholicism, Afro-Mexicans obviously still revel in the rhythm of drum and related music and dance. Andrews (2004, 29) provides support in his assertion that

> one of the central messages of African music is that rhythm lifts us out of the daily grind by transforming consciousness, transforming time, transforming and heightening our experience of the moment. And that consciousness-altering effect is entirely purposeful: in Africa and its New World diaspora, rhythm and music were an essential part of religious observance, particularly in creating the emotional and spiritual conditions for the gods to manifest themselves by possessing and "mounting" their worshippers. Drumming and dance were fundamental elements of African religious ritual; and as Africans adopted Christianity and turned it to their uses, a final way in which they transformed Iberian Catholicism was to inject it with the power of African drums.

We have seen then the various ways in which Afro-Mexicans construct identity, by creating "figured worlds" in both oral and lyric poems. Reality is presented as they understand it and as they want the wider Mexican society to perceive them. Different cultural identities are performed in the "figured worlds" to manipulate the images projected by Afro-Mexicans of themselves and their region to others. The regions predominantly inhabited by Afro-Mexicans are owned as "spaces of authoring" to allow a range of selected identities – "positional identities" – to be created for Afro-Mexicans to assert their own cultural and racial self-fashioning, debunk the myths about who they are, and unsettle erroneous accounts of their lack of contributions to and place in the Mexican nation. The suggestions of harmony and connectivity between Afro-Mexicans and the land or region seem to imply the possibility of a similar type of unity and harmony between Afro-Mexicans and the rest of Mexican society.

Furthermore, the asserted identities serve to debunk the concept of *mestizaje* as defended by Mexico in its official definition of nation and identity in terms of homogeneity. Their emphasis, furthermore, on affirming blackness and regionalism as they speak the one to the other, provides ample support to Benítez-Rojo's (1996, 26) claim that "*mestizaje* is nothing more than a concentration of differences". This is to say that the poems, with their various revelations of Afro-centrality, belie Mexico's claim of *mestizaje* as a synthesis or homogeneity. They reveal a significant level of racial consciousness among the performers and writers of Afro-Mexican poems, and an even greater awareness of the link between the places occupied by Afro-Mexicans and their representation of themselves as being irrefutably Mexican.

5.

Afro-Mexico in the Context of a Caribbean Literary and Cultural Aesthetics

There are performers who were born in the Caribbean and who are not Caribbean by their performance; there are others who were born near or far away and nevertheless are.
—Antonio Benítez-Rojo, *The Repeating Island*

The Caribbean constitutes in fact, a field of relationships . . . a threatened reality that nevertheless stubbornly persists.
—Édouard Glissant, *Caribbean Discourse*

In the 1970s Mexico, under the leadership of President Luis Echeverría (1970–76), expounded a new political stance with regard to the Caribbean. This new position – that Mexico is also Caribbean – was further buttressed in the 1980s when Mexico declared itself Caribbean, based on the shared historical past and similarities between the cultures.

Mexico, like the Caribbean, was the site of fierce combat and contestation as European expeditioners fought to take control of territories. Slavery ensued in both regions once it was established that the regions were extremely useful for the production of cattle, sugarcane and other agricultural products. Mexico's relationship with Jamaica, in particular, existed from as early as the colonial period. According to Laura Muñoz (1990, 89): "Durante el resto de la época colonial y después de la conquista y colonización inglesa de Jamaica, las relaciones entre ésta y la Nueva España se desarrollaron, fundamentalmente, en torno a tres aspectos: el tráfico de esclavos, los asedios de piratas y el comercio ilegal practicado por los ingleses en las costas del Golfo de México." (During the remainder of the colonial period and after the conquest and English colonization in Jamaica, relations between the latter and New Spain developed fundamentally with respect to three factors: the slave trade, the assaults of pirates and the illegal trade practised by the English on the Gulf of Mexico.) In 1713, this relationship was further fortified when the English were given the sole right to provide slaves to the Spanish colonies. This was done through the port of Veracruz and later on Campeche (Aguirre Beltrán 1946, 348). Jamaica functioned as the main point of contact between Mexico and the Caribbean region in the colonial period. There was constant communication among the governors general of Veracruz, Yucatán and Jamaica regarding matters related to peace in the region and the presence of the English in waters considered to belong to Spain, among other controversial issues (Muñoz 1990, 90). The relationship between Mexico and the Caribbean was also bolstered by the launch of the first Mexican consulate in the region, in Jamaica in 1857. This consulate monitored the movement of various persons as well as trading and maritime activities including the passage of merchant ships in the port of Veracruz between the two corridors, throughout the region and in the port of Kingston.

Migration played a central role in instituting and strengthening ties between the Caribbean and Mexico. In its attempts to achieve economic independence, the Porfirio government in the nineteenth century endeavoured to attract foreigners to work in the agricultural sector in Mexico. Some foreigners were also recruited to work in the manufacturing of whisky and beer, in meat preservation and in the mining industry. The workers who were favoured by both federal and privately owned companies were purported to be Cubans, Puerto Ricans and Jamaicans. As a result, hundreds of Caribbean workers travelled to Mexico to work in these jobs, which were expected to build the Mexican economy. The majority of the workers were Jamaicans, who were seeking to improve their own standard of living. In 1882 approximately three hundred Jamaican workers went to work on the railway line in Tampico – San Luis Potosí–Tampico del Ferrocarríl Central, which served to link Mexico City and the coast (Muñoz 1990, 91).

In 1889, the railway company again contracted Jamaicans to work in the wharves (González Navarro 1960). This was so because Jamaicans had proved themselves to be hard-working people, even though they worked in untenable conditions to construct the railway line. Different companies, as well as Mexican governments, continued to recruit Jamaicans to work in areas ranging from agriculture to the unloading of coal, a task which indigenous Mexicans had proved not strong enough to undertake. In 1905, a mining company in Guanaceví recruited three hundred Jamaicans to Mexico to work in the mines, despite protests from some Mexicans who believed the Jamaicans were taking their jobs (*El imparcial*, 6 April 1905, 1). Muñoz (1990, 94) argues that "a pesar de las condiciones adversas, la capacidad de oposición y resistencia de estos trabajadores contra la nueva forma de esclavitad que constituía su relación laboral fue extraordinaria". (In spite of the adverse conditions, the level of opposition and resistance of the workers against the new form of slavery that constituted this labour relations were extraordinary.) Certainly Caribbean people, Jamaicans in the main, have made significant contributions to the historical, social, economic and cultural development of Mexico. It is highly improbable that they did not also leave the imprints of their own Afro-derived culture on Mexican society, even though the research has not recorded this aspect of the result of the many years of interaction, exchanges and collaborations between the Caribbean region and Mexico.

This chapter pivots in part on the knowledge of the undeniable historical and cultural connections between the Caribbean and Mexico, to suggest that Afro-Mexican cultural forms can also be located within a broad Caribbean cultural and literary aesthetics. Research bears testimony that some Afro-Jamaican religious herbal art survived in Mexico in the early twentieth century when many wealthy Mexicans sought the help of a Jamaican herbalist with their illnesses and problems relating to their romantic affairs. Furthermore, as Muñoz (1990) observes, if Jamaicans could take music, dance and other cultural forms to London and other parts of the world, then without doubt there must be some traces of Caribbean inferences that have been left behind in Mexican culture.

The chapter will extend the debate beyond historical and cultural links, heritage or legacy to examine the ways in which Afro-Mexican culture itself can be located within a Caribbean cultural aesthetic. I will examine a selection of poems from the collection *Alma cimarrona*. In their endeavour to elicit Afro-Mexicans' participation in the project to collect these poems, cultural anthropologists convinced them of the urgent need to rescue both themselves and their culture from obscurity and resist the homogenizing principle of *mestizaje*. The analyses will reveal that these poems problematize the traditional configuration of nationality in Mexico. My intention is to argue that the diversity that these poems add to Mexican culture and the definition of Mexican nation places them within the broad discourse of Caribbean literary and cultural aesthetics. This is so in the first place because Caribbean literary and cultural aesthetics have traditionally been "expressions of the search for national identity in opposition to Europe's cultural inventions" (Forbes 2005, 4). I will also examine the extent to which these poems may be placed in the tradition of Caribbean discourse, which has come full circle since José Martí extolled "the idea of the Caribbean as part of the Americas, as creole and heterogeneous" (Dash 1998). At the end of the twentieth century Glissant (1989, 19) characterized the Caribbean as a "space marked by diversity and cross-culturality" and Benítez-Rojo (1996, 4) characterized it as "not a common archipelago, but a meta-archipelago". Both Glissant and Benítez-Rojo offer terms which suggest that the geographical as well as the cultural definitions of the Caribbean may be expanded. For his part, Glissant proposes a geographical space which encompasses the Caribbean and its surrounding rimlands. Benítez-Rojo's concept of an expanded Caribbean may be a more metaphorical venture, but both definitions work in tandem to project the Caribbean as a broader cultural space than has traditionally been conceptualized.

It is arguable that the case for Afro-Mexican literary and cultural production to be located within a Caribbean cultural space is less applicable to the Costa Chica than to the city of Veracruz, which is considered to be in the Caribbean Basin. In fact, the city itself has adopted as its motto the definitive claim "Veracruz también es Caribe" ("Veracruz is Caribbean too") to highlight the extent to which this city shares historical as well as cultural ties with the Caribbean. However, Veracruz itself also does not state this claim exclusively because of its geographical location, but attributes this to various aspects of the African heritage which have survived in the city and the Caribbean. In 1990, the city held its second forum under the same motto with the firm insistence that "pensamos que el concepto Caribe, desborda la visión geográfica... y que su vecindad le ha permitido impregnarse de este proceso histórico y cultural" (Juárez Hernández 1990, 7). (We think that the concept of the Caribbean extends beyond geographical borders and its geographical vicinities to include the historical and cultural process.) Among these Afro-derived cultural forms are the religious rites and practices and various aspects of the oral tradition, such as those discussed in the previous chapter. The performance of these African-derived forms has been discussed as being pivotal to the construction of identities that are shaped by an African consciousness and presence.

Alma cimarrona, which has previously been discussed, comprises two sections: the first includes *coplas* – popular compositions which were recorded, but do not belong to an individual author; and the second includes lyric poems written by individual poets. In the previous chapter we defined the *copla* as a popular lyrical composition or ballad of Spanish origin that ranges in length, as stanzas may vary from three to five lines of eight to twelve syllables each. The project to compile Afro-Mexican *coplas* brings to mind a similar one undertaken in the Esmeraldas region of Ecuador by the writer Luz Argentina Chiriboga (2001), who believed that this central Afro-Ecuadorian cultural form was being threatened with extinction. Like the Afro-Ecuadorian ones, the Afro-Mexican *coplas* are typified by assonance and by rhyming even lines, in keeping with the oral tradition from which they are drawn. They underline the centrality of the oral tradition to definitions of Afro-Mexicanness as they engage each other in an interactive definition of self. The *coplas* are arranged in thematic groups such as *Escolares* (School Verses), *Amor y piropos* (Love and Flirtation), *Ofensivos* (Offensive Verses) and *Groserías* (Rude Verses). The content of each section graphically corresponds with the title. For instance, the section *Amor y Piropos* features attempts at courtship, endearment and flirting between male and female personae as is evidenced in the following verses:

Bendito sea Dios, Negrita	Blessed be God, black woman
que linda y hermosa te ha hecho,	how pretty and beautiful he made you,
delgadita de cintura	thin around the waist
y abultadita del pecho.	and with a large bosom.
(*Alma cimarrona*, 24)	

The very rhythmic movement of the lines, the strong vowel sounds and the repetition of the internally and externally pronounced *A* sound create an appealing tone of bold, barefaced flattery.

In the section *Groserías* (Rudeness), we find the following verses which reveal the level of banter and benign disparagement and depreciation often expressed in the *copla*:

Yo le pregunté a Cúpido	I asked Cupid
que si había mujer honrada	if an honest woman existed
y me respondió afligido	and he painfully said
que en este mundo no hay nada,	that in this world there is none,
pa' putas, todas son putas,	talking about whores, all are whores
mayormente las casadas,	especially the married ones,
y también quieren hablar	and they want to talk
hijas de siete chingadas.	of the seven screwed women also.[1]
. . . Eres puta y eres puta,	. . . You are a whore and you are a whore,
tienes la cara de res,	you have the face of a cow,
cómo dices que eres monja	how do you say that you are a nun
y te manejas a tres,	and manage to have three at a time,
y tu marido es un rependejo	and your husband is a halfwit
que no te lo echa de ver.	who doesn't realize.
(*Alma cimarrona*, 45–46)	

The Caribbeanness of these *coplas* lies in the first place in their orality, an orality which derives from bold graphic words, rhythm, rhymes and natural musicality. I would suggest further that they exhibit certain aspects of "true orality" as explained by Phillip Nanton (1995, 89–90), who claims that "true orality has long used tricks and humour to set alight the power of the word . . . and [relies on] word-play as well as making jokes about 'serious things'". Here, serious issues of adultery and sexual immorality are presented in a manner which evokes humour, even if it is sardonic. Indeed we see that while there is no extensive use of imagery, the poems rely heavily on humour and the force of simple direct language, employed in a rhythmic manner derived from their use of assonance and rhyme and more importantly on the graphic meaning and shock effect of some words.

Some *coplas* are exchanges between two speakers, most often a male and a female who try to outdo each other in a verbal exchange of insults or in self-praise. In some, females disparage males who are guilty of infidelity and sexism, while in others the male speaker exhibits a strong *machista* attitude. In some *coplas*, the male and female characters are clearly identified, as in the following in which they both engage in an exchange of derogatory comments. These seem to be done in a manner reminiscent of extempo calypso war performances. Extempo refers to an improvised form of competitive calypso performance in Trinidad and Tobago. It involves the improvisation or invention of words and verses in a calypso before an audience. Performers use it with ridicule, flattery and ingenuity to outperform a competitor as in the following example:

El:	He:
Las mujeres son . . .	Women are . . .
son como el demonio,	are like the devil
parientes del alacrán,	the cousins of the scorpion,
nomás ven al hombre pobre	as soon as they see that the man is poor
paran la cola y se van,	they move their tail and leave
pero si los ven con dinero,	but if they see them with money,
hasta les abren el zaguán.	They even open the front hall.

Ella: *She:*
Los hombres dicen que   *Men say*
son el demonio las mujeres   *that women are the devil*
y por dentro están pidiendo   *and are wishing within*
que el demonio se los lleve.   *that the devil may take them away.*
(*Alma cimarrona*, 41)

These *coplas* are intended to entertain an audience, but the humour is often abusive and insulting as in the previous lines. The gender dynamics in these *coplas* are indeed interesting because – despite the obvious *machismo* and misogyny displayed in some of the coplas – the women are seen to be equally articulate in their performance of a range of *coplas*, in which they often outdo the men in their bold insults and mockery. Our reaction may be either laughter or criticism of the undermining of each other by both male and female personae. But regardless of the value system that we may use to respond to the tone or message, the fact is that these exchanges reveal an aspect of a community's way of life and provide an indication of how, in an obviously marginalizing context, they engage in redefinition of themselves. Even some of the most flippant, tactless or offhanded *coplas* reveal perhaps an unconscious commitment to race and consciousness of self as evidenced by frequent use of the terms *negra, negro, negrita*:

Me puse a bañar un negro	I began to bathe a black man
a ver qué color tenía	to see what colour he was

entre más se lo tallaba	the more I worked on him
más negro se le ponía	the blacker he got.
("Groseros", *Alma cimarrona*, 45)	

What at the surface level may elicit mere humour, at a deeper level seems to bespeak the recognition of a stubborn commitment to an Afrocentric ideology. In his discussion of true orality, Nanton (1995, 89) further states that in the oral poem, "when we make a joke we are not really making a joke". The humour reveals, however, an ability to poke fun at oneself while simultaneously communicating a deeper and more sober meaning.

In this context, we might usefully recall Édouard Glissant's (1989, 104) theorizations on the importance of the form of expression employed in the articulation of identity: "The literary activity that is part of . . . a collective consciousness in search of itself is not only a clarification of the community but also a reflection on (and concern with) the specific question of expression. This form of discourse is not satisfied with mere expression but articulates at the same time why it uses that form of expression and not another." Similarly, the dramatic and performative nature of the *coplas* finds resonance in Benítez-Rojo's (1996, 307) assertion that Caribbeanness "functions in a carnivalesque manner", which, as Forbes (2005, 11) explains, "means it is an endlessly performative cultural space. Carnivalesque performance is ritualization of identity." Indeed, in reading these poems one imagines or visualizes the performative space in which they were presented and ritualized. It may be said, then, that the *coplas* embody Caribbeanness as they are typified by this "carnivalesque performance". Furthermore, the focus on their experiences, the poignancy of the oral literature, draws attention to their collective values and identity and establishes the cultural consciousness of the community in a manner which is in consonance with Caribbean sensibilities. It seems then that while there may be substance to the widely held view that Afro-Mexicans lack an understanding of themselves as blacks, the project, which produced the poems in the collection, indicates that some have maintained communal ties which reveal that the spoken word has been transferred through generations. Indeed, the performance of oral forms encourages an interactive definition of self that has helped to establish an independent collective identity for them. Furthermore, the *coplas* underline the function of memory and orality as communal recovery and gives voice to those who have been silenced under definitions of nation that did not include them, despite their presence (Feracho 2001, 36). *Coplas* reveal furthermore, that there has been a communal space in which they have preserved an Afro-Mexican identity. It seems reasonable to suggest, moreover, that in their performances they simultaneously redefine – or should redefine – our understanding of Mexicanness, since the cultural frame of references is at times very clearly Mexican (as for instance when one of the *coplas* refers to the *chingadas*). The term *chingadas* is derived from the verb *chingar*, which is widely used in Spanish-speaking countries. In Mexico, however, it is uniquely used to reflect the definition offered by Octavio Paz (1997) in his book *El laberinto de la soledad* to refer to the savage rape of native women by Spanish conquerors on their arrival in Mexico. These women, according to Paz's definition, became the first *chingadas*, and as a result Mexicans are commonly referred to as *"los hijos de la chingada"*.

The oral poems of the first half of the collection contrast with the single-authored lyric poems of the second half of the collection that is entitled *Poemas regionales* (*Regional Poems*). These lyric poems are written by several writers who interrogate, explore and express their own responses to their Afro-Mexicanness. The title of the section, as well as the content of the poems, emphasizes the importance of the region or place to the authors in shaping their understanding of themselves as Mexicans. The poems express a range of ideas, sentiments, responses and contrasts in tone with the broad-talking, signifying nature of the *coplas*, but all function as texts which the writers consciously or subconsciously use as sites of self-assertion and self-construction as they seem to speak to each other and resonate with interactively constituted meanings.

The poem "Caminos" (Roads) by Francisco J. Zárate Arango (1999a, 51) constitutes an intriguing tribute to roads employed as a metaphor of the Afro-Mexican's very existence – past, present and future. Roads link communities on a literal level: Afro-Mexican communities are remote settlements along the Costa Chica and roads are therefore important for connecting Afro-Costa Chicans to the outside world. But roads also speak to the undeniable links between remote Afro-Mexican communities and larger, more developed areas of Mexico. Tiny roads eventually lead to wider, more developed ones which eventually lead to Mexico City and Guadalajara and all the parts of Mexico that enjoy more recognition. So the roads symbolically embed Afro-Mexican communities into that larger complex network of Mexican roads and by extension Mexican society or nation:

Caminos tiene la tierra	The earth has roads
que peinan su geografía,	that comb its geography,
tienen caminos las ferias	festivals have roads
caminos tiene la vida.	life has roads.
Esos hilos que nos unen	These threads that unify us
a negros, blancos e indios	blacks, whites and indigenous people
son como ríos que fluyen	are like rivers that flow
buscando el mismo destino.	searching for the same destiny.
(Ibid.)	

The poetic persona asserts the heterogeneity of Mexican society by emphasizing that the roads lead in different directions and bring different experiences, establishing contacts among different ethnic groups. Furthermore, roads allow people to retrace their tracks to somewhere; and so it is this meditation on roads that allows the poetic persona to point to the history of the establishment of *palenques* by their Maroon forebears, such as Nyanga Yanga, the great seventeenth-century black rebel leader discussed in the introduction to this book. Attention is drawn to the fact that some blacks occupied different places not as victims or slaves but as free people:

Como el camino que llega	Like the road that arrives
cruzando selvas y mares,	crossing forests and seas,
llegó nuestra raza negra	our black race arrived
a poblar estos lugares	to people these sites
Raza indómita de bronce	Irrepressible race of bronze
no todos venían cautivos	not all came as captives
si Yanga lo dijo entonces	Yanga said it then
tratan el mismo camino.	they came on the same road.
(Ibid.)	

This is an attempt to write a history of rebellion that for the most part has repeatedly been omitted from official Mexican discourse. The road metaphor both emphasizes the cultural contributions of the Afro-Mexicans and implicitly points to the absence of progress and development in the region as the persona evokes the need to construct more roads. Roads are necessary for the dispersed communities of the Costa Chica to maintain consensus on keeping their cultural traditions intact. Interestingly, there is also an appeal for community members to participate in the construction of roads for their own internal progress and unity:

Teniendo costumbres bellas	Having beautiful traditions
hemos forjado destinos	we have forged destinies
y para unir nuestros pueblos	and to unite our peoples
nos hace falta caminos.	we need roads.
No importa dónde te encuentres	It doesn't matter where you are
hermano negro te pido	black brother I ask you
para unir a nuestra gente	in order to unite our people
construyamos más caminos.	let's build more roads.
(Ibid.)	

Again the figure of speech functions on a very pragmatic level, but also on a symbolic and philosophical level to highlight the need to facilitate collaboration and unity among Mexicans in general, but also among black Mexicans in particular.

Two further poems by Zárate Arango (1999b, 1999c), "Canto a la costa mía" (Song to My Coast), "Radiografía costeña" (Coastal X-ray), as well as Álvaro Carillo's (1999) "Costa Chica mía" (My Costa Chica), construct Afro-Mexican identity as rooted specifically in the Costa Chica region. It is the place they regard as home and the base of Afro-Mexican life and culture. The firm and lasting impression made by the poetic voice of these poems is the need for recognition of these black settlements.

In Zárate Arango's "Canto a la costa mía" (1999b, 52) the subject's construction of a Caribbean identity is intricately linked to and understood through loyalty to the coastal region similar to the way the sea and the coast have been treated by Caribbean poets such as the Afro-Cuban Cos Causse. The poetic subject explicitly defines him or herself first as a *costeño* (inhabitant of the coast), and within these parameters all considerations of nation are understood. The persona seems to question the importance of the Mexican nation in the construction of identity and to privilege the critical region as the site of its construction:

Del palmar surgió una voz	From the palm grove rose a voice
que a gritos me lo pedía	that asked me, yelling,
que le cantara a mi tierra	that I should sing to my land

a la Costa Chica mía.   to my Costa Chica.
(Ibid.)

The poetic persona projects a panoramic view of the area naming several Afro-Mexican towns in Guerrero along with their respective characteristics – natural beauty, festivals, dances, brave men, beautiful black women. The use of the terms *costeño* and "Costa Chica" clearly establishes the sense of region and expresses sentiments of pride and ownership of a regional identity. Simultaneously, the poem seems to call for an interrogation of the concept of Mexican statehood that excludes this particular region.

The poem laments the neglect of the region as a place that has produced some of the bravest and most beautiful people in Mexico: "La cuna de hombres valientes y de morenas bonitas" (ibid.). (The birthplace of valiant men and beautiful black women.) The fact that the region's beauty and achievements are not lauded is also bemoaned:

Nadie te cantó jamás	No one ever sang to you
y me parece horroroso,	and I think this is horrible
ni versos de Rubén Mora	nor did the verses of Rubén Mora
le dieron luz a tu rostro,	illuminate your face,
por eso te canto yo	therefore I sing to you
Cuajinicuilapa hermoso.[2]	beautiful Cuajinicuilapa.

(Ibid.)

Read in conjunction with Zárate Arango's other poems, this claiming of the region is synonymous with the agenda to establish right of place for Afro-Mexicans in a country that has attempted to erase blacks from national memory. The poetic persona's connection to the land underlines the importance of belonging, as a theme in the postcolonial Caribbean context, and illustrates Glissant's (1992) claim that landscape is a character rather than merely background in Caribbean literature. This is an extension of the theme already seen in the previous chapter, but with a greater focus on how this speaks to the Caribbean context in which the poems may be placed.

Álvaro Carrillo's (1999, 56–57) "Costa Chica mía" (My Costa Chica) is a similarly assertive poem that emphasizes the extent to which a sense of self and belonging is shaped by location or place. Through short, strong phrases, the poetic persona praises the indomitable and enduring nature of the region that becomes synonymous with Afro-Mexicans as the land is described as a "morena serrena", modifying the old conquistadorial trope of the land as a woman's body:

Morena serrena de cuerpo cenceño	Proud black woman with a thin body
y alma cimarrona,	and a maroon soul
Costa Chica mía,	my Costa Chica
deja que mi estro,	let my inspiration,
tripulando en sueños,	steering in dreams,
pase el rubicón	take the risk
de hablar tu poesía;	of speaking your poetry;
tu poesía que es nube	your poetry that is cloud
y es golpe roqueño,	and stony blow,
tristeza, jolgorio,	sadness, revelry,
paz y rebeldía;	peace and rebelliousness,
deja que lo diga porque soy costeño,	let me say it because I am from the coast,
porque yo la llevo,	because I carry it within,
Costa Chica mía.	my Costa Chica.
(Ibid.)	

Poetry is here inherent in the land itself and thus emerges almost organically from it. Origin becomes constitutive of selfhood, as the speaker declares that he carries it within him- or herself. As the poem proceeds, it highlights the importance of the region's culture, its dances, songs and fights:

No, tú nunca mueres,	No, you never die,
porque estás brillante en los cascabeles de tus tradiciones,	because you are shining in the small bells of your traditions,
porque hasta el brebaje	because even the potion
de tus aguardientes	of your alcoholic drinks
deja gotas bellas para mis canciones,	leaves beautiful drops for my songs,
para la chilena que es,	for the *chilena* [coastal *son*] that is,
entre tus sones,	amongst your *sones* [popular music]
el arpegio cumbre que bailan los dioses,	the summit of music that the gods dance
aquí en el Olimpo de mis pretensiones.	here in the Olympus of my hopes.

No, tú nunca mueres,	No, you never die,
tu pueblo ha surgido de tus	your people have surged from your
peñascales, como águila brava,	slopes, like a fierce eagle,
como salta un rayo	jumps like a ray
partiendo las brumas nubes fantasmales	parting the mist, ghostly clouds
que alzan cataclismos en el mes de mayo	that raise cataclysms in the month of May
Yo soy de este pueblo, ingenuo,	I am from this people, candid,
bravero, yo me rifo todo	fierce, not afraid of anything
cuando suelto un gallo y, en los jaripeos,	when I release a cockerel, and in the rodeos,
yo soy el primero que le entra	I am the first one to enter the brawls
a los jaleos, jineteando un toro,	riding a bull
montando un caballo,	mounting a horse
arrastrando el vértigo de una vaquilla,	dragging the vertigo of a heifer
en la serpentina de una lechuguilla.	in the ribbons of an agave.
(Ibid.)	

In Álvaro Carrillo's poem, the Costa Chica region functions as a model of black strength, pride and triumph. Furthermore, the poem challenges the monolithic construction of Mexican national identity as the poet's people are described as having "surgido de tus peñascales, como águila brava". The eagle – which to the Aztecs represented the sun god Huitzilopotchli – is an important national symbol and has been integrated into the Mexican coat of arms. Thus, Álvaro Carrillo forcefully challenges the myths of Mexican nationalism by pointing to the country's multiethnicity. Identity in the poem is doubly inscribed (as referencing the nation and the region).

The suggestion that Afro-Mexican identity and understanding of nation are shaped by geography and place is further conveyed in another poem, "Radiografía costeña" (Coastal X-ray) by Zárate Arango (1999c, 74–77). In this poem, the poetic persona has subjected the region to a metaphorical X-ray that exposes the physical, social and cultural degeneration that has taken place. Environmental pollution, the younger generation's loss of interest in their cultural heritage and the resulting discontinuity of some traditional foods, practices and customs are threatening the regional environment and transforming it in an unwelcoming manner:

¡Oh! Costa	Oh! Costa
has perdido la sonrisa cristalina	you have lost the crystalline smile
y hoy me embarga una tristeza sofocante	and today a suffocating sadness seizes me
pues tus suelos	because your lands
ya semejan a mil ruinas	already resemble a thousand ruins
Y tus playas	And your beaches
no son limpias como antaño	are not clean like in days gone by
pues reciben de tus ríos desperdicios	because they receive from your rivers waste
que transportan de drenajes,	that they transport from drainage,
de los caños.	from brooks.
¡Oh! Costa . . .	Oh! Costa . . .
ya no eres la risueña de aquel tiempo	you are no longer cheerful as you once were
la que Álvaro Carrillo idolatraba	the Costa that Álvaro Carrillo idolized
y en su chilena	and in his song
te hiciera un monumento	built a monument for you
Los cerros que aprietan tu cintura	The hills that sit tightly around your waist
ya no lucen aquel verde esmeralda,	no longer shine with that emerald green,
tus pueblos van perdiendo su cultura,	your peoples are forgetting their culture,
sus jorongos, sus trenzas, sus enaguas.	their ponchos, their braids, their skirts.
Ya no en sus fandangos regionales,	No longer do their regional *fandangos* [folk music and dance] exist
sus bodas alegres de enramadas	their weddings, cheerful in *enramadas*
sus moles, arroz y sus tamales,	their *moles,* rice and their *tamales*[3]
sus carnes, barbacoa sepultada.	their meats, their underground barbeques.
Ya no están los abuelos que lo hacían,	The grandparents that cultivated the traditions are not here anymore,
nuestros padres perdieron por completo	our fathers have completely lost

las costumbres tan bonitas que tenían,	the beautiful traditions that they had
ya no hay nada que heredar a nuestros nietos.	there is nothing to bequeath to our grandchildren anymore.
. . . .	. . . .
Te mueres poco a poquito	You die little by little
¡Oh! Costa chica mía	Oh! My Costa Chica
te han robado tus colores	they have robbed your colours
tus fandangos, tus tradiciones;	your *fandangos*, your traditions;
tus chilenas y tus sones.	your *chilenas* and your *sones*.
(Ibid.)	

The poetic persona clearly lacks the optimism seen in Carrillo's poem. While the focus on the physical features of the Costa Chica again illustrates the need for imaginatively taking possession of the homeland, this is here offset by the overwhelming sense of loss heightened through anaphoric repetition. The poem's structure ties the physical deterioration of the land to the loss of traditions. The emphasis on how the beaches and rivers have been polluted by waste water highlights the contamination of the area and points to the neglect of the African-derived people. Yet despite its emphasis on the loss of culture, the poem establishes the region as a space of Afro-Mexican difference.

Another noteworthy way in which the official discourse on nation in Mexico – while enunciating a familiar Caribbean problematic – is challenged by the collection is evidenced by the poem "El negro" (Black Man), by Joaquín Álvarez Añorve (1999, 59–60). This poem, which is written in a type of Afro-Mexican dialect, draws attention to the fact that the reconstruction of Mexican national identity also requires the acknowledgement of the ethno-linguistic identity of Afro-Mexicans. This unique linguistic mode typical of Afro-Mexicans, challenges the official discourse that denies linguistic expressions that do not reflect a particular mode:

Soy negro chiriquí y tengo	I am a black man from Chiriquí and I have
patitas de zanatilla	little black legs
pué nací en una cuadrilla	because I was born in the barracks
muy cerquita del Tamale,	very close to the Tamale
mi cuna jué una canajtilla	my cradle was a basket
con varitas de cauyagüe.	with sticks of *cauyagüe*.[4]

Mi mamá cuando nací	When I was born, my mother
me llevó a San Nicolá,	took me to San Nicolás,
pa' bujcá un padrino allá	to look for a godfather
que me juera a bautizá,	who would baptize me,
pa' que en la fiesta mercara	so that during the celebration
mucho aguardiente y mezcal.	he would buy lots of alcohol and *mezcal*.[5]
De chiquito fui timbón	From when I was small I had a big stomach
choco chimeco y chando	hunchback
siempre andaba sin calzón	I always walked without pants
porque no tenía pa' cuando	because I didn't have money for that
y cuando tenía cotón	and when I had garments
ere rojo y pa'l juandango.	they were red and for the *fandango*.
(Ibid.)	

The Afro-Mexican is presented in a space typified by difference – a linguistic difference – presented from the perspective of an Afro-Mexican poetic voice. This use of dialect constitutes linguistic marronage and an assertion of the fact that Afro-Mexicans have not been totally assimilated into the mainstream culture and that Mexican identity and issues related to the nation require an engagement with this linguistic difference. The first person voice, moreover, gives authenticity to the claims asserted in the verses.

The poem overwhelmingly draws attention to the poverty in which the black child grows up in Mexico. The striking image of his birthplace – a basket for a cradle – his lack of clothes and his impecunity, corroborates the claim usually made about the living conditions of blacks, such as Alva Moore Stevenson's (n.d., 4) assertion that Afro-Mexicans remain largely marginalized and occupy places at the lowest rung of the economic ladder.

The final poem I will consider is a very memorable and arresting one, "Negro y blanco" (Black and White) by Fidencio Escamilla (1999, 70). Through its simplicity, this poem problematizes the issue of race and the discourse on Mexican nation. The poetic voice is that of a seemingly bewildered child. It is evident that he or she has suddenly lost all innocence about race relations as she or he is affected by the racist stereotyping and depreciation of blacks in the country. The overt simplicity conveyed through the child's voice ironically heightens the senselessness of the situation: the child discovers he or she is not allowed to socialize with whites who are supposedly superior:

> Mamita,
> mamita que vengo,
> que triste vengo del campo
> porque dijeron que un negro
> no se revuelve con los blancos.
>
> Que yo parecía un chamuco
> venido desde el infierno,
> que como yo, había muchos,
> que me pusieran los cuernos.
>
> Que a todos los niños blancos
> se los lleva Dios al cielo,
> y que a los negros, el diablo,
> se los lleva a los infiernos.
> (Ibid.)

> Mamita,
> mamita I come to you
> how sad I am as I come from the countryside
> because they said that a black person
> does not mix with whites.
>
> That I looked like a devil
> straight from hell,
> that there were many just like me,
> and they would put horns on me.
>
> That all white children
> are taken by God to heaven
> and that all the black ones, the devil
> takes to the fires of hell.

The child, gullible and impressionable, is ready to accept the demeaning identity created by others. The child's emotional and psychological struggle with this discovery suggests a reality of brainwashing and socialization that fosters the perpetuation of stereotypical caricatures of blacks in the wider society. This leads to self-loathing and a desire to be white:

> Mamita
> quiero ser blanco,
> porque los blancos son buenos,
> que los negros apestamos
> y nos comparan con perros.
>
> Que no tenemos conciencia
> que los negros somos malos,
> mamita de mí ten clemencia
> ¡que quiero ser niño blanco!
> (Ibid.)

> Mamita
> I want to be white,
> because whites are good,
> because we blacks smell
> And they compare us with dogs.
>
> That we do not have a conscience
> that blacks are bad
> Mamita have mercy with me
> I want to be a white child!

Of course the cardstacking fallacy advanced by the discourse of hegemony escapes the innocent child, but the poem's exposure of the flaws and material weaknesses of the discourse that denies the existence of blacks in Mexico should not be missed. The official discourse on nation is challenged since if there is but one race, there would be no racial difference and a child could/would not experience rejection on the basis of race. Self-assertion is achieved through an overtly innocent but covertly subversive strategy which exposes racial inequality and simultaneously questions the claim that there is no racial (or rather: ethnic) diversity. In other words, "Negro y blanco" problematizes and brings into question this proclaimed synthesis of races. Benítez-Rojo (1996, 26) has denounced the synthesizing logic that accrues to the concept of *mestizaje*: "The high regard for the *mestizaje,* the *mestizaje* solution, did not originate in Africa or Indoamerica or with any People of the Sea. It involves a positivistic and logocentric argument, an argument that sees in the biological, economic, and cultural whitening of Caribbean society a series of successive steps toward 'progress'. And as such it refers to conquest, to slavery, neocolonialism, and dependence." While it must be emphasized that Benítez-Rojo was not referring specifically to Mexico, it is also important to highlight his call for a different understanding of *mestizaje* which would allow for the co-existence of differences: "Within the realities of a rereading, *mestizaje* is nothing more than a concentration of differences" (ibid.).

"Salta pa'trás" (Step Back) is a sarcastic and unapologetic poem of self-assertion that was penned by Zárate Arango (2012). It may be seen as a forceful repudiation of self-deprecatory attitudes, such as that exhibited by the naïve child-persona of the poem "Negro y blanco" that was previously discussed. This persona employs the term *salta pa'trás* (step/jump back) that is reminiscent of a well-known maxim in the Caribbean: "If you are brown, step around / If you are black, step back." Both expressions speak firmly to the ways in which blacks are regarded in many multiracial societies as belonging to the back of the line or the bottom of the social ladder. This adult poetic voice, however, turns the specious assertions and the concept of black inferiority upside down by rejecting all stereotypical representations of blacks.

Moreover, the poetic voice articulates pride in the beauty and regality of his black skin to even insinuate that others are envious of this skin colour. A high level of understanding of the ethno-racial dynamics of his country is made evident through a series of rejections of attempts to denigrate him on the basis of racial phenotype and through his firm declaration of his unequivocal acceptance of his identity as a black person. He undermines the scorn and ridicule often directed towards blacks, including insinuations of a correlation between blackness and a lower level of intelligence, and rejects the general tendency to place a higher premium on people of white descendancy. The message of self-worth is undergirded by the celebratory and grandiloquent tone, without being tendentious:

Salta pa'tras

Ayer me gritaron negro	Yesterday they shouted at me "Blackey"
con un tono despectivo	in a disrespectful tone
pero bajo esta piel tengo	But below this skin
un corazón que es tan lindo.	I have a beautiful heart
Que ya quisieran tenerlo	They wouldn't mind having it,
los blancos y anglosajones	the whites and Anglo-Saxons
no me apena el color negro	I am not ashamed of my black colour
me enorgullecen sus dones.	Its gifts fill me with pride
Porque me acepto cual soy	Because I accept who I am
me siento tan orgulloso	I feel so very proud
bajo los rayos del sol	Below the rays of the sun
mi cuerpo es maravilloso.	my body is glorious.
¿Con gritos . . . ? No me denigran	With their shouts . . . Do they belittle me?
ni con palabras hirientes	Not even with offensive words
yo sé, que el ser más blanquitos	I know that being whiter
no los hace inteligentes.	doesn't make them smarter.
Andamos de boca en boca	We are the talk of the town
por tener la piel oscura	For having dark skin
ignoran que nuestra ropa	They don't know that our clothes
quita a mi piel su hermosura.	hide the beauty of my skin.
¿Qué ayer me gritaron negro?	That yesterday they shouted "Blackey!"
no ha sido casualidad	Wasn't by chance
así como soy me acepto	Just as I am, I accept myself
yo sí tengo identidad.	I have an identity.
Alguno que otro blanquito	Some white man or the other
a mí se me quiere igualar	Wants to be like me
lo blanco no quita lo indito	The whiteness doesn't take away the Indianness
tampoco el salta pa'tras.	Neither does jump back/step back.

An unmistakable position of self-authoring and self-definition is declared in the poem "Yo soy mexicano" (I Am Mexican), also by Zárate Arango (2012). It becomes a statement of self-definition that is inserted into the broader conversation about identity and nation. Both title and content convey a sense of belonging and nationhood which are not just rooted in Mexico, but extend beyond its borders to the wider American/Latin American region. The poetic voice is bolstered by individual pride and confidence which allow him to advance a claim that has no room for challenges or rebuttals:

¡Yo soy mexicano!	I am Mexican!
Dueño de este continente	Owner of this continent
quizá soy navajo	Maybe I am Navajo
pies negros o cheroqui	Blackfoot or Cherokee
no soy desplazado	I will not be moved
¡Soy americano!	I am American!

These two preceding poems seem to make a final summation of the position that is being advanced as one that is beneficial to Afro-Mexicans who need to assert self and proclaim an identity that defies all the ways in which they have been homogenized and derogated. Together they present a self-portraiture that debunks all portraits of them presented by others. These self-representations, moreover, seem to loom larger than the broad Mexican narrative about blacks in Mexico and leaves no room for ambiguity about the identity of this specific black Mexican.

Several features of these Afro-Mexican poems situate them within a broad postcolonial Caribbean context as well as help to reconfigure our understanding of the Mexican nation. The oral and written poems are simultaneously different and similar. They present the Afro-Mexican community at two different points in its existence – the one an oral folk context, the other a literate or more formal one – but both constructions of identity emphasize their Caribbean-ness because they corroborate the fact that Mexican identity and Caribbean cultural identity in general are neither static nor can they be reduced to any one aspect or fixed experience, context or category. It is evident that Vasconcelos's (1925) concept of *mestizaje* constructs a false national identity through its claims of homogeneity.

The oral tradition of the *coplas*, their carnival poetics, and the preoccupation with claiming the region and redefining self and its ethnic identity all highlight the ways in which Afro-Mexican poetry embodies Caribbeanness. These poems – both oral and written – serve as sites of stability and empowerment as they reveal that Afro-Mexicans seem to establish their geographical/cultural identity and difference. Indeed, the poems are located in a context which is undeniably Mexican, especially in their reference to Mexican place names, Ometepec and Costa Chica, and in the explicit reference to the Afro-Mexican hero Yanga in "Caminos". The explicit assertions of blackness in "El negro" and the use of the Afro-Mexican dialect are also deliberate attempts to place distinctive Afro-Mexican features in the poems. This way the poems forcefully project a regional construction of identity which challenges and extends national ones.

Finally, Caribbeanness as cultural identity involves diversity, such as that brought to Mexican identity by the Afro-Mexican oral and lyric poems. Without question Mexican governments need to modify the official discourse on nation and acknowledge the ways in which Mexican culture is enriched by the black contribution. Moreover, there is an imperative to move beyond the limited construction of the Mexican nation to establish a characterization that includes a section whose literary and cultural contribution is unique because it may simultaneously be placed fully within Caribbean literary and cultural aesthetics, while being uniquely Costa Chican or Mexican, produced in Mexico by Mexicans. This is particularly important at a time when globalization is geared towards homogenizing cultures; it is important for all nations to recognize those elements that contribute to their uniqueness and distinctiveness on local, national and global levels – that is, both within and beyond the nation.

Conclusion

"The great sweep of world history that we call the African diaspora contains many important components. Foremost are the contributions to art and technology, religion and literature, music, science and material civilization in the Western world."
—Michael Conniff and Thomas Davis, *Africans in the Americas*

At the heart of this research was an agenda to promote the globalization of the local and localization of the global. Indeed, the literary and cultural production of a small group of persons whose presence in Mexico continues to be controverted for the most part, in that country and elsewhere, has provided a superb opportunity for this agenda to be fulfilled. The folktales, *décimas*, *coplas*, *corridos* and lyric poems need to be promoted among the global public and certainly, the research and critical analyses will further this goal. The analyses broadcast a wide range of distinctions of Afro-Mexican society, including their general cultural legacy, traditions, values and various ways of expressing ethnic and cultural identity and subjectivities.

This representation of a small body of cultural and literary material has been probed through the lenses of cultural studies, gender studies, feminism and other globally established academic theories to make evident the ways in which this production that is known on a very small local scale can be disseminated in order to be given global acknowledgement. The main theoretical frame, established by postcolonial criticism and broad postmodernist approaches which have global relevance, has uncovered the role of Afro-Mexican oral tradition in establishing cross-cultural connections and identities that are grounded in cultural and geographical specificities. All of this moreover, aids the agenda of locating Afro-Mexican cultural production within a broad Caribbean aesthetic; in consequence, contributing to the expansion of the Caribbean as a broader cultural and historical space which includes Central and Latin America. This extending of the concept of Caribbean simultaneously points to the centrality of Afro-Mexican cultural production in global affairs.

These globally relevant critical approaches also accentuate the extent to which cultural production unfolds as significant repositories of memory, which have evolved in consonance with a particular belief system and the convergence of history and place. All this becomes strikingly reminiscent of Wilson Harris's (1999, 239) assertion that "popular culture is shaped by history as the outcome of the slaves' and subsequent immigrants' suffering and struggles for survival". It forcefully recalls too, Harris's further claim, made in reference to the limbo, but applicable to other cultural items, that at the core of "culture as a whole – lies the displacement of peoples. The cultural perspective offered by the dance necessitates the interrogation of narration of the past and the nation" (ibid.). Indeed, the study allows for a deeper understanding of diasporic peoples, their cultural heritage, literary expression and their role in establishing themselves within the nation and beyond, as argued by Kerstin Oloff (2009, 240), who shares Harris's view, that art that is fundamentally "displaced", is by necessity relational (that is, anti-essentialist and aware of its situatedness in the global order) but anchored in local culture.

Among the many revelations uncovered by these analyses is the unmistakable response of the Afro-Mexicans to issues of race/ethnicity and even to racism itself. Indeed, the works serve as testimony to the inherent understanding of self, identity and place that are not readily considered or anticipated by those of us who are outsiders to Afro-Mexican spaces. We witness the unmistakable rejection, through verses and stories that suggest a distinctive cultural and ethnic group, of the generally held view that Afro-Mexicans lack a consciousness of self and of themselves as African descendants. This position is firmly stated by González (2010, 2): "While Africans and their descendants have lived in Mexico for centuries, many Afro-Mexicans do not consider themselves to be either black or African. Instead, members of this ethnic population blend into the national imagination of Mexico, as a mixed-race country." However, the folk narratives, the lyric poems, the performance of *corridos* and the powerful use of a language of subversion, speak otherwise. This is a fact that González (2010, 2) herself concedes and so, despite her generalizations, she forcefully declares that "African descendants in the Americas generally maintain a discrete body of performance practices that attest to their presence". Indeed, the identities established of some cultural forms such as *corridos* are encased in the posturing, in the language usage, in the images and pictures painted and the general performance and even bold declarations of community, self-definition, self-certainty and connections to a particular history and community – a political and ideological consciousness. This acknowledgement of self-awareness is reinforced by Father Glyn, who expressly states:

> Two qualities have deeply impressed me. Firstly, their apparent and often commented indifference to "race" and to the "racism directed against them" hides a deeper sense of hurt and injustice they all carry below their skin. Furthermore, once given the opportunity they are prepared to address that situation. In the second place, there is a sense of family, of belonging to a larger community that is constantly referred to and celebrated. The term *pariente* is quite common as a form of greeting. (Personal interview, July 2013)

It is undeniably clear that, as the literary and cultural production of the small towns of the Costa Chica imply, Afro-Mexicans are a people held together by several bonds that unite them as a cohesive group. Perhaps it is these bonds that allow them to produce lyric poems and re-narrate folktales, *coplas* and *corridos* that serve as evidence of a distinctive black/diasporic presence. All the forms of production reveal a cohesive group with kinship, *compadrazco*, belonging to a region, a particular landscape and a particular relationship with this land. This research has also undoubtedly established that there is a community of Afro-Mexicans united by their understanding of themselves, their commitment to their land and region and a strong sense of kinship. They are not just a random sprinkling of people without anchor, but are also engaged in creating self-referential identities and affirming black consciousness. Ironically, *Memín Pinguín*, Mexico's favourite comic character, who, though not produced by Afro-Mexicans, undermines Mexico's claims of homogeneity. Memín is the caricature of an African-derived person who is often disparaged along lines which intimate racial and ethnic biases, despite the claims of his innocent comic appeal. He reveals, more importantly, the difficulty in claiming or pretending to have a Mexico without blacks. Memín, therefore, becomes a significant index of Mexico's need for cultural decolonization and rejection of the legacy of colonial ideas regarding race.

The critical scrutiny of gender issues and of the portrayal of black male-female relationships puts forward the view that Afro-Hispanic society is inherently sexist, given the various performances of male dominance and the ambivalent manner in which both masculine and feminine identities are negotiated. This intimates that at some level there is a need to understand how inequality affects all genders so that marginalized Afro-Mexican women should also be projected as asserting agency and subjectivity. But the failure to address this in popular cultural forms implies that the negotiations of Afro-Mexican identities in general are complex. At the same time, the performance of some types of hegemonic gender positions seems necessary, in particular in the *corridos* in which males employ violent language, violence and even wit to "restore the ego" by ridiculing and belittling the dominant other, who is always regarded as an ominous threat. Perhaps the most striking observations reside in the discovery or disclosure of the extent to which the discourse on nation, gender and race intersect, making evident the degree to which issues that affect Afro-Mexicans in general are influenced by hegemonic power positions.

The research has provided the opportunity to disturb Mexico's concept of *mestizaje*, to reveal cultural diversity and to puncture the Mexican hegemonic concept of a monolithic society. Indeed, the world view, the sense of self and history which emerge in these literary and cultural productions, implies the shift in Afro-Mexican identities, self-definition and the movement towards rejecting the perception of themselves as *gente corriente*. Father Glyn attests to the transformation he noted thirty years after being told that "un negro no puede ser sacerdote, somos gente corriente, somos para el machetero" (a black man cannot be a priest, we are ordinary people, we are for machete work) (personal interview, July 2013). They now affirm, similar to the works they have preserved throughout the years and the new poems they now create –"Somos negros" (We are blacks). Indeed, their understanding of their blackness may not be connected to any wider organized project related to blackness or consciousness-raising, but rather to an inherent consciousness which is obviously growing. Father Glyn commented on this clear indication of how Afro-Mexicans' perception of their identity is shifting as he reflects on his time living and working among them: "The best part of it for me was seeing people who had been indifferent before, not openly rejecting their blackness or trying to escape it; slowly taking a hold of themselves and using the words 'Somos negros' (We are blacks) with some sort of ownership" (ibid.). The work of Father Glyn in helping to raise awareness of self among the people of Costa Chica cannot be ignored. However, there is still much to be done to get many persons to embrace this understanding of self. This has become evident from the work of a small group of persons who, following the teachings and consciousness-raising achieved through workshops previously conducted by Father Glyn, now understands their identity as people of African heritage. This group, which has denominated itself *México Negro*, held its fifteenth symposium in November 2014. Established in 1997, its members openly and repeatedly acknowledge the work of Father Glyn in sowing the seeds of their knowledge of Afro-Mexican heritage and helping them to understand themselves as a distinctive ethnic group in Mexico. Their main objective is to obtain constitutional recognition from the federal government of Mexico and a commitment to the development of their region with good roads, a good education system and social amenities. Indeed, more than twenty years after early researchers working in the region wrote of the abject poverty and appalling conditions of neglect and squalor in which the people lived, many of these conditions persist in the twenty-first century in a country with reasonable resources.

México Negro is also concerned about the preservation of their traditional Afro-derived cultural forms and the elimination of all types of discrimination against black Mexicans in all areas of Mexico. The group organizes annual conferences aimed specifically at educating Afro-Mexicans about their racial heritage and history, their civic rights and the importance of redefining themselves as persons who are integral to Mexican society. Perhaps their biggest challenge to the Mexican government is for the inclusion of Afro-Mexicans in the national census so that there will be an official record of the number of black persons in the country.

Current president of the organization Sergio Peñaloza has expressed his vision of a Mexico in which the social and governmental invisibility of blacks does not exist. He also explains the difficulty involved in getting many Afro-Mexicans to define themselves as blacks since thay have been taught for centuries that they are *mestizos* and have, furthermore, been taught racist stereotypes about blacks that have evoked feelings of ignominy and humiliation among them (personal interview, November 2014). *México Negro* is committed to continuing the struggles of a Trinidadian priest who went to work for and with them in the 1980s and helped them to understand themselves as black people with connections to a broader history and cultural heritage.

The globalizing of matters related to Afro-Mexico will and should also be the result of actions within Mexico itself and not just the result of academic projects, or the work of well-meaning outsiders. It is important to note that, only as recently as June 2013, the Oaxacan legislature indicated a willingness to recognize the presence of the Afro-Mexican people in the state:

> The Oaxacan state legislature modified the constitution to give political, social, cultural, and economic rights to its Afro-descendant population. Similar debates are taking place in the neighbouring state of Guerrero, as well as at the federal level. Underlying this, there is an ongoing movement towards greater awareness of the ingrained racism within Mexican society as this affects Afro-Mexicans. There are, however, no clear signs that this movement is finding strong support among *mestizo* and indigenous groups. This may be a reflection of the inability of the Afro-Mexican sector to carry their fight into other sections of society. It may also reflect the marginal status given by society (outside the academic sector) to problems affecting the black minority in Mexico. Within the population, at least on the Pacific Coast, there is growing acceptance of the validity of the struggle. The huge task ahead is the mobilization of Afro-Mexicans towards consolidating their movement, and towards fighting for the implementation of the promises offered by the recent political changes. "When the state legislature, a few weeks ago, made the declaration, in one day, I got five or six emails from people celebrating and they were pointedly saying – "Padre valía la pena" (Father it was worth it). (Personal interview with Father Glyn Jemmott Nelson, 19 July 2013)

In 2014, the legislature of Guerrero followed the example of Oaxaca and made an official declaration that blacks were constitutionally recognized as an ethnic group in the state. This shift in the attitude of officials in Oaxaca and Guerrero is a significant achievement, particularly for those persons who have worked to correct the misconceptions about Mexican identity and presence.

This development at the local level notwithstanding, the need to end the invisibility of Afro-Mexicans is not any less urgent. An Associated Press release dated 16 August 2013 exposed the chronic ignorance about Mexico's ethnic/racial composition that still exists, even among some who are concerned about racial and social equality. The release critiqued the discriminatory language of the advertisement that was placed by an Aeroméxico recruiting agency, which specified it wanted "nobody dark-skinned" (Gomez Licon 2013).

Ironically, Adriana Gomez Licon (2013), who condemns the inappropriate language, simultaneously reveals her own embracing of *mestizaje* and the exclusion of the "real dark-skinned" people in Mexico. The faulty and sweeping generalization is made that Mexico's population is "largely dark-skinned". Of course, Mexico's population comprises a range of complexions and the "dark-skinned" are by no means in the majority. The writer further claims that "Indians have suffered persistent racial discrimination since the Spanish conquest" – citing a survey in which "ninety-three percent . . . said they believed discrimination against Indians exists" (Gomez Licon 2013). It is lamentable that no mention is made of blacks or Afro-Mexicans and their condition of marginalization, poverty and invisibility in Mexico. The article reinforces their total exclusion from the conversations about Mexican racial heritage and continues to advance the view that only Indians are victims of discrimination in Mexico – this in the year 2013.

Indeed, there is much more work to be done to collect, preserve and publicize Afro-Mexican literary and cultural production and rescue them from obscurity. The Consejo Nacional para la Cultura y las Artes, Instituto Guerrerense de la Cultura and the Dirección General de Culturas Populares have all done a commendable task of collecting and recording many of the oral narratives and lyric poems that were studied for this project. However, much more needs to be done in Mexico to ensure that they will not be lost from public memory. This book has by no means exhausted all aspects of the literary material produced by Afro-Mexicans, and so there is a need for ongoing study.

The undeniable changes to be realized in this community will continue at both the local and global levels. The attempts at self-authoring and the establishment of positional identities will remain abiding testimonies of Afro-Mexicans' attempts to promote self both within and outside of Mexico and to set the records straight about their undeniable contributions to the Mexican nation and the multiculturalism of Mexican heritage.

Figure 13. Afro-Mexican girl (Courtesy of María Elisa Velázquez, president of Comité Científico Ruta del Esclavo UNESCO)

Figure 14. Woman from El Ciruelo (P.A. Ramsay)

Figure 15. Policeman in the town of Santo Domingo (P.A. Ramsay)

Figure 16. Resident of El Ciruelo (P.A. Ramsay)

Figure 17. Young girl from El Ciruelo (P.A. Ramsay)

Figure 18. Young girl from Santo Domingo (P.A. Ramsay)

Figures 19–20. Women in El Ciruelo (P.A. Ramsay)

Figure 21. Afro-Mexican woman in Punta Maldonado selling typical Costa Chican *champurrado* (made from corn and chocolate/cacao) (P.A. Ramsay)

Figure 22. Policeman in Santo Domingo (P.A. Ramsay)

Figure 23. Afro-Mexican boy in El Ciruelo (courtesy of Father Glyn Jemmott Nelson)

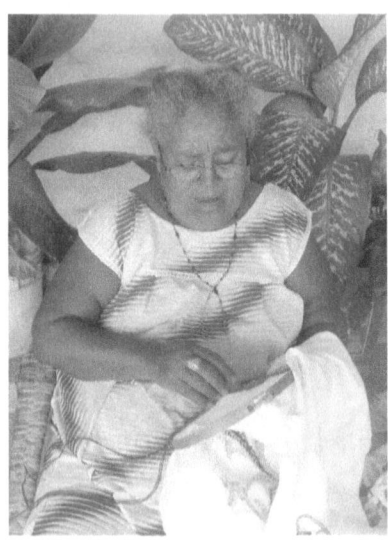

Figure 24. Afro-Mexican woman teaching traditional craft (Courtesy of Father Glyn Jemmott Nelson)

Figure 25. People at workshop in Lagunillas (Courtesy of Father Glyn Jemmott Nelson)

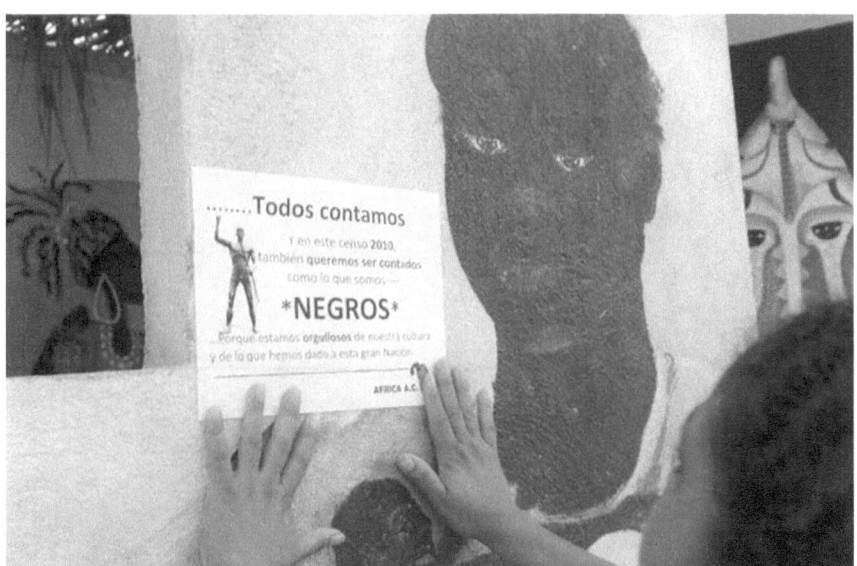

Figure 26. Petition made by *México Negro* for black Mexicans to be counted in the 2010 census as a distinct ethnic group

Figure 27. Entrance to the town of El Ciruelo (P.A. Ramsay)

Figure 28. Entrance to the town of Santo Domingo Armenta (P.A. Ramsay)

Figures 29–32. Scenes from Cuajinicuilapa in the state of Guerrero (P.A. Ramsay)

Figure 33. Current president of *México Negro*, Sergio Peñalosa

Figure 34. Father Glyn Jemmott Nelson with Paulette Ramsay

Figures 35–36. Traditional houses in Tapextla (P.A. Ramsay)

Figure 37. Vendor in Cuajinicuilapa (P.A. Ramsay)

Figure 38. Banner on display in the XI *Encuentro de pueblos* (P.A. Ramsay)

Figure 39. Woman in the street in Lagunillas (Courtesy of Father Glyn Jemmott Nelson)

Figure 40. Women in workshop (P.A. Ramsay)

Figure 41. Small library with information on the black heritage of Afro-Mexicans located in the town of El Ciruelo (P.A. Ramsay)

Notes

Note about Translations

While I have done most of the translations, I must thank Karen Henry and Peter Bailey for their help with some translations, and Kerstin Oliff and Michael Nibbel for their translation of a few verses in chapter 4 as indicated.

Introduction

1. *Ladinos* were Spanish-speaking Africans who lived in the Iberian Peninsula; in the sixteenth century there were more than fifty thousand *ladinos* in Spain.
2. The *encomienda* was a system of tributary labour developed as a means of securing a cheap labour supply. It was first used over the conquered Moors and then taken to Latin America. The *ecomienda* system began on Columbus's third voyage to Hispaniola. See *The Ecomienda in New Spain* (Simpson 1966) revised and enlarged edition.
3. Older Africans who were Latinized in the Spanish culture and Castilian language (as the Moors in Spain) were also called *ladinos*.
4. The more pejorative term, *bozales* was given to new Africans because they were perceived as "semi-salvaje" (half-savage).
5. The Treaty of Tordesillas (1494) was an agreement between Spain and Portugal in which the lands explored by Columbus were divided between Spain and Portugal. The lands to the east were given to Spain and those to the west were given to Portugal.
6. Congo Kings collaborated with São Tomen slavers to supply European traders but because they were unable to meet the demands they developed alliances with some tribal rulers.

7. For more, see Love (1967, 93), "Negro Resistance to Spanish Rule in Colonial Mexico". Yanga is another black hero as well as a notable figure in the history of Mexico. Famously known for his distinctiveness as a Negro during slavery in Mexico, Yanga made history by setting precedence: he established the first free town of the Americas or, as some say, the first free territory on American soil. Yanga was an African of noble and royal lineage: "pertenecía al tribu de los Yang-bara, del Alto Nilo . . . de sangre real" (Herrera Casasús 1991, 87), cultured in the Mohammedan tradition.
8. *Indigenismo* in Latin America is a political ideology that privileges the Indian populations – it sets them apart from non-indigenous groups in a manner that favours them. In Mexico the policies/ideologies emphasize the importance of Mexico's native heritage even though these policies were implanted to improve the condition of the Indian populations. See the *Oxford Encyclopedia of Mesoamerican Cultures* (Carrasco 2001) for more.

Chapter 1

1. Juan Angel Serrano (2005). A black Mexican cattle farmer as quoted by Clarence Page in the article "The *Memín Pinguín* Controversy": "[Other Mexicans] just don't see us. People ask us where we are from. They say we can't be from México." See also Guillermo Bonfil Batalla's *México profundo: una civilization negada* (1987).
2. Term borrowed from Norman Whitten Jr (1981, 45–94), "El Mestizaje: An All Inclusive Ideology of Exclusions".
3. For more on this response to the series see the article by Marco Katz (2007) "Tiras, timbres y estereotipos: El negro Memín Pinguín y la manipulación de la cultura popular con representaciones étnicas".
4. During the late colonial period, people of indigenous or African descent in Mexico were allowed to buy the title of *blanco*. Such was the case for José María Morelos y Parón, who was a general in the War of Independence and played a major role in winning Mexico's independence from Spain. For more on this issue, see Muhammad (1995).
5. Vicente Guerrero, also known as the "poor people's champion", as well as, "El Negro Guerrero", was the second president of Mexico and the first of African descent. He fought along with Morelos and other well-known blacks who were fighting not for only liberation from Spain but also for the end of slavery and ethnic segregation (Muhammad 1995, 168).

Chapter 2

1. For more on the ideological framing of the folktales, see Díaz Pérez (1993). See also Yuval-Davis (1997, 70–79) for her firm theorizing of the intersections between gender and nation.
2. Baugh is here drawing on Simone de Beauvoir's (2010, 6) elaboration in *The Second Sex* of the Sartrian thesis of man's insistence on establishing himself as self and woman as other.

Chapter 3

1. Fanon (1970, 7–8) is regarded as having advanced the thesis of how black men have been emasculated by the process of colonialism.
2. See Connell's (1995, 70–71) well-debated arguments in which he systematically questions each category for its weaknesses and inconsistencies. All four categories are as follows:
    1. essentialist, which draws on Freud's theories of the contrast between masculinity and femininity, focused on certain traits which were attributed to men (aggressive, risk taking);
    2. positivist definitions which are based on "what men really are" (p. 69);
    3. normative definitions based on the argument that there is a "norm" or standard of what men should be; and
    4. semantic approaches, which define masculinity "through a system of symbolic differences in which masculine and feminine places are contrasted" (p. 70).
3. My translation of Octavio Paz's (1994) statement on Mexicaness.
4. See also Herrera-Sobek (1990) who examines the archetype of the female soldier and women in the Mexican Revolution. The discussions are based on how concepts of the *soldadera*, which was not really conceptualized as women in actual battles, existed in the religious structures and the minds of in the Aztec nation.
5. Tomás Marín

    | Les voy a cantar un corrido | I will sing you a *corrido* – |
    | señores, perdonaran, | gentlemen, forgive me; |
    | este corrido es compuesto | this *corrido* is composed |
    | del pueblo de San Nicolás. | from the town of San Nicolás. |
    | | |
    | El pueblo de San Nicolás | The town of San Nicolás |
    | ya se esta poniendo el plan, | is already making a plan; |
    | allí pagaban dos mil pesos | there they paid two thousand pesos |
    | que agarraran a Tomás. | so they would capture Tomás. |

Ese caso estuvo serio por la fiesta de un rosario, el andaba muy confiado porque andaba en los rezados.	That case was a serious one at a rosary celebration, he went around without worry, as he was among those praying.
Así es que ya estaba preso luego mandaron a ver, que ya Tomás estaba preso que lo fueran a traer.	And so he was already captured; they told them to come and see that Tomás was already captured; they should come and take him away.
Allí los ricos de Tapextla ya les prestaban dinero, que lo lleven a Tomás para el estado de Guerrero.	There the rich people of Tapextla now they were lending them money, so they would bring Tomás into the state of Guerrero.
De Tapextla lo sacaron pa'l pueblo de San Nicolás, porque llegando a la raya allí lo iban a matar.	They took him from Tapextla to the town of San Nicolás, because, arriving at the border there they were going to kill him.
Cuando le estaban tirando el sargento se sonrió, ya todos ya le tiraron cuantas penas se recibió.	When they were firing at him the sergeant was all smiles; then they all shot at him; so many wounds he received.
El se sacó la pistola y un tiro le disparó, le tiró a la mera frente comoquiera no le dio.	He took out his pistol and fired one shot at him he fired right at his forehead; even so, he didn't get him.
Allí dieron la media vuelta, todititos la risada: "Ahora si, Tomás Marín, ya te cargó la fregada."	There they spun around, all of them laughing loudly: "Now for sure, Tomás Marín, now your goose is cooked."
Asi que ya se habian ido Tomasito hasta se rio: "Mama, no se ha de espantar todavía estoy vivo yo."	Then when they had all left Tomás even let out a laugh: "Mother, you need not worry for I am still alive."
Ese Pipino Noyola llego hasta San Nicolás:	That Pipino Noyola arrived at San Nicolás:

"Ahora que Tomás murió ¿que si hacemos un fandango?"	"Now that Tomás is dead let's have ourselves a party."
Dijo Alfredo Fuentes pero con una apureza: "Si Tomás ya se murió dispararemos cerveza."	Alfredo Fuentes said, but in a tremendous hurry: "If Tomás is dead let's go toss down some beers."
ando le llega una carta que Tomás no estaba muerto, que Tomás no estaba muerto, lo que estaba solo herido.	When he receives a letter it seems Tomás was not dead, it seems Tomás was not dead, that he was only wounded.
Allí dijo Alfredo Fuentes: "Que se termine este baile, si Tomás no se murió que si lo barre con el."	There Alfredo Fuentes said: "Let this dance be done; if Tomás did not die maybe we should finish him off."
Allí dice Tomás Marín: "Traigo la sangre caliente, la muerte de mi papa me la paga Alfredo Fuentes."	There says Tomás Marín: "My blood is boiling over; the death of my father will be paid by Alfredo Fuentes."
Ya me voy a despedir – señores, perdonaran, aquí termina el corrido de Alfredo Fuentes y Tomás.	Now I will take my leave – gentlemen, forgive me; here ends the corrido of Alfredo Fuentes and Tomás.

6. The cult of the Virgin de Guadalupe had its beginnings in a general climate of religious distrust and religious heterogeneity and syncretism. The early period of colonization, with its diverse ethnic populations, inevitably produced an explosive clash of religious beliefs. The intense missionary zeal of the Spaniard to Christianize the Indian and other *no creyentes* (nonbelievers) forced an underground movement of beliefs that fermented into a sputtering of fanatic prophets, visionaries and other cult-oriented religious leaders who sought to liberate the masses from Spanish and creole political hegemony. No doubt both the political and religious instability of the times helped nurture the Virgen de Guadalupe (Herrera 37).

Chapter 4

1. For more reading see Muhammad (1995). See also Díaz Pérez (1992).
2. For more of my discussion of the *corrido* and Afro-Mexican folktales, see Ramsay (2003, 2001).
3. Hidalgo was an Afro-Mexican priest who, following the revolt of blacks in Veracruz, initiated the attempts to challenge the cause for social, economic and political equality in Mexico for Afro-Mexicans. He denounced the caste laws and called for the abolition of slavery. He was killed in 1813, but his death was met with apathy by the ruling class (Vincent 1994, 259). See also Carroll (2001, 152–53).

Chapter 5

1. "*Chingar* . . . is to do violence to another. The verb is masculine, active, cruel: it stings, wounds, gashes, stains. And it provokes bitter, resentful satisfaction. The person who suffers the action is passive, inert and open, in contrast to the active, aggressive and closed person who inflicts it. The *chingón* is the *macho*, the male; he rips open the *chingada*, the female, who is pure passivity, defenseless against the exterior world" (Paz 1994).
2. *Cuajinicuilapa* is a municipality on the Costa Chica in the Mexican state of Guerrero. The largest concentration of Afro-Mexicans is to be found in the remote villages in this area.
3. *Enramadas* is outdoor space for social activities; moles and tamales are typical Mexican foods.
4. *Cauyagüe* is a type of wood indigenous to Mexico.
5. *Mezcal* is a distilled alcoholic beverage (tequila) made from the maguey plant native to Mexico.

References

Aguirre Beltrán, Gonzalo. 1946. *La población negra de México 1519–1810.* México: Ediciones Fuente Cultural.

———. 1972. *La población negra de México: Estudio etnohistórico.* México: Fundo de Cultura Económica.

Álvarez Añorve, Joaquín. 1999. "El negro". In *Alma cimarrona: versos costeños y poesía regional,* edited by Angustia Torres Díaz and Israel Reyes Larrea, 59–60. Oaxaca, Mexico: Dirección General de Culturas Populares.

Andrade Aguirre, David. 1999. Introduction. In *Palenque: Décimas,* by Luz Argentina Chiriboga. Quito, Ecuador: Editorial Instituto Andino de Artes Populares.

Andrews, George. 2004. *Afro-Latin America, 1800–2000.* Oxford: Oxford University Press.

Apodaca, Manuel. 2008. "The Dance of the Devils of the Costa Chica: Afro-Mexican Performance of Identity and Resistance". *Publication of the Afro-Latin/American Research Association (PALARA)* 12 (Fall): 51–70.

Aramoni, Aniceto. 1965. *Psicoanálisis de la dinámica de un pueblo.* Mexico City: Universidad Nacional Autónoma de México.

Archibold, Randall. 2014. "Negro? Prieto? Moreno? A Question of Identity for Black Mexicans". *New York Times,* 26 October. http://www.nytimes.com/2014/10/26/world/americas/negro-prieto-moreno-a-question-of-identity-for-black-mexicans.html.

Ashcroft, Bill, Garth Griffiths, and Helen Tiffin. 2005. "Feminism". In *The Post-Colonial Studies Reader,* edited by Bill Ashcroft, Garth Griffiths and Helen Tiffin, 233–34. London: Routledge.

Bakhtin, Mikhail. 1981. *The Dialogic Imagination: Four Essays.* Translated by Michael Holquist; edited by Carl Emerson. Austin: University of Texas Press.

Barthes, Roland. 1964. *Elements of Semiology.* Translated by Annette Lavers and Colin Smith, 1968. New York: Hill and Wang.

Bartolomé, Miguel Alberto. 1997. *Gente de costumbre y gente de razón: las identidades étnicas de México.* Mexico City: Siglo Veintiuno.

Baugh, Edward. 1991. "Lorna Goodison in the Context of Feminist Criticism". *Journal of West Indian Literature* 4 (1): 1–13.
Beckles, Hilary. 2004. "Black Masculinity in Caribbean Slavery". In *Interrogating Caribbean Masculinities: Theoretical and Empirical Analysis*, edited by Rhoda Reddock, 225–43. Kingston: University of the West Indies Press.
———. 1999. *Centering Women: Gender Discourses in Caribbean Slave Society*. Kingston: Ian Randle.
Benítez-Rojo, Antonio. 1996. *The Repeating Island: The Caribbean and the Postmodern Perspective*. Translated by James Maraniss. 2nd ed. Durham, NC: Duke University Press.
Bennett, Herman L. 2005. *Africans in Colonial Mexico*. Bloomington: Indiana University Press.
Bhabha, Homi. 2012. *The Location of Culture*. London: Routledge.
———. 1994. *The Process of Creating Culture from the Interstitial, Hybrid Perspective*. http://rowenasworld.org/essays/newphil/bhabha.htm.
"Blanca Flor". 1993. In *Jamás fandango al cielo: narrativa afromestiza*, by María Cristina Díaz Pérez, Francisca Aparicio Prudente and Adela García Casarrubias, 75–85. San Angel, Mexico: Dirección General de Culturas Populares.
Bonfil Batalla, Guillermo. 1987. *México profundo: una civilization negada*. Mexico City: Random House Mondadori.
Brand, Dionne. 1998. *No Language Is Neutral*. Toronto: McClelland and Stewart.
Carrasco, David, ed. 2001. *Oxford Encyclopedia of Mesoamerican Cultures: The Civilizations of Mexico and Central America*. New York: Oxford University Press.
Carrilo, Alvaro. 1999. "Costa chica mía". In *Alma cimarrona: versos costeños y poesía regional*, edited by Angustia Torres Díaz and Israel Reyes Larrea, 56–57. Oaxaca, Mexico: Dirección General de Culturas Populares.
Carroll, Patrick. 2001. *Blacks in Colonial Veracruz: Race, Ethnicity, and Regional Development*. Austin: University of Texas Press.
CERD (Committee for the Elimination of Racial Discrimination). 1965. "International Convention on the Elimination of All Forms of Racial Discrimination". http://www.ohchr.org/EN/ProfessionalInterest/Pages/CERD.aspx.
Chiriboga, Luz Argentina. 2001. *Coplas Esmeraldeñas*. Esmeraldas, Ecuador: L.A. Chiriboga.
Connell, R.W. 1995. *Masculinities*. 2nd ed. Berkeley: University of California Press.
Connif, Michael, and Thomas Davis. 1994. *Africans in the Americas: A History of the Black Diaspora*. New York: St Martin's.
Dash, Michael. 1998. *The Other America: Caribbean Literature in the New World Context*. Charlottesville: University Press of Virginia.
Davidson, David. 1973. "Negro Slave Control and Resistance in Colonial Mexico, 1519–1650". In *Maroon Societies: Rebel Slave Communities in the Americas*, edited by Richard Price, 84–104. New York: Anchor.

De Beauvoir, Simone. 2010. *The Second Sex*. New York: Vintage.
Del Toro, A. 1921. "Influencia de la raza *negra* en la formación del pueblo mejicano". *Eltios*, 8–12.
Díaz Pérez, María Cristina. 1993. Introduction. In *Jamás fandango al cielo: narrativa afromestiza,* edited by María Cristina Díaz Pérez, Francisca Aparicio Prudente and Adela García Casarrubias, 19–26. San Angel, Mexico: Dirección General de Culturas Populares.
———. 1992. Introduction. In *Cállate burrita prieta: poética afromistiza,* edited by Francisca Aparicio Prudente, Adela García Casarrubias and María Cristina Díaz Pérez, ix–xii. Chilpancingo, Mexico: Dirección General de Culturas Populares.
Díaz Pérez, María Cristina, Francisca Aparicio Prudente and Adela García Casarrubias, eds. 1993. *Jamás fandango al cielo: narrativa afromestiza*. San Angel, Mexico: Dirección General de Culturas Populares.
Dietrich, Elise. 2010. "Ziraldo's *A turma do Pererê*: Representation of Race in a Brazilian Children's Comic". *Afro-Hispanic Review* 29: 143–60.
Domínguez, Melquíades. 1990. "Yoatzin". In *Jamás fandango al cielo: narrativa afromestiza,* edited by María Cristina Díaz Pérez, Francisca Aparicio Prudente and Adela García Casarrubias. 1993. San Angel, Mexico: Dirección General de Culturas Populares.
Eckert, Penelope, and Sally McConnell-Ginel. 2007. *Language and Gender.* Cambridge: Cambridge University Press.
Edwards, Tim. 2006. *Cultures of Masculinity.* London: Routledge.
"El Caballito de virtud". 1993. In *Jamás fandango al cielo: narrativa afromestiza*, edited by María Cristina Díaz Pérez, Francisca Aparicio Prudente and Adela García Casarrubiasm, 98–108. San Angel, Mexico: Dirección General de Culturas Populares.
Escamilla, Fidencio. 1999. "Negro y blanco". In *Alma cimarrona: versos costeños y poesía regional*, edited by Angustia Torres Díaz and Israel Reyes Larrea, 70. Oaxaca, Mexico: Dirección General de Culturas Populares.
Fairclough, Norman. 2013. *Language and Power.* London: Routledge.
Fanon, Frantz. 1970. *Black Skin, White Masks.* London: Paladin.
Feracho, Lesley. 2001. "Women's Diasporic Dialogues: Redefining Afro-Caribbean and Afro-Latin American Identity in Rojas' *Elculumpio de Rey Spencer* and Chiriboga's *Jonatás y Manuela". Publication of the Afro-Latin/American Research Association (PALARA)* 5 (Fall): 32–41.
Finnegan, Ruth. 1992. *Oral Traditions and the Verbal Arts: A Guide to Research Practices.* London: Routledge.
Forbes, Curdella. 2005. *From Nation to Diaspora: Samuel Selvon, George Lamming and the Culture Performance of Gender.* Kingston: University of the West Indies Press.
Foucault, Michel. 1980. *History of Sexuality.* Vol. 1: *An Introduction.* New York: Vintage.
Gilroy, Paul. 2001. *Black Identity.* London: Hansib.
Glissant, Édouard. 1989 *Caribbean Discourse.* Charlottesville: University Press of Virginia.

Gomez Licon, Adriana. 2013. "Aeromexico Apologizes for Light-Skinned Casting Call". *USA Today*, 16 August. http://www.usatoday.com/story/todayinthesky/2013/08/16/mexico-airline-apologizes-for-light-skin-casting/2666355/.

González, Anita. 2009. "Imaging the Darker Brother: Critical Performances of Racialized Dance in Mexico". Paper presented at the Latin American Studies Association conference. Rio de Janiero, Brazil, 11–16 June.

———. 2010. *Afro-Mexico: Dancing between Myth and Reality*. Austin: University of Texas Press.

González Navarro, Moisés. 1960. *La colonización en México: 1877–1910*. Mexico: Talleres de impresion de estampillas y valores.

Graber, Davis. 1981. "Political Language". In *Handbook of Political Communication*, edited by Dan Niomo and Keith Saunders. Los Angeles: Sage.

Griffin, Susan. 1997. "Eco-feminism and Meaning". In *Eco-feminism: Women, Culture, Nature*, edited by Karen J. Warren, 213–26. Bloomington: Indiana University Press.

"Groseros". 1999. In *Alma cimarrona: versos costeños y poesía regional*, edited by Angustia Torres Díaz and Israel Reyes Larrea, 45–46. Oaxaca, Mexico: Dirección General de Culturas Populares.

Habana Zárate, Rodrigo. 1990. "Tontosoy". In *Jamás fandango al cielo: narrativa afromestiza*, edited by María Cristina Díaz Pérez, Francisca Aparicio Prudente, and Adela García Casarrubias, 139–43. San Angel, México: Dirección General de Culturas Populares.

Habekost, Christian. 1993. *Verbal Riddim: The Politics and Aesthetics of African-Caribbean Dub Poetry*. Amsterdam: Rodopi.

Harris, Wilson. 1999. *Selected Essays of Wilson Harris: The Unfinished Genesis of the Imagination*, edited by Andrew Bundy. London: Routledge.

Hernández Cuevas, Marco Polo. 2004. "La población negra de México: parte del discurso blanqueador para poner al negro en su lugar". *Afro-Hispanic Review* 23 (1): 3–9.

Herrera Casasús, María Luisa. 1991. *Piezas de Indias: La esclavitud negro en México*. Veracruz, México: Instituto Veracruzano de Cultura.

Herrera-Sobek, María. 1990. *The Mexican Corrido: A Feminist Analysis*. Bloomington: Indiana University Press.

Hill Collins, Paricia. 1999. *Black Feminist Thought: Knowledge, Consciousness and the Politics of Empowerment*. 2nd ed. London: Routledge.

Holland, Dorothy, et al. 2003. *Identity and Agency in Cultural Worlds*. Cambridge, MA: Harvard University Press.

hooks, bell. 2000. *Feminism Is for Everybody: Passionate Politics*. Cambridge, MA: South End.

Hudson-Weems, Clenora. 1993. *Africana Womanism: Reclaiming Ourselves*. Troy, MI: Bedford.

Jant, Fred, and Heather Hurdley. 2007. "Intercultural Dimensions of Communicating Masculinities". *Journal of Men's Studies* 15 (2): 216–31.

Johnson, Sally, and Ulrike Hanna Meinhof, eds. 1997 *Language and Masculinity*. Oxford: Blackwell.

Juárez Hernández, Yolanda. 1990. Introduction. *2o foro Veracruz también es Caribe*. Veracruz, Mexico: Insituto Veracruzano de Cultura.

Katz, Marco. 2007. "Tiras, timbres y estereotipos: el negro *Memín Pinguín* y la manipulación de la cultura popular con representaciones étnicas". *Culturas Populares. Revista Electrónica* 5 (July–December). http://www.culturaspopulares.org/textos5/articulos/katz.htm.

Kimmel, Michael, and M. Messner. 1995. *Men's Lives*. New York: Allyn and Bacon.

Krause, Enrique. 2005. "The Pride in *Memín Pinguín*". *Washington Post*. 12 July, A21.

Lakoff, Robin. 1973. "Language and Woman's Place". *Language and Society* 2: 45–80.

Legler, Gretchen. 1997. "Eco-feminist Literary Criticism" In *Eco-feminism: Women, Culture, Nature,* edited by Karen J. Warren, 227–38. Bloomington: Indiana University Press.

Love, Edgar F. 1967. "Negro Resistance to Spanish Rule in Colonial Mexico". *Journal of Negro History* 52 (2): 89–103.

Martínez Montiel, Luz María. 1992. *Los negros en México*. Mexico City: Madfire.

McClintock, Anne. 1995. *Imperial Leather: Race, Gender and Sexuality in the Colonial Context*. New York: Routledge.

McDowell, John. 2000. *Poetry and Violence: The Ballad Tradition of Mexico's Costa Chica*. Champaign: University of Illinois Press.

Méndez Tello, Donají. 1999. "Pa' mi Nicolasita". In *Alma cimarrona: versos costeños y poesía regional,* edited by Angustia Torres Díaz and Israel Reyes Larrea, 72. Oaxaca, Mexico: Dirección General de Culturas Populares.

Meza Herrera, Malinali. 1992. Foreword to *Cállate burrita prieta: poética afromistiza,* edited by Francisca Aparicio Prudente, vii–viii. Chilpancingo, Mexico: Dirección General de Culturas Populares.

Mirandé, Alfredo. 1997. *Hombres y Machos: Masculinity and Latino Culture*. Boulder: Westview.

Molina Enríquez, Andrés. 1909. *Los grandes problemas nacionales*. México: Impr. de Carranza e Hijos.

Monsivaís, Carlos. 2005. "De las tribulaciones de *Memín Pinguín*". http://hemisphericinstitute.org/hemi/es/e-misferica-52/monsivais.

Moore Stevenson, Alva. N.d. "Blacks in Mexico". http://www.blueroadrunner.com/default.htm.

"Morena". 1993. In *Jamás fandango al cielo: narrativa afromestiza,* edited by María Cristina Díaz Pérez, Francisca Aparicio Prudente and Adela García Casarrubias, 109–19. San Angel, Mexico: Dirección General de Culturas Populares.

Muhammad, Jameelah, ed. 1995. "Mexico and Central America". In *Afro-Latin Americans Today: No Longer Invisible*, 163–80. London: Minority Rights Publications.

Muñoz, Laura. 1990. "La presencia del Caribe en México: Una retropectura historia". In *20 foro Veracruz también es Caribe*, 87–94. Veracruz, Mexico: Insituto Veracruzano de Cultura.

Nanton, Phillip. 1995. "Making Space for Orality on Its Own Terms". In *The Pressures of the Text: Orality, Texts and the Telling of Tales*, edited by Stewart Brown, 83–90. African Studies Series, no. 4. Birmingham, UK: Centre of West African Studies.

Nurse, Keith. 2004. "Masculinities in Transition: Gender and the Global Problematique". In *Interrogating Caribbean Masculinities: Theoretical and Empirical Analysis*, edited by Rhoda Reddock, 3–33. Kingston: University of the West Indies Press.

Oloff, Kerstin D. 2009. "Wilson Harris, Regionalism and Postcolonial Studies". In *Perspectives on the "Other America"*, edited by Michael Niblett and Kerstin Oloff, 233–56. Amsterdam: Rodopi.

Ong, Walter J. 2000. *Orality and Literacy*. London: Routledge, Taylor and Francis.

Palmer, Colin. 1990. "Africa's Legacy in Mexico: A Legacy of Slavery". http://www.smithsonianeducation.org/migrations/legacy/almleg.html.

Patatán Mariche, Luis. 1991. "Juaniquito el oso". In *Jamás fandango al cielo: narrativa afromestiza*, edited by María Cristina Díaz Pérez, Francisca Aparicio Prudente and Adela García Casarrubias, 86–92. San Angel, México: Dirección General de Culturas Populares.

Paz, Octavio. 1994. *The Labyrinth of Solitude: The Other Mexico, Return to the Labyrinth of Solitude, Mexico and the United States, the Philanthropic Ogre*. New York: Grove.

———. 1997. *El laberinto de la soledad*. New York: Penguin.

Pérez Fernández, Rolando Antonio. 1990. *La música afromestiza mexicana*. Veracruz, Mexico: Universidad Veracruzana.

Ramchand, Kenneth. 2004. "Calling All Dragons: The Crumbling of Caribbean Masculinity". In *Interrogating Caribbean Masculinities: Theoretical and Empirical Analyses*, edited by Rhoda Reddock, 309–25. Kingston: University of the West Indies Press.

Ramírez, Rafael. 1993. *Dime Capitán: Reflexiones sobre la Masculinidad*. Rio Pierdras, Puerto Rico: Ediciones Huracán.

Ramsay, Paulette A. 2001. "Establishing an Independent Identity: Afro-Mexican Oral Narratives in the Context of Post-Colonial Criticism". *Langston Hughes Review* 16 (1–2): 8–17.

———. 2003. "History, Violence and Self-Glorification in Afro-Mexican *corridos* from Costa Chica de Guerrero". *Publication of the Afro-Latin/American Research Association (PALARA)* 7 (Fall): 62–78.

———. 2009. "Cross-Cultural Poetics: Debating the Place of Afro-Mexican Poetry in the Context of Caribbean Literary and Cultural Aesthetics". *Perspectives on the Other*

America: Comparative Approaches to Latin American Culture, edited by Michael Niblett and Kerstin Oloff, 197–220. Amsterdam: Rodopi.

Reddock, Rhoda, ed. 2004. *Interrogating Caribbean Masculinities: Theoretical and Empirical Analyses*. Kingston: University of the West Indies Press.

Reyes Larrea, Israel. 1999. "Negrita cimarrona". In *Alma cimarrona: versos costeños y poesía regional*, edited by Angustia Torres Díaz and Israel Reyes Larrea, 69. Oaxaca, Mexico: Dirección General de Culturas Populares.

Robles, Jesús. 1990. "La mojarrita de tres colores". In *Jamás fandango al cielo: narrativa afromestiza*, edited by María Cristina Díaz Pérez, Francisca Aparicio Prudente and Adela García Casarrubias, 204–5. San Angel, Mexico: Dirección General de Culturas Populares.

Rohlehr, Gordon. 2004. "I Lawa: The Construction of Masculinity in Trinidad and Tobago". *Interrogating Caribbean Masculinities: Theoretical and Empirical Analysis*, edited by Rhoda Reddock, 326–403. Kingston: University of the West Indies Press.

Said, Edward. 2005. "Resistance, Opposition and Representation". In *The Post-Colonial Studies Reader,* edited by Bill Ashcroft, Garth Griffiths and Helen Tiffin, 95–98. London: Routledge.

Sanders, Edith R. 1969. "The Hamitic Hypothesis: Its Origin and Functions in Time Perspective". *Journal of African History* 10 (4): 521–32.

Serrano, Juan Angel. 2005. "The Memín Pinguín Controversy – And What We Could Learn from Mexico", by Clarence Page. *History News Network*. 15 July. http://historynewsnetwork.org/article/13198.

Simpson, L.B. 1966. *The Encomienda in New Spain*. Revised and enlarged edition. Berkeley: University of California Press.

Slemon, Stephen. 1988. "Post-Colonial Allegory and the Transformation of History". *Journal of Commonwealth Literature* 23 (1): 157–68.

———. 2005. "Post-Colonial Allegory and the Transformation of History". In *The Post-Colonial Studies Reader*, 2nd ed., edited by Bill Ashcroft, Garth Griffiths and Helen Tiffin, 102–6. London: Routledge.

Stam, Robert, and Louise Spence. 2005. "Colonialism, Racism and Representation". In *The Post-Colonial Studies Reader*. 2nd ed., edited by Bill Ashcroft, Garth Griffiths and Helen Tiffin, 109–12. London: Routledge.

Tang, R. 1999. "The Place of Culture in the Foreign Language Classroom: A Reflection". *Internet TESL Journal* 8. http://iteslj.org/articles/Tang-culture.html.

Tiffin, Helen. 2005. "Post-Colonial Literatures and Counter-Discourse". In *The Post-Colonial Studies Reader*, 2nd ed., edited by Bill Ashcroft, Garth Griffiths and Helen Tiffin, 99–101. London: Routledge.

Torres Díaz, Angustia, and Israel Reyes Larrea, eds. 1999. *Alma cimarrona: versos costeños y poesía regional*. Oaxaca, Mexico: Dirección General de Culturas Populares.

Valles, Luis. N.d. "Memín Pinguín en el divan del siconalista". http://gmoaguilera.tripod.com/memin.html

Valencia Valencia, Enrique. 1993. Preface. In *Jamás fandango al cielo: narrativa afromestiza*, edited by María Cristina Díaz Pérez, Francisca Aparicio Prudente, Adela García Casarrubias, 13–17. San Angel, México: Dirección General de Culturas Populares.

Van Sertima, Ivan, ed. 1992. *African Presence in Early America*. London: Transaction.

Vargas Dulché, Yolanda. 2008a. *Memín Pinguín: aventura emocionante*. Edición Homenaje, vol. 153. Mexico: Grupo Editorial Vid.

———. 2008b. *Memín Pinguín: buscando una ilusión*. Edición Homenaje, vol. 154. Mexico: Grupo Editorial Vid.

———. 2010a. *Memín Pinguín: el nuevo pianista*, vol. 415. Mexico: Grupo Editorial Vid.

———. 2010b. *Memín Pinguín: desmelenados*. Edición Homenaje, vol. 248. Mexico: Grupo Editorial Vid.

———. 2010c. *Memín Pinguín: en guardia, faralones*. Edición Homenaje. Vol. 249. Mexico: Grupo Editorial Vid.

———. 2010d. *Memín Pinguín: viva el amor*. Edición Homenaje, vol. 251. Mexico: Grupo Editorial Vid.

———. 2010e. "*Memín Pinguín: tomo 23*. Vol. 221–30. Mexico: Grupo Editorial Vid.

Vasconcelos, José. 1925. *La raza cósmica: misión de la raza iberoamericana*. Madrid: Agencia Madrid de Librería.

Vaughn, Bobby. 2004. "Los negros, los indígenas y la diáspora: una perspectiva etnográfica de la Costa Chica". In *Afroméxico: el pulso de la población negra en México: una historia recordada y vuelta a recordar*, edited by Ben Vinson III and Bobby Vaughn, 74–96. Mexico City: Fondo de Cultura Economica.

Vaughn, Bobby, and Ben Vinson III. 2005. "Memín Penguin: Changing Racial Debates and Transnational Blackness". *La jornada*. http://hemisphericinstitute.org/hemi/en/e-misferica-52/vaughnvinson.

Velázquez Gutiérrez, María Elisa. 2005. "Memín Pinguín: Tres años después". *La jornada*. http://hemisphericinstitute.org/hemi/en/e-misferica-52/velazquezgutierrez.

Villegas Zapata, Efraín. 1999. "Costa". In *Alma cimarrona: versos costeños y poesía regional*, edited by Angustia Torres Díaz and Israel Reyes Larrea, 53. Oaxaca, Mexico: Dirección General de Culturas Populares.

Vincent, Ted. 1994. "The Blacks Who Freed Mexico". *Journal of Negro History* 79 (3): 257–76.

Vinson III, Ben. 2001. *Bearing Arms for His Majesty: The Free-Coloured Militia in Colonial Mexico*. Palo Alto, CA: Stanford University Press.

———. 2004. "La historia del estudios de los negros en Mexico". In *Afroméxico: el pulso de la población negra en México: una historia recordada y vuelta a recordar*, edited by Ben Vinson III and Bobby Vaughn, 19–74. Mexico City: Fondo de Cultura Economica.

Vinson III, Ben, and Bobby Vaughn. 2004. *Afroméxico: el pulso de la población negra en*

México: una historia recordada y vuelta a recordar. Mexico City: Fondo de Cultura Economica.
Webb, Barbara. 1992. *Myth and History in Caribbean Fiction.* Amherst: University of Massachusetts Press.
White, Elizabeth. 2009. "Bakhtinian Dialogism: A Philosophical and Methodological Route to Dialogue and Difference". Paper presented at the thirty-eighth annual conference of the Philosophy of Education Society of Australasia. http://www.hawaii_peanconf/zpdfs/16white.pdf.
Whitten, Norman Jr, ed. 1981. *Cultural Transformation and Etnicity: Urban Ethnicity in Modern Ecuador.* Champaign: University of Illinois Press.
Williams, Eric. 1994. *Capitalism and Slavery.* Chapel Hill: University of North Carolina Press.
Yuval-Davis, Nira. 1997. *Gender and Nation.* Los Angeles: Sage.
Zárate Arango, Francisco J. 2012. *Memoria y canto desde la Costa Chica: Poemas.* Mexico City: Palabra en Vuelo.
———. 1999a. "Caminos". In *Alma cimarrona: versos costeños y poesía regional*, edited by Angustia Torres Díaz and Israel Reyes Larrea, 51. Oaxaca, Mexico: Dirección General de Culturas Populares.
———. 1999b. "Canto a la costa mía". In *Alma cimarrona: versos costeños y poesía regional*, edited by Angustia Torres Díaz and Israel Reyes Larrea, 52. Oaxaca, Mexico: Dirección General de Culturas Populares.
———. 1999c. "Radiografia costeña". In *Alma cimarrona: versos costeños y poesía regional*, edited by Angustia Torres Díaz and Israel Reyes Larrea, 74–77. Oaxaca, Mexico: Dirección General de Culturas Populares.

Corridos

"Chicharrón". 2000. In *Poetry and Violence: The Ballad Tradition of Mexico's Costa Chica* by John McDowell, 221–23. Champaign: University of Illinois Press.
"Corrido de Martín Díaz". 1990. In *The Mexican Corrido: A Feminist Analysis* by María Herrera-Sobek, 47–48. Bloomington: Indiana University Press.
"Corrido de los Zapatistas de San Nicolás". 1975. *Traigo una flor hermoso y mortal: Los Cimatrones Band.* Sound Recording.
"El Zanatón". 1975. *Traigo una flor hermoso y mortal: Los Cimatrones Band.* Sound recording.
"Fan (Juan) Chanito". 1975. *Traigo una flor hermoso y mortal: Los Cimatrones Band.* Sound recording.
"La Gallinita". 2014. Letras Musicales. http://www.letrasmusicales.ws/la-gallina-banda-arkangel-r-15/.

"La Mula Bronca". 1975. *Traigo una flor hermoso y mortal: Los Cimatrones Band.* Sound recording.
"Pedro el Chicharrón". 2000. In *Poetry and Violence: The Ballad Tradition of Mexico's Costa Chica,* by John McDowell, 227–31. Champaign: University of Illinois Press.
"Prisco Sanchez". 1975. *Traigo una flor hermoso y mortal: Los Cimatrones Band.* Sound recording.
"Tomás Marín". 2000. In *Poetry and Violence: The Ballad Tradition of Mexico's Costa Chica,* by John McDowell, 220–21. Champaign: University of Illinois Press.

Index

Acapulco, xii, 127
Acapulco Tropical, 20
Aéromexico, recruiting language, 162
Africana Womanism, 67–70
Africans
    compensation awarded, 3, 175n2
    interbreeding with indigenous Indians, 5–6
    physical/psychological denigration of blacks, 6–7
    role in conquest of Mexico, 2–3
    social ranking of in New Spain, 3, 175nn3–4
Afro-Cuban Cos Causse, 145
Afro-Latin America (Andrews), 1
afromestizo, 16–17
Afro-Mexican communities, xii
    Collantes, 21
    Cuajinicuilapa, xii, 127, 146, 180n2
    El Coyolillo, 20
    living conditions, 13–14
Afro-Mexican heritage
    cultural contributions, 19–20
    cultural preservation of, 132–33
    drums, response to, 119–23
    government research, 11–12
    Nuestra Tercera Raíz (Our Third Root), 13

Afro-Mexicans
    agricultural production, 19
    black phenotype, 120–21
    caste laws (*sistema de castas*), 6, 9
    colonial race relations, 6–7
    in contemporary political landscape, 14–16
    derogation of Afro-Mexican characters, 23, 31, 34, 59–60
    as distinctive black/diasporic presence, 159
    ethno-linguistic identity of, 150–51
    exclusion from Mexican national discourse, 10, 59–60, 162–63
    Guerrero recognition of, 162
    as *jarocho*, 20
    mestizaje, aesthetic eugenics of, 10–11
    Mexican ignorance of, 19
    non-recognition of, 126–27, 162–63
    Oaxacan recognition of, 162
    official Mexican position on, 12
    omission of black men in Mexican definitions of masculinity, 76–79
    post-independence, 9–11
    recognition of, 13, 161–62
    understanding of self, identity and place, 158–59
Afroméxico (Vinson, Vaugn), 1

agency, 23
    assertion of, 86–87
    in Black Feminist thought, 67–68
    of eco-feminism, 71
    speaking, act of by women, 57
    of women, 53–54, 160
Aguirre Beltrán, Gonzalo, xii, 107
    Cortés, and importation of slaves, 2
    Costa Chica, living conditions, 13–14
    La población negra de México, 2, 11
    Maroon descendants, of Costa Chica, 84
Alma cimarrona (Maroon Soul), 12, 110–12, 129
    blackness, self-affirmation of, 112–14, 115
    "Caminos" (Roads), 143–45, 156
    "Canto a la costa mía" (Song to My Coast), 145–46
    and Caribbean cultural aesthetic, 137, 145–46
    coplas. See coplas
    "Costa Chica mía" (My Costa Chica), 145, 146–48
    "El negro" (Black Man), 150–51, 156
    lyric poems, 143–45
    "Negrita cimarrona" (Little Black Maroon), 119–23
    "Negro y blanco" (Black and White), 151–53
    "Pa' mí Nicolasíta" (For my Nicolasita), 123–25
    "Radiografía costeña" (Coastal X-ray), 145, 148–50
    "Salta pa'trás" (Step Back), 153–54
    "Yo soy mexicano" (I Am Mexican), 155
Álvarez Añorve, Joaquín, "El negro" (Black Man), 150–51, 156
Andrade Aguirre, David, 112

Andrews, George, 5, 132–33
    Afro-Latin America, 1
Aparicio Prudente, Francisca, 111
Aramoni, Aníceto, 77
Archibold, Randall, 14, 16
Ashcroft, Bill, 51
authoring, of identity, 24–25, 108, 109, 129, 133–34
Aztec society, *machista* tendencies of, 76–78

Bakhtin, Mikhail, dialogism, 109
Barthes, Roland, and visual rhetoric, 31
Bartolomé, Miguel Alberto, 10
Baugh, Edward, 61, 177n2
Beckles, Hilary, 75
belonging, and consciousness of connections, 71
Benítez-Rojo, Antonio, 107, 133–34, 135
    Caribbean as meta-archipelago, 138
    carnivalesque performance of *coplas*, 142
    on *mestizaje*, 153
Bennett, Herman, 11
Bhabha, Homi, 33, 42, 96
black ethnicity
    afromestizo, 16–17
    dehumanization of, 35
    indigenismo, as exclusion of, 16–17
    invisibility of, 12, 19, 30
    Memín Pinguín stamp controversy, 29–30
    and myth of uncivilized black people, 39–42
    negative characterization of, 37
    objectification of, 42
    parental violence, inferences of, 40–41
Black Feminist thought, and woman consciousness, 67–68, 69

INDEX   *193*

blackness
   assertions of, 156
   elevation of the black male, 114–15
   inferiority of, 4, 38, 153
   as political and social risk, 15–16
   positive images of, 125
   self-affirmation of, 112–15, 133–34, 160–61
"Blanca Flor" (White Flower), 50, 65–67
blanco, 176n4
bote, 21
bozales, 3, 175n4
Brand, Dionne, 73
Bruno, Catalina, 49, 50, 68, 70
Bush, George W., 30

Cállate burrita prieta (*Be Quiet Little Black Donkey*)
   black women, respect for, 117
   blackness, self-affirmation of, 113–15
   compilation of, 110–12
calypso, Trinidadian
   as expression of masculinity, 79
   extempo calypso, 140–41
   The Mighty Sparrow, 104
   phallocentric masculinity, 103
"Caminos" (Roads), 156
Campeche, 136
"Canto a la costa mía" (Song to My Coast), 126–29, 145–46
Caribbean
   Afro-derived cultural forms, 138–39
   Afro-descendant populations, xii–xiii
   Afro-Jamaican religious herbal art, 137
   as creole and heterogeneous, 138
   cross-culturality of, 137–38
   cultural whitening of, 153
   expansion of as cultural space, 158
   and Mexican labour migration, 136–37
   and Mexico, shared historical past of, 135–36
   step back (maxim), 153
Caribbean masculinities, 75
   political power as symbol of "manhood", 82
Carillo, Álvaro
   "Costa Chica mía" (My Costa Chica), 145, 146–48
Carroll, Patrick, 2, 3, 5, 8, 9, 11
Casteñon, Guadelupe, 11
charrasca, 21
chilena music, 20
chingadas, 140, 143, 180n1
Chiriboga, Luz Argentina, 139
Cisneros, René Juárez, 15–16
citizenship
   Mexican omission of Afro-Mexicans, 59–60
   racial consciousness of belonging, 108
colonialism
   feminist critique of, 60–61
   identity, hierarchal notions of, 46
   imposition of identity on minorities, 45–46
   masculinity, and racial hierarchies, 78
Connell, Robert
   masculinity, and gender relations, 73–74, 77, 78, 96, 177n2
   self-attribution, 89
Conniff, Michael, 157
Consejo Nacional para la Cultura y las Artes, 163
coplas, 112
   Amor y piropos (Love and Flirtation), 139

coplas (continued)
  assonance, 139
  blackness, self-affirmation of, 114–15
  Caribbeanness of, 140–41, 142
  carnivalesque performance of, 142
  as communal recovery, 142–43
  defined, 139
  Escolares (School Verses), 139
  exchanges between speakers, 140–41
  gender relations in, 141
  Groserías (Rude Verses), 139–40, 180n1
  Ofensivos (Offensive Verses), 139
  orality in, 140
  positional identity of women, 115–18
  repetitition as discursive strategy, 117
  rhyming patterns, 114–16, 139
  women, queenly quality of, 118
"Corrido de los Zapatistas de San Nicolás, 80, 81–82
"Corrido de Marín Díaz", 99–100
corridos
  African influence on, 20
  betrayed male image, 96–97
  correlation between *machismo* and self-praise, 97–98
  "Corrido de los Zapatistas de San Nicolás, 80, 81–82
  "Corrido de Marín Díaz", 99–100
  as discourse of the powerless, 80–82
  discursive language strategies, association with power, 83
  "El Zanatón", 81, 84–86, 92
  ethnic pride, of male hero, 89–90
  "Fan (Juan) Chanito", 90–92
  female figures in, 78–79, 96–97, 98–99, 102
  and feminist masculinity, 104–6
  Great Mother archetype, 99–100
  hero as sacrificial lamb, 92
  "La gallinita" (Little Chicken), 90, 93–94
  "La mula bronca" (The Wild Mule"), 97, 100–101, 103
  language, and masculinity, 82–83, 84, 86–87
  language choice, 92–93
  Los cimarrones, 12
  loyalty to community, 89–90
  "Lupe Baños", 102
  male audiences, 95–96
  male bravado, 82, 87, 88
  masculinity, power and language, 79–82
  mother figures, 99–100, 177n4
  "Pedro el Chicharrón", 87–89, 93, 101, 103–4
  performance competitions, 20
  performance of masculinity in, 24, 78–79
  phallocentric masculinity, 103–4
  "Prisco Sánchez", 98–99
  problematic representations of masculinity, 95–99
  regional language as linguistic code, 89–90
  "Tomás Marín", 101–2, 177–79n5
  Triago una flor hermosa y mortal, 78, 96–97
  violence, and language, 84–95, 160
Cortés, Hernán, 2, 76
Cortés, Juan, 2, 3
"Costa" (Villegas Zapata), 129–32
"Costa Chica mía" (My Costa Chica), 145, 146–48
Costa Chica region
  Afro-Mexican communities, xii
  blackness, and Afro-Mexicans, 17–19
  constitutional recogniton, 161–62
  corridos of, 20, 78

indigenismo, and *afromestizo*, 16–17
living conditions, 13–14
local speech of, 89–90, 112
Maroon descendants of, 7–12, 84
Mexican neglect of, 146
as model of black strength, 146–48
mortality rates, 14
oral verse of, 111–12
performance art, 132–33
recitation events, 112
regional environment, 148–50
regionalism, of oral verse, 126–29, 130–31
social services, development of, 14
women, distinctiveness of in place of origin, 127–29
creative revisionism, 110
Cuajinicuilapa, xii, 127, 146, 180n2
cultural identity, 23
and displacement of peoples, 158
repression of plurality, 10
cultural studies, 108

dances
in Afro-Mexican cultural expression, 122
chilena dancers, 127
as cultural expression, 132–33
El baile del Toro (Dance of the Bull), 112
El Son de Artesa, 21, 22
as form of self-expression, 23
instruments used, 21
La Danza de la Tortuga (Turtle Dance), 21, 122–23
La Danza del Diablo (Dance of the Devil), 21, 23, 122–23
masks in, 21
and recitation events, 112
Davidson, David, 6

Davis, Thomas, 157
de las Casas, Bartolomé, 4
de Narváez, Pánfilo, 2
décimas, poetic form of, 112–13
Derbez, Luis Ernesto, 30
Detriech, Elise, 45
dialogism, as response to authoritative discourses, 109
diaspora, as double consciousness, 64
diasporic reunion of Afro-descendant populations, xii–xiii
Díaz Pérez, María Cristina, 111
  Jamás fandango al cielo (*Never Again a Party in the Sky*), 48, 49
difference
  official attitude toward racial difference, 30
  as undesirable, 23–24, 29
  visual images, impact on children, 45
Dirección General de Culturas Populares, 12, 163
Domínguez, Melquíades, 55
double consciousness, 64

eco-feminism
  and female empowerment, 54–61
  resistance to male tyranny, 66
  social construction of gender and nature, 65–67, 71
Ecuador, *coplas* of, 139
Edwards, Tim, 73, 78
"El Caballito de virtud", 50
El Ciruelo, xii
"El negro" (Black Man), 150–51, 156
El Son de Artesa, 21, 22
  performances of, 22
"El Zanatón", 81, 84–86, 92
emasculation theory, 73, 177n1
empowerment, politics of, 54–61, 71–72
encomienda system, 3, 175n2

Escamilla, Fidencio
    "Negro y blanco" (Black and White), 151–53
essentialist definitions of masculinity, 177n2
ethnicity, 23
    in construction of identity, 107–10
    and cultural identity, 129–32
extempo calypso, 140–41

Fairclough, Norman, 94
"Fan (Juan) Chanito", 90–92
Fanon, Frantz, 73, 177n1
femininity
    construction of in Caribbean societies, 75
    in folktale constructions, 49
    language as 'performing gender', 83
    parental violence, inferences of, 40–41
    representation of in *Memín Pinguín*, 43–45
    as social construction, 24
feminism
    Africana Womanism, 67, 68–70
    Black Feminist thought, 67–68
    critique of colonialism/imperialism, 60–61
    and female empowerment, 54–61
    feminist masculinity, 104–6
    and oral narrative, 24
figured worlds, 108, 129
    of Afro-Mexican identity, 133–34
    of oral poems, 24–25
    "Pa' mí Nicolasíta" (For my Nicolasita), 123–25
film, 23
folktales, 23
    "Blanca Flor" (White Flower), 50, 65–67
    derogation of Afro-Mexican characters, 59–60
    "El Caballito de virtud", 50
    female characters, presentation of, 49, 50–51
    "fixed" structure of, 49
    gender, in shaping of narrative perspective, 48–49
    gender relations, portrayals of, 47
    Jamás fandango al cielo (*Never Again a Party in the Sky*), 12, 47–48, 55
    journey/travel motif, 63
    "Juaniquito el oso" (Little John the Bear), 62–65
    "La mojarrita de tres colores" (The Three-Coloured Bream), 50, 51–54
    "La ranita" (Little Toad), 70–71
    male characters as protagonists, 49, 51–54
    "Morena" (Black Woman), 50–51, 68–70
    patriarchal ideologies, representations of, 51–54
    patriarchal system, stereotypes of, 49
    power and authority of maleness, 50–51
    "Tontosoy", 50, 53–54
    "Yoatzin", 55–61
Forbes, Curdella, 73
Foucault, Michel, 79–80, 81, 82

García Casarrubias, Adela, 111
Garrido, Juan, 3
gender, 23
    intersection with nation and race, 71
    and nature, eco-feminist view of, 65–67
    and nature, power relations of, 55–61
    patriarchal constructions of, 52
    representations of in oral narrative, 24

in shaping of narrative perspective, 48–49
social construction of, 54–55, 74
gender relations
  binary opposition, patterns of, 62–64
  and construction of nation, 59
  in *coplas*, 140–41
  folktale portrayals of, 47
  male/female characterizations, 49–54
  male/female collaboration, 68–72
  and masculinity, 73–74, 177n2
  oppositionality, principle of, 68
  sexism of Afro-Hispanic society, 160
Gilroy, Paul, 64
Glissant, Édouard, 135
  cross-culturality of Caribbean, 138
  on diversity, 28
  expression, in articulation of identity, 142
  landscape as character, 146
globalization of the local, 157
Gomez Licon, Adriana, 162–63
González, Anita, 22, 123, 132, 158, 159
Graber, Davis, 92–93
Granada War, Treaty of Tordesillas, 4, 175n5
Griffin, Susan
  eco-feminism, and nature, 54–55
  on rape metaphor, 63–64
Griffiths, Garth, 51
Guerrero, state of
  Afro-Mexican communities, xii, 17, 18, 19
  recognition of Afro-Mexicans, 162
Guerrero, Vicente (*El Negro Guerrero*), 8–9, 30, 176n5

Habana Zárate, Rodrigo, 53
Harris, Wilson, 158
hegemonic masculinity, 74

Hernández Cuevas, Marco Polo, 11
Herrera Casusús, María Luisa, 9–10
Herrera-Sobek, María, 99–100
Hidalgo, Miguel, 9
Hidalgo, Pluma, 131, 180n3
Hidalgo rebellion, 8
hierarchy, and rituals of power, 24
Hill Collins, Patricia, 47
Holland, Dorothy, 108–9
homogeneity
  imperialistic myth of, 33
  as political exclusion, 14–16
hooks, bell, 105
Hudson-Weems, Clenora, 67–68, 69
Hymes, Dell, 82

identity
  Caribbeanness of, 155–56
  contexts of construction, 108–9
  cultural identity, 23, 158
  expression, in articulation of identity, 142
  figured worlds, 108
  place, role of in identity formation, 125–34
  and racial consciousness, 108, 125, 126–29
images, use of in persuasion, 31–32
imperialism
  civility as characteristic of dominance, 42
  feminist critique of, 60–61
  racial/cultural homogeneity as strategy of control, 33
indigenismo, and exclusion of black ethnicity, 16, 176n8
indigenous peoples, 163
  enslavement of, 4, 5
  treatment of in settler/invader societies, 45–46

Instituto Guerrerense de Cultura
 (Guerrero Cultural Institute), 107
Instituto Guerrerense de la Cultura, 163
Instituto Oaxaqueño de la Cultura
 (Oaxacan Cultural Institute), 111
interdisciplinary analyses, 23–24
isolation, 23
Iturralde Nieto, Gabriela, 11

Jackson, Jesse, 29–30
Jamaica, relationship with Mexico,
 135–37
Jamás fandango al cielo (*Never Again a Party in the Sky*). *See* folktales
Jemmott Nelson, Father Glyn, 14, 162
 blackness, and Afro-Mexicans, 17–18
 on perception of identity, 160–61
 role of in self-awareness of Afro-
  Mexicans, 108, 159, 161
Johnson, Sally, 83, 89–90
"Juaniquito el oso" (Little John the
 Bear), 62–65

Katz, Marco, 44–45
Kimmel, Michael, 75, 95–96
Krause, Enrique, 30

La Danza de la Tortuga (Turtle Dance),
 21, 122–23
La Danza del Diablo (Dance of the
 Devil), 21, 23, 122–23
"La gallinita" (Little Chicken), 90, 93–94
"La mojarrita de tres colores" (The
 Three-Coloured Bream), 50, 51–54
"La mula bronca" (The Wild Mule"), 97,
 100–101, 103
La población negra de México (Aguirre
 Beltrán), 2, 11
"La ranita", 70–71
ladinos, 2, 3, 175n1, 175n3
land, trope of, 147

language
 "anti-language", 95
 as culture, 32
 discursive language strategies,
  association with power, 83
 hegemonic constructs in
  deconstruction of, 32–33
 language, and masculinity, 82–83
 name-calling strategies, 94
 as "performing gender", 83
 political language, purposes of,
  92–94
 power relations, and oppression,
  94–95
 regional language as linguistic code,
  89–90, 112
 use of in cultural forms, 159
 violent language of *corridos*, 160
 visual rhetoric as, 32
Latin America
 African musical influence, 20
 Afro-descendant populations, xii–
  xiii, 1
Legler, Gretchen, 54
localization of the global, 157
Los cimarrones, 12
"Lupe Baños", 102
lyric poems
 "Caminos" (Roads), 143–45
 "Negrita cimarrona" (Little Black
  Maroon), 119–23

Machiavelli, Niccolo, 79
machismo, 52, 76–77
mala raza (bad race), 122, 127
mala sangre (bad blood), 122, 127
marginality, 23, 78–79
Maroons, and marronage, 7–12, 21, 84,
 144
Martí, José, 138

Martínez Montiel, Luz María, 2, 7, 11
Marx, Karl, 79
masculinity
    Caribbean masculinities, 75, 79
    categories for defining, 74, 177n2
    and deception, 66
    emasculation theory, 73, 177n1
    as expression of resistance, 79
    feminist masculinity, 104–6
    in folktale constructions, 49–54
    and gender relations, 73–74
    hegemonic masculinity, 74
    language as "performing gender", 83
    machismo, 52, 76–77
    male characters as protagonists, 51–54
    and male identity, 73–74
    in Mexican context, 76–79
    myth of male power, 96
    phallocentric masculinity, 103–4
    political power as symbol of "manhood", 82
    postcolonial context of, 75
    problematic representations of in *corridos*, 95–99
    and self-attribution, 89
    as social construction, 24, 74
    stereotypes of, 55
    subordinate masculinity, 74, 75
    super machismo, 76
    white masculinity, 75, 76, 78
McDowell, John, 95
McKay, Claude, "If We Must Die", 100
Meinhof, Ulrike Hanna, 83, 89–90
Memín Pinguín
    affectionate condescension towards, 33–34
    arrogance of as boaster, 37–38
    Aventura emocionante, 34–37, 40
    cultural decolonization, need for, 46, 159–60
    as cultural icon, 43–44
    depiction of mother, 31, 40–41, 42
    derogation of Afro-Mexican characters, 23, 31, 34
    hegemonic constructs of, 32–34
    image of violent black persons, 39–42
    inferior position of, 38–39
    Memín as object of mockery, 36–37
    moral/religious protests against, 31
    objectification of black ethnicity, 42
    outsiderness, representation of, 35
    racism, and racial marginalization, 44
    self-validation, craving for, 34–37
    stamp controversy, 29–30, 43
    stereotypical behaviours of, 29
    visual rhetoric, 31–32, 45
memory, as repository of culture, 142–43, 158
Méndez Tello, Donají, "Pa' mí Nicolasíta" (For my Nicolasita), 123–25
Messner, M, 75, 95–96
mestizaje
    aesthetic eugenics of, 10–11
    as concentration of difference, 107, 133–34, 153
    false national identity of, 155–56
    and homogenization of ethnicities, 10–11
    as ideology of exclusion, 28, 176n1, 176n2
    as national policy, 17, 137–38, 152–53, 160
    as process of racial/cultural whitening, 1
    racial construct of, 121–22
mestizo, 161
    as national identity of Mexico, xi, xii, 10, 28
    non-white ethnic groups, 11–12

Mexican Consejo Nacional para la Cultura y las Artes (Mexican National Council for Culture and Arts), 110
Mexican identity, Eurocentric view of, 23
Mexican Revolution, 10
Mexican War of Independence, 8–9
Mexico. *See also* New Spain (colonial Mexico)
    Afro-Mexican communities, xii, 13–14, 20, 21, 127, 146, 180n2
    as Caribbean, 135
    and Caribbean labour, 136–37
    contemporary political landscape, 14–16
    Dirección General de Culturas Populares, 12
    ethnicity and identity, construction of, 107–10
    Eurocentric self-image of, 33
    exclusion of ethnicities in census data, 1, 161
    Hidalgo rebellion, 8
    ignorance of black communities, 19, 126–27, 162–63
    indigenismo, discourse of, 16, 176n8
    mestizaje, ideology of, 1, 10–11, 17, 28, 107, 121–22, 133–34, 152–53, 155–56, 160, 176n1, 176n2
    mestizo identity of, xi, xii, 10, 28
    as mixed-race country, 158
    multiculturality of, 48, 125
    non-recognition of Afro-Mexicans, 126–27
    non-white ethnic groups, 11–12
    official position on Afro-Mexicans, 12
    popular culture, use of by government, 44–45
    pre-Columbian African presence, 2
    recruitment of foreign labour, 136–37
    relationship with Jamaica, 135–37
    War of Independence, 8–9

México Negro, goals of, 161–62
Meza Herrera, Malinali, 111
mining industry, 136, 137
Ministry of Education (Mexico) Multicultural Mexico Project, 13
Mirandé, Alfredo, 76
miscegenation, 5–6, 12
Monsiváis, Carlos, 43–44
Morelos, José María, 8, 9, 30, 176n4
"Morena" (Black Woman), 50–51
    Africana Womanism of, 68–70
Muhammad, Jameelah, 6, 11, 20, 116
Multicultural Mexico Project, 13
multiculturalism, 48, 125
Muñoz, Laura, 135–36, 137
music, 13
    Acapulco Tropical, 20
    in Afro-Mexican cultural expression, 122
    chilena, 20
    corridos. *See corridos*
    as cultural expression, 132–33
    influence of African culture on Mexican music, 19–20
    son jarocho, 20
    tropical, 20

Nanton, Phillip, 140, 142
Nariela, Adriana, 11
nation, constructions of, 59, 71
nationalism
    as constitutive of gendered identities, 97–98
    and Mexican national identity, 148
    regional pride of people and place, 128, 129
nature
    and gender, eco-feminist view of, 65–67, 71
    as "other", 54
    in "Yoatzin", 55–61

"Negrita cimarrona" (Little Black Maroon), 119–23
"Negro y blanco" (Black and White), 151–53
New Spain (colonial Mexico)
    African labour, preference for, 2, 4–5
    black auxiliaries, role in conquest of Mexico, 2–3
    caste laws (*sistema de castas*), 6, 9
    enslavement of indigenous Indians, 4
    expulsion of Spanish, 9
    integration of blacks into Spanish colonial culture, 3, 175nn3–4
    miscegenation, and population expansion, 5–6
    physical/psychological denigration of blacks, 6–7
    race relations, 6–7
    relationship with Jamaica, 135–36
    slave freedom of expression, limitations to, 7
    slave labour, demand for, 5–6, 175n6
    Tenochitlán, conquest of, 2–3
normative definitions of masculinity, 177n2
Nuestra Tercera Raíz (Our Third Root), 13
Nurse, Keith, 95, 96, 97
Nyanga Yanga, 7, 144, 156, 176n7

Oaxaca
    Afro-Mexican communities, xii, 17, 18, 19
    recognition of Afro-Mexicans, 162
Oloff, Kerstin, 158
Ong, Walter, 113
oppression, politics of, 24
oral tradition, 13
    cross-cultural connections of, 157–58
    as cultural/community process, 113
oral verse, 23
    alliteration, 130
    Alma cimarrona (Maroon Soul), 110–14, 115, 119–23, 129
    anaphoric repetition, 150
    audience, response of, 112–13
    availability of Afrocentric poetry, 25
    Cállate burrita prieta (Be Quiet Little Black Donkey), 110–12, 113–15, 117
    "Canto a la costa mía" (Song to My Coast), 126–29
    coplas. See coplas
    "Costa", 129–32
    décimas, 112–13
    in definition of self, 142–43
    figured worlds of, 24–25, 133–34
    forms of, 112–13
    musicality of, 132–33
    racial consciousness of, 109
    recitation events, 112
    regionalism in, 126–29
    rhyming patterns, 114–16
orality
    in *coplas*, 140, 142
    as cultural/community process, 113
    true orality, 140, 142
Orozco y Berra, Manuel, 2
others, and otherness
    nature as "other", 54
    objectification of, 33
    and subordinate masculinity, 95–96
    of women, 51, 104
outward appeal, considerations of, 70–71

"Pa' mí Nicolasíta" (For my Nicolasita), 123–25
Palmer, Colin, 11, 12
Paredes Martínez, Carlos, 11
Partido Revolucionario Institucional (Institutional Revolutionary Party), 15
patriarchy
    and gender relations, 47

as gender subordination, 51
and male entitlement, 69
in objectification of women, 66–67
outward appeal, considerations of, 70–71
representations of in *corridos*, 95
representations of in oral narrative, 24, 51–54
subversion of, 70–71
as system of unequal power, 63
women as "other", 50–51, 104
Paz, Octavio
chingadas, 143
"cult of *machismo*", 76–77
El laberinto de la soledad, 143
The Labyrinth of Solitude, 76–77
"Pedro el Chicharrón", 87–89, 93, 101, 103–4
Peñaloza, Sergio, 161
Pérez Fernández, Rolando, 19
Petatán Mariche, Luis, 62
phallocentric masculinity, 103–4
pirates, 136
place, and belonging, 23
regional particularism of, 126–29
role of in identity formation, 125–34
poetry. See *coplas*; oral verse
political language, purposes of, 92–94
positional identities, 24–25, 108–9, 117, 129, 133–34
positivist definitions of masculinity, 177n2
postcolonial criticism in dismantling of European codes, 32–34
postcolonialism
binary opposition, patterns of, 62–64
and neocolonial domination, 45–46
and oral narrative, 24
resistance and reconstruction, process of, 45–46
women as "other", 50–51

power relations
"cult of *machismo*", 76–77
and discursive language strategies, 83
domination as two-way process, 61
of gender, and nature, 55–61
jurídico/political conceptions of power, 79
language, and oppression, 94–95
postcolonial binaries, 62–64
power, definitions of, 79–80
and powerlessness, 96
and subjectivity, 79–80, 81
"Prisco Sánchez", 98–99

race relations, colonial Mexico, 6–7
racial awareness, in construction of identity, 107–10
racial caricatures, portrayal of, 23–24
racial consciousness
and citizenship, 108
in *coplas*, 141–42
and identity, 108, 125, 126–29
in oral verse, 109, 115
racism, and racial marginalization, 44
"Radiografía costeña" (Coastal X-ray), 148–50
Ramchand, Kenneth, 75, 79
Ramírez, Lupe, "El diablo", 92
Ramírez, Rafael, 74
Ramsay, Paulette, 84
Reddock, Rhoda, 82
relational identities, 24–25, 108–9, 117, 129
religion, and religious beliefs, 3, 6, 13, 133
Reyes Larrea, Israel, 111, 119, 120–21
road metaphor, 143–45
Robles, Jesús, 51
Roeder, Jonathan, 14
Rohlehr, Gordon, 79, 104

Salinas, Julian, 22

"Salta pa'trás" (Step Back), 153–54
Salvador, Gabriel, 19
San Lorenzo de los Negros, 7–8, 176n7
Sanders, Edith, 6
Santos, María, 22
self-definition, of Africana Womanism, 68
semantic approaches to masculinity, 177n2
semiotics, theory of, 31–32
sexuality
    Costa Chican view of, 129
    in dance, 122–23
    in folktales, 47
    in *Groserías* (Rude Verses), 140, 180n1
    rape metaphor, 63–64
    representations of in oral verse, 24
sistema de castas (caste laws), 6, 9
slavery
    African labour, preference for, 4–5
    African trade in, 5, 175n6
    allegorical treatment of in "Juaniquito el oso", 63–65
    black auxiliaries, role in conquest of Mexico, 2–3
    bozales, 3, 175n4
    Caribbean/Mexican history of, 136
    colonial labour needs, 5–6
    of indigenous Indians, 4, 5
    ladinos, 2, 175n1
    slave labour, reliance on, 5
slaves, perceptions of, 6–7
Slemon, Stephen, 110
social constructionism, and masculinity, 74, 78
social stratification, caste laws (*sistema de castas*), 6
son jarocho, 20
Spain
    black auxiliaries, role in conquest of Mexico, 2–3

black inferiority, ideology of, 4
defeat of Moors, 4
ladinos in, 2, 175n1
masculinity in cultural heritage of, 76
Treaty of Tordesillas, 4, 175n5
Spence, Louise, 33
Stam, Robert, 33
stereotypes
    of black females, 43
    in folktales, 47
    mala raza (bad race), 122, 127
    mala sangre (bad blood), 122, 127
    negligient black men, 124–25
    of patriarchal system in folktales, 49
    racial caricatures, 23
    women, as fearful and timid, 53
subordinate masculinity, 74, 75
    and subjectification of the "other", 95–96

Tang, R., 32
Tiffin, Helen, 51
tigrera, 21
Todos Santos (All Saints Day), 21
"Tomás Marín", 101–2, 177–79n5
"Tontosoy", 50, 53–54
Torres Díaz, Augustía, 111, 122
traditional medicine, 13
Traigo una flor hermosa y mortal (*I Bring Beautiful and Deadly Flowers*), 12
tropical music, 20
true orality, 140, 142

UN Committee for the Elimination of Racial Discrimination, 13
Unidad Regional de Guerrero de Cultura Populares (Guerrero Regional Unit for Popular Culture), 48, 111
United States
    Memín Pinguín stamp controversy, 29–30, 43

Valencia Burgos, Sixto, 40
Van Sertima, Ivan, 2
Vargas Dulché, Yolanda, 29
Vasconcelos Calderón, José, 10, 28, 155
Vaughn, Bobby, 11, 15–16, 20
   Afroméxico, 1
Velasquez, Luz María, 11
Velázquez, María Elisa, 11
Velázquez Gutiérrez, María Elisa, 44
Veracruz, 17, 20, 136, 138
Villegas Zapata, Efrain, "Costa", 129–32
Vinson, Ben, III, 4, 11, 17
   Afroméxico, 1
violence
   in language of *corridos*, 84–95, 160
   in *Memín Pinguín*, 39–42
Virgin de Guadalupe, 101–02, 179n6
visual rhetoric
   and child protagonist, 45
   elements of, 31–32

White, Elizabeth, 109
white superiority, 151–53
   rejection of, 121–22
   and self-worth, 153–54
Williams, Eric, 5
woman consciousness, 67–68
women
   agency of, 53–54, 57, 67–68, 71, 160
   in *coplas*, 115–18, 140–41
   defeminism of, 64
   derogation of in *corridos*, 78–79, 98–100, 177n4
   distinctiveness of Costa Chican women, 127–29
   eco-feminism, and nature, 54–55, 70
   empowerment of, 54–61, 71–72
   as fearful and timid sex, 53
   fearlessness, and spirit of resistance, 121
   female as betrayer, 100–102
   female characters, presentation of, 31, 49
   Great Mother archetype, 99–100
   male dominance, rejection of, 57–59
   marriageability of, 53, 70–71
   myth of oversexuality, 116
   narrative perspective of, 48–49
   objectification of, 42, 51, 53–54, 68, 70–71
   as "other", 50–51, 104
   parental violence by, 40–41
   queenly quality of, 118
   rape metaphor, 63–64
   restitutive role, 116
   self-invention of, 61, 177n2
   self-realization, 66–67
   slave/woman slave master relationship, 64–65
   speaking, as expression of selfhood, 57
   subjugation of, 62–64

Yanga (Maroon community), 7–8, 176n7
Yanga (Maroon warrior), 7, 144, 156, 176n7
"Yo soy mexicano" (I Am Mexican), 155
"Yoatzin", 55–61

Zárate Arango, Francisco J., 107
   "Caminos" (Roads), 143–45, 156
   "Canto a la costa mía" (Song to My Coast), 145–46
   "Radiografía costeña" (Coastal X-ray), 145, 148–50
   "Salta pa'trás" (Step Back), 153–54
   "Yo soy mexicano" (I Am Mexican), 155

www.ingramcontent.com/pod-product-compliance
Lightning Source LLC
Chambersburg PA
CBHW021840220426
43663CB00005B/339